THE LAW AND ETHICS OF MEDICAL RESEARCH

INTERNATIONAL BIOETHICS AND HUMAN RIGHTS

Cavendish
Publishing
Limited

London • Sydney • Portland, Oregon

THE LAW AND ETHICS OF MEDICAL RESEARCH

INTERNATIONAL BIOETHICS AND HUMAN RIGHTS

Aurora Plomer, BA, LLB, MA, PhD
Lecturer in Law
University of Nottingham

U.W.E.L.
LEARNING RESOURCES

ACC No. 2354229

CONTROL 185941687x

DATE -8. MAY 2005   SITE WV

CLASS 325

174.
28

PLO

SLS

Cavendish
Publishing
Limited

London • Sydney • Portland, Oregon

First published in Great Britain 2005 by
Cavendish Publishing Limited, The Glass House,
Wharton Street, London WC1X 9PX, United Kingdom
Telephone: + 44 (0)20 7278 8000   Facsimile: + 44 (0)20 7278 8080
Email: info@cavendishpublishing.com
Website: www.cavendishpublishing.com

Published in the United States by Cavendish Publishing
c/o International Specialized Book Services,
5824 NE Hassalo Street, Portland,
Oregon 97213-3644, USA

Published in Australia by Cavendish Publishing (Australia) Pty Ltd
45 Beach Street, Coogee, NSW 2034, Australia
Telephone: + 61 (2)9664 0909   Facsimile: + 61 (2)9664 5420
Email: info@cavendishpublishing.com.au
Website: www.cavendishpublishing.com.au

© Plomer, A 2005

All rights reserved. No part of this publication may be reproduced, stored in a
retrieval system, or transmitted, in any form or by any means, electronic, mechanical,
photocopying, recording, scanning or otherwise, without the prior permission in
writing of Cavendish Publishing Limited, or as expressly permitted by law, or under
the terms agreed with the appropriate reprographics rights organisation. Enquiries concerning
reproduction outside the scope of the above should be sent to the
Rights Department, Cavendish Publishing Limited, at the address above.

You must not circulate this book in any other binding or cover
and you must impose the same condition on any acquirer.

British Library Cataloguing in Publication Data
Plomer, Aurora
The law and ethics of medical research: international bioethics and human rights
1 Medicine – Research – Law and legislation
2 Medicine – Research – Moral and ethical aspects   3 Bioethics
I Title
174.2'8

Library of Congress Cataloguing in Publication Data
Data available

ISBN 1-85941-687-X
ISBN 978-1-843-14677-3

1 3 5 7 9 10 8 6 4 2

Printed and bound in Great Britain by
Biddles Ltd, Kings Lynn, Norfolk

For Seumas and Fiona

ACKNOWLEDGMENTS

This book was originally prompted by my involvement in *Euricon*, a multi-disciplinary pan-European project on parental consent to the inclusion of neonates in clinical trials funded by the European Commission. The project got underway just after the Council of Europe's Convention on Human Rights and Biomedicine (1997) had been adopted, thus providing me with a unique opportunity to reflect about biomedical research from a human rights perspective. I owe much to Chris Megone for inviting me to take part in the project in the first instance and also for commenting on an early version of Chapter 2, which appeared in a collection which he edited with Su Mason on *European Neonatal Research* (Ashgate, 2001), and which was selected by the American Philosophical Association for inclusion in a collection of papers on their centenary conference on Morality in the Twenty-First Century. Roger Crisp too added his philosophical acumen and valuable insight into several chapters of the book, whilst Roger Stenger offered considerable support and comments on US law. I am grateful to colleagues at the University of Nottingham, most notably Alastair Mowbray, Robert McCorquodale and Stephen Bailey, for having taken the trouble to read several chapters and offered invaluable advice and support. I would also like to thank all those who commented on earlier versions of Chapters 5 and 6, which were delivered at the University of Sheffield and King's College London respectively.

My final thanks go to Claire Jennings for providing ever efficient and enthusiastic secretarial support, Helen Stevens for stepping in to help in the last stages of formatting and editing the manuscript and finally to the editors at Cavendish Publishing for their support and patience.

CONTENTS

TABLE OF CASES

INTRODUCTION

Medical research is needed in order to uncover the causes of ill health or to discover new ways of treating or alleviating pain or illness. In the last decades, however, the pace of scientific advances in the application of biotechnologies has forced a global and international revision of ethical and legal controls in biomedicine, particularly in the field of research involving human subjects.[1] In the fast developing field of research involving the application of new biotechnologies such as stem cell research or research on human tissue, the formulation of the applicable ethical and legal principles tends to lag behind the science. There is often a legal vacuum as policy makers strive to reach a consensus on the guiding principles of regulation.

This book analyses the evolution and changes in form and content of international instruments regulating the conduct of biomedical research from the Declaration of Helsinki to the Council of Europe's Convention on Human Rights & Biomedicine (CHRB) (Oviedo, 1997) and highlights some of the most difficult ethical and legal challenges posed by globalisation and the use of new biotechnologies in medical research in the 21st century. A central claim of the book is that the increasing globalisation of medical research is heightening the tension between the aspiration to universality of ethics driven regulation and the emerging reality of the diversity of moral cultures in democratic societies and the need to respect plurality and ethical diversity. I suggest that ethics driven regulation is limited both by the underdeterminacy of general ethical principles and by the weak legal effect of purely 'ethical' guidelines which have no direct legal force. In this light, a significant achievement of the CHRB[2] is to have shifted the focus of international debates on the protection of human subjects in research from the realm of ethics to the realm of legal enforceable human rights in biomedicine. The book thus systematically explores the strengths and weaknesses of the CHRB and its ability to deliver a legal framework which will safeguard the fundamental rights of the individual in some of the most controversial areas of biomedical research today.

Chapter 1 begins with an examination of the origins of modern bioethics and landmark international codes such as the Declaration of Helsinki (1964). The evolution of the Declaration of Helsinki is set against the global growth of the bioethics movement, its impact on public policy and the emergence of national and international bioethics committees. The limitations of ethics driven regulation as against human rights based regulation are discussed. The chapter draws on philosophical theories[3] to highlight the fundamental underdeterminacy of ethical principles, their logical compatibility with divergent moral theories and the consequent difficulties in ascertaining the scope of application of fundamental principles outside their 'core meaning'. I examine the extent to which legal principles suffer from similar difficulties and conclude with an overview of the CHRB. I argue that, in spite of some shared

---

1   See for instance Taylor, 1999.
2   On the history of the drafting of the Convention see Zilgalvis, 2001, pp 31–47. On the legal status and legal scope of the Convention see Plomer, 2001a, pp 313–30.
3   Particularly Wittgenstein, 1984.

weaknesses, the shift from ethics to human rights driven regulation represents a fundamental change which has the potential to provide greater, more certain and more effective protection for participants in medical research.

Chapter 2 illustrates the theoretical difficulties in ascertaining the determinate meaning and status of ethical and legal principles in the field of biomedical research. The drafters of the CHRB sought to identify universal principles which could bind all States, irrespective of their particular moral or political persuasion. Hence, they opted for general definitions and deferred the specification of key concepts to later protocols. They calculated that this would maximise the chances of avoiding outright divisions and of reaching a consensus on broad, overarching principles which would allow States which were reluctant to sign up to common European human rights law a wide margin of appreciation when implementing the Convention's provisions. However, in so doing, the drafters also opened themselves to the charge that the Convention would drive down ethical standards and would either be an empty text, devoid of substantive meaning, or a 'conceptual muddle' glossing over sharp ethical divisions. By comparing the principles contained in the CHRB with the principles identified a year earlier in the US by the Advisory Committee on Human Radiation Experiments (ACHRE),[4] it is possible to determine the extent to which the CHRB has the capacity to avoid these charges and realise its aspiration to universality.

Not all principles or fundamental rights contained in international codes or instruments admit of the same degree of indeterminacy or uncertainty regarding their meaning and/or scope of application. Indeed, the 'core' meaning of general principles may be well settled, notwithstanding varying degrees of indeterminacy on their boundaries. Chapter 3 focuses on the rules on 'consent' contained in the Convention, where arguably the 'core' meaning of the related underlying principle of respect for individual autonomy and bodily integrity is not indeterminate or in dispute, but where questions arise instead in respect of the degree of protection offered by the Convention. By comparing Convention principles with UK domestic law and Canadian and US jurisprudence on the protection of participants in non-therapeutic medical research, it is possible to determine whether the Convention offers a higher or lower level of protection. The analysis specifically focuses on the Porton Down experiments in the UK and compares the UK legal framework with the litigation surrounding the radiation experiments in the US. I highlight the weaknesses of the tort system as against judicial acknowledgment of the fundamental nature of the rights to autonomy and bodily integrity and their constitutional protection in the US. I conclude with an examination of the strengths and weaknesses of European human rights law.

---

4   Advisory Committee on Human Radiation Experiments, 1996.

Chapter 4 discusses the ethical and legal principles applicable to research on human embryos and illustrates the underdeterminacy of fundamental principles beyond their core meaning. Embryonic stem cell research is generating global controversy. Much of the debate so far has focused on the ethical legitimacy of such research and on the search for an ethical consensus. This chapter focuses instead on the extent to which ethical arguments about human dignity and the right to life translate into legal protection for the human embryo in human rights instruments, most notably the CHRB and the European Convention on Human Rights (ECHR) 1950. I review the interpretation and application of the right to life and human dignity specified in these instruments by Constitutional courts in Europe and analyse the US cases on 'custody' of frozen embryos. I suggest that both the ethical and legal concept of human dignity is underdetermined, and encompasses a plurality of ethical perspectives which are in turn compatible with a diversity of views on the right to life.

Could fundamental principles and rights on biomedical research which are normally attributed only to the living be extended to individuals who are no longer alive, but dead? Chapter 5 considers just such a question. The removal of body parts and organs from corpses of children without the parents' consent at the Bristol and Alder Hey hospitals in the UK has caused enormous grief and public concern.[5] The consensus emerging from the Scottish and England & Wales official enquiries was that the medical profession's (mal)practice may have been partly assisted by substantial lacunae and uncertainties in domestic law, now under revision through the adoption of a Human Tissue Bill currently going through Parliament. This in turn raises the question of the extent to which domestic law on the removal and use of body parts for research purposes was compliant with human rights law. This chapter reviews the scope of application of fundamental principles, such as bodily integrity and dignity, to persons who are no longer alive. The chapter begins with an examination of ethical perspectives on the moral status of dead bodies, and the normative implications of the profound cultural and moral schism which emerged from the Bristol and Alder Hey scandals between the medical establishment's perception of the human body and that of relatives and the rest of society. The weaknesses of the then existing domestic law are examined in this light. The chapter concludes with an exploration of how the ECHR could be extended to secure adequate

5   *Interim Report: Removal and Retention of Human Material,* May 2000, Bristol Royal Infirmary Inquiry; *Report of the Royal Liverpool Children's (Alder Hey) Inquiry,* January 2001, HC (Redfern Report); *The Removal, Retention and Use of Human Organs and Tissue from Post-mortem Examination,* Advice from the Chief Medical Officer, 2001; *Report of a Census of Organs and Tissue Retained by Pathology Services in England,* Advice from the Chief Medical Officer, 2001; *Report of Content Analysis of NHS Trust Policies and Protocols on Consent to Organ and Tissue Retention at Post-mortem Examination and Disposal of Human Materials in the Chief Medical Officer's Census of NHS Pathology Services,* 2000, all accessible on www.doh.gov.uk. For Scotland, see *Report of the Independent Review Group on the Retention of Organs at Post-mortem,* January 2001 (McLean Report).

legal protection of the dead whilst recognising the public interest and legitimacy of some forms of interference with and research on human corpses and body parts.

Chapter 6 reviews new international and regional ethical guidelines on research in developing countries and their compatibility with fundamental principles of human rights law. Developing countries are facing a humanitarian crisis of catastrophic proportions caused by the AIDS epidemic. The crisis has prompted the international community into a re-evaluation of the ability of established international guidelines such as the Declaration of Helsinki adequately to address issues of justice and exploitation in research. In 2000, the Declaration of Helsinki was revised following years of international controversy prompted by the failure of US researchers sponsored by the National Institutes of Health (NIH) to follow Helsinki guidelines on the use of placebo controls in developing countries in the zidovudine (AZT) trials. This chapter reviews and compares the 2000 revision of Helsinki with new ethical guidelines on research in developing countries developed by Council for International Organizations of Medical Sciences (CIOMS) and the options canvassed by the World Medical Association (WMA) in response to the continuing controversy over the text of the 2000 revision. The legal implications of the rift from Helsinki are evaluated and the compatibility of the new guidelines with human rights law as codified in the CHRB are considered. The chapter analyses the extent to which the new guidelines are consistent with the fundamental principle of international human rights law of respect for the equal dignity of all human beings and the prohibition on discrimination. The conclusion highlights the need to enhance procedures and widen access to courts, to enable participants in research whose rights have been breached to secure a remedy and to achieve transnational justice.

As this book goes to press, the Committee of Ministers of the Council of Europe has just adopted a new protocol to improve the protection of patients involved in biomedical research: Additional Protocol to the Convention on Human Rights & Biomedicine Concerning Biomedical Research, Strasbourg, 30 June 2004. To be effective, the Protocol has yet to be opened for signature and four member States have expressed their consent to be bound by the Protocol. The scope of the Protocol is limited and does not address some of the controversial questions/issues discussed in this book (for example, embryo research *in vitro* or research on human tissue removed from the dead). Where the expanded provisions on biomedical research contained in the Protocol add something new to the Convention on Human Rights and Biomedicine on the questions discussed in this book, for example, in the field of research in developing countries, these new provisions have been analysed in detail.

CHAPTER 1

FROM BIOETHICS TO HUMAN RIGHTS IN BIOMEDICINE

Landmark international codes on medical research, such as the Declaration of Helsinki (1964) and the growth of the modern bioethics movement, were prompted by the appalling abuse of human lives during the Holocaust.[1] In the last decade, however, it is the pace of scientific advances in the application of biotechnologies which has forced a global and international revision of ethical and legal controls in biomedicine, particularly in the field of research involving human subjects.[2] This chapter provides an overview and analysis of the evolution and changes in form and content of international instruments regulating the conduct of biomedical research from the Declaration of Helsinki to the Council of Europe's Convention on Human Rights & Biomedicine (CHRB) (Oviedo, 1997). The chapter begins with an analysis of the Declaration of Helsinki, its history, changes and controversy over its substantive norms and its limitations as regards legal enforcement. The evolution of the Declaration of Helsinki is set against the global growth of the bioethics movement, its impact on public policy and the emergence of national and international bioethics committees. A central claim of this chapter is that the increasing globalisation of medical research is highlighting the tension between the aspiration to universality of ethics driven regulation and the emerging reality of the diversity of moral cultures and the need to respect plurality and ethical diversity in democratic societies. I suggest that ethics driven regulation is limited both by its weak legal effect and by the underdeterminacy of general ethical principles and their potential compatibility with a diversity of moral values and theories. The chapter concludes with an overview of the CHRB and argues that the shift to human rights driven regulation represents a fundamental change in the form of regulation of biomedicine which has the potential to offer greater protection to human subjects.

1.1   THE ORIGINS OF INTERNATIONAL BIOETHICS

The origin of modern international bioethics has been traced to the brutal abuse of human lives in the Holocaust.[3] At the Nuremberg 'Doctors Trial' (1946–47) medical researchers were convicted of 'crimes against humanity' on the basis of 10 ethical principles which were said to be fundamental and universally applicable to all eras and cultures.[4] In the decade that followed, increasing efforts were made to formalise and codify a set of principles which would command international approval.

---

1   Annas and Grodin, 1992.
2   See, for instance, Taylor, 1999, pp 451–79.
3   Annas and Grodin, 1992.
4   See discussion in Annas and Grodin, 1992.

The World Medical Association (WMA) was founded in 1947 to represent physicians and to promote medical ethics and professional freedom worldwide. In 1948, the WMA issued the Declaration of Geneva,[5] the first international document stating the ethical duties of physicians to their patients. The Declaration consists of a Physician's Oath 'not to use my medical knowledge contrary to the laws of humanity' and an undertaking to 'practise my profession with conscience and dignity; the health of my patient will be my first consideration'. The Declaration of Geneva was followed in 1949 by the adoption of the first International Code of Medical Ethics.[6] The 1949 Code contains a brief statement of a doctor's duties, which include an obligation to ensure that 'any act or advice which could weaken physical or mental resistance of a human being may be used only in his interest', 'complete loyalty to the patient', 'absolute secrecy on all he knows about his patient' and a list of practices relating to conflicts of interest and monetary benefits which are deemed unethical. The International Code was amended twice in 1968 and last in 1983.[7] The most notable amendments are to the language, where categorical prescription 'a physician *shall*' replaces the original normative language of 'should' and 'ethical duties'. The 1983 revision of the Code also introduces a requirement that the rights of patients and colleagues shall be respected.[8] However, in terms of practical impact, it is the Declaration of Helsinki adopted by the WMA in 1964 which has had and continues to have the greatest influence on the international regulation of biomedical research.

1.1.1 The Declaration of Helsinki: content and evolution of norms

The Declaration of Helsinki was originally adopted in 1964. Like the earlier codes, it is intended 'as a statement of ethical principles to provide guidance' to physicians and others conducting medical research on human subjects. In terms of its content, the values evinced in the original Declaration look somewhat outdated today. For instance, an assumption of paternalistic benevolence is evident in the relaxed approached to informed consent adopted in the context of therapeutic research. Paragraph II.I states that: 'If at all possible, consistent with patient psychology, the doctor should obtain the patient's freely given consent after the patient has been given a full explanation.'[9]

---

5   The Declaration was adopted just three months before the UN General Assembly adopted the Universal Declaration on Human Rights (1948).

6   World Medical Association, 1949, pp 109, 111.

7   International Code of Medical Ethics, WMA. Adopted by the 3rd WMA General Assembly, London 1949 and amended by the 22nd WMA General Assembly, Sydney, Australia, 1968 and the 35th WMA General Assembly, Venice, Italy, 1983.

8   Also, the obligation to preserve human life from conception onwards is replaced by a weaker requirement to 'always *bear in mind* the obligation of preserving human life'.

9   Paragraph II.I also states that: 'In case of legal incapacity, consent should also be procured from the legal guardian; in case of physical incapacity the permission of the legal guardian replaces that of the patient.'

The Declaration has undergone five revisions since it was originally adopted in 1964.[10] The last two revisions (1996 and 2000) in particular have been the subject of fierce international disagreement from within and without the medical profession.[11]

The distinction between therapeutic and non-therapeutic research in the original 1964 version was declared to be 'fundamental'.[12] Section II(2) of the 1964 Declaration further added that: 'The doctor can combine clinical research with professional care, the objective being the acquisition of new medical knowledge, *only* to the extent that clinical research is justified by its therapeutic value for the patient' (emphasis added). However, the distinction between therapeutic and non-therapeutic research was removed in the 2000 version after a protracted debate and amidst concerns from critics that the removal of the distinction would lower the protection of research participants.[13] The terms 'therapeutic' and 'non-therapeutic' have been avoided in new human rights instruments such as the CHRB but, as will be seen, not the related conceptual and normative issues (see Chapter 2).

Controversy also continues to rage over the standards set by Helsinki in relation to the 'export' of clinical trials to underdeveloped countries by large pharmaceutical corporations in the fast increasing globalisation of medical research. An audit of external sponsoring of research in developing countries carried out by the US Food and Drug Administration (FDA) in 2001 showed a steep increase in the number of foreign researchers carrying out research in the decade 1990–2000. Numbers grew from 271 in 1990 to 4,458 in 1999. The FDA survey also reveals that the number of countries conducting research increased threefold from 28 to 79 in the same period, with the largest growth occurring in Latin America and Eastern European countries.[14] The controversy over Helsinki standards was prompted by the trials of the drug zidovudine (AZT) to prevent

---

10   WMA, *Declaration of Helsinki* adopted by the 18th WMA General Assembly, Helsinki, Finland, June 1964 and amended by: the 29th WMA General Assembly, Tokyo, Japan, October 1975; the 35th WMA General Assembly, Venice, Italy, October 1983; the 41st WMA General Assembly, Hong Kong, September 1989; the 48th WMA General Assembly, Somerset West, Republic of South Africa, October 1996; and the 52nd WMA General Assembly, Edinburgh, Scotland, October 2000. A Note of Clarification on para 29 was added by the WMA General Assembly, Washington 2002.

11   Macklin, 2001; Roman, 2002; Bland, 2002; Rosenau, 2000; Levine, 1999; Todres, 2000; Nicholson and Crawley, 1999; Forster, Emanuel and Grady, 2001; Schuklenk and Ashcroft, 2000; Wendler, 2001; de Zulueta, 2001; Singer and Benatar, 2001.

12   'In the field of medical research a distinction must be recognised between clinical research in which the aim is essentially therapeutic for a patient and the clinical research, the essential object of which is purely scientific and without therapeutic value to the person subjected to the research' (*Declaration of Helsinki*, 1964).

13   McGinn, 2001; Vastag, 2000; McGinn, 2000.

14   DHHS Office of Inspector General, 2001. The significance of these figures is discussed in the Nuffield Council on Bioethics' Report, *The Ethics of Research Related to Healthcare in Developing Countries*, 2001, p 23.

mother to child transmission of HIV. The trials were conducted in Africa under the aegis of the Joint United Nations Programme on HIV/AIDS (UNAIDS) and the World Health Organization (WHO). Previous trials had already established that long courses of the drug reduced transmission of the virus, but the cost of the drug was outside the reach of local populations. The new trials were designed to test the efficacy of shorter and more affordable courses. The shorter courses of zidovudine were tested against a placebo instead of the 'best proven treatment' which could not be afforded locally. A furious exchange took place through the pages of the *New England Journal of Medicine*, following allegations in an editorial that the trials were unethical and exploited populations who were already vulnerable.[15] The dispute centred on the question of whether the standards set in the Declaration are universal or whether they should be adjusted to reflect local circumstances, particularly socio-economic constraints affecting developing countries lacking the health resources available to the industrialised world.[16]

The strength of the language used on both sides and accusations by developing countries that it is 'ethical imperialism' for outsiders to dictate what sort of research is ethical or unethical[17] have raised questions not only about the universality of Helsinki principles but about the ability of the WMA genuinely to represent an international spectrum of opinion and to achieve the broad consensus required to legitimate its authority.

In addition to the controversies surrounding the relative or universal status of Helsinki norms, increasing concerns have been voiced about the process through which revisions of the Declaration are adopted by the WMA. Both the content of the 1996 revision and the process by which the revisions were made were challenged by the American Medical Association (AMA) which produced its own alternative draft within a year. The WMA rejected the AMA's draft and produced a new draft which was issued for worldwide public consultation for the first time ever in response to criticisms about the WMA's lack of accountability.[18] In an international climate where globalisation has prompted concerns about democratic accountability, the authority of the WMA will inevitably become increasingly dependent on its ability to satisfy concerns about public scrutiny and accountability.

---

15 Angell, 1997; Lurie and Wolfe, 1997. See also Schuklenk, 1998; Schuklenk and Ashcroft, 2000; Crouch and Arras, 1998; Glantz, Annas, Grodin and Mariner, 1998. An editorial critical of the 'ethics industry' also appeared in *The Lancet* 350:897.

16 Levine, 1998; Levine, 1999; Brennan, 1999.

17 For instance, Ruth Macklin reports that the chairman of the AIDS research committee in Uganda wrote a letter to the US National Institutes for Health defending the placebo-controlled trials and stating that 'It is a wrong assumption that we do not have the vision to deal with such issues' (letter from Edward K Mbidde to director of NIH, 8 May 1997). Cited in Macklin, 2001. The expression 'ethical imperialism' had appeared a decade earlier in an editorial of the *New England Journal of Medicine* (Angell, 1988), defending the universality of the concept of informed consent.

18 WMA, 2000.

1.1.2 Helsinki's legal status

From a purely legal perspective, the authority of the Declaration is weak and limited. As the language of the Declaration itself makes clear, it is a statement of professional *ethical* principles or ideals issued by members of the medical profession to other members of the medical profession. The preamble to the original Declaration (1964) stressed that: '... the standards as drafted are *only a guide* to physicians all over the world. Doctors are not relieved from criminal, civil and ethical responsibilities under the laws of their own countries' (emphasis added).

The practical contribution of the Declaration of Helsinki lies primarily in the influence that it can carry in the area of professional self-regulation in the elaboration of professional codes of practice or alternatively in the drafting of legal instruments which endorse its principles.[19] The Declaration of Helsinki has often been traced as a core influence on the development of many international and national codes governing research on human subjects,[20] but where the Declaration has been invoked in legal proceedings, a close analysis of the court rulings reveals that the legal force of the Helsinki Declaration is severely limited by local procedural and substantive rules of law.

The Declaration has been invoked in a series of cases heard by US courts, where it has been cited along with the International Covenant on Civil and Political Rights (ICCPR) as a guide to international legal principles on the conduct of medical experiments.[21]

For instance, in the *Pfizer* case,[22] a claim relying on international law in the US courts had to be founded on an alleged breach of a domestic statute – 'The Aliens Tort Claims Act' – in addition to other general rules contained in s 404 of the US Restatement (Third) prescribing the conditions under which claims for breach of international law can be brought by an individual against another private party or the State.[23] The pharmaceutical company Pfizer was alleged by the claimants to have embarked on a medical experiment involving the new and untested antibiotic Trovan which resulted in the deaths of 11 children and caused serious injury to other children including paralysis, deafness and blindness. The children

---

19 Eg, Codes of practice incorporating the Declaration, CIOMS guidelines, Clinical Trials Directive (2001), etc.

20 Annas and Grodin, 1992.

21 *Abdullahi v Pfizer Inc*, 2002 WL 31082956 (SDNY, 17 September 2002) (NO 01 CIV 8118), *Robertson ex rel Robertson v McGee*, 2002 WL 535045 (ND Okla, 28 January 2002) (NO 01CV60), *Grimes v Kennedy Krieger Institute Inc*, 366 Md 29, 782 A 2d 807 (Md, 16 August 2001) (NO 128 SEPT TERM 2000, 129 SEPT TERM 2000), *Johnson v Arthur*, 65 Ark App 220, 986 SW 2d 874 (Ark App, 3 March 1999) (NO CA98-660, CA98-661), *Whitlock v Duke University*, 637 F Supp 1463, 33 Ed Law Rep 1082 (MDNC, 16 June 1986) (NO C-84-149-D), *Pierce v Ortho Pharmaceutical Corp*, 84 NJ 58, 417 A 2d 505, 115 LRRM (BNA) 3044, 12 ALR 4th 520, 101 Lab Cas P 55,477, 1 IER Cases 109 (NJ, 28 July 1980).

22 *Abdullahi v Pfizer Inc*, 2002 WL 31082956 (SDNY, 17 September 2002) (NO 01 CIV 8118).

23 As far as the substance of the claimant's claim was concerned and the legal status of Helsinki in particular, the NY District Court accepted that international Treaties or 'non-self executing agreements' such as the ICCPR evidenced principles of international law (II.4).

selected were aged between one and 13 and exhibited symptoms of meningitis. Pfizer treated half the children with Trovan. The other half was treated with ceftriaxone, an FDA approved drug shown to be effective in treating meningitis but allegedly 'purposely low dosed' to enhance the comparative results of Trovan. Parents were not informed that the treatment was experimental, or that other organisations offered conventional treatment free of charge.[24] The claimants alleged that FDA approval for the export of Trovan had been circumvented by Pfizer and only sought retrospectively through the Nigerian government which had allegedly acted in concert with Pfizer and falsified FDA documents in order to gain approval for the sale and marketing of the drug to the US consumers.

The New York (NY) District Court found that while claimants need not rely on the ICCPR to provide a private right of action, they may look to that Treaty to allege that Pfizer's conduct violated 'well-established, universally recognised norms of established international law'.[25] Although the Declaration of Helsinki lacks the status of a Treaty since it is not an agreement between States, the court accepted that it too could be invoked as evidence of well-established principles of international law. The court held that, as a private actor, Pfizer could be liable for breach of international law. However, breaches of international law committed by private actors must be of 'universal concern'. The NY District Court then relied on the disturbing finding of several US courts that torture, summary execution, genocide and religious and racial discrimination did not satisfy the 'universal concern' criterion.[26] The NY Court found that, by comparison, Pfizer's alleged conduct, however reprehensible, fell short of constituting a s 404 violation of 'universal concern'. Hence, the claimants' claim for breach of international law against Pfizer – as a private actor – failed. However, the Court accepted the claimant's alternative claim that the breach had been committed by a 'State actor'[27] because the Nigerian government had acted in concert with Pfizer by providing a letter of request to the FDA to authorise the export of Trovan, arranging for Pfizer's accommodation in the area of the epidemic, assigning Nigerian physicians to work with Pfizer and backdating an 'approval letter' that international protocol required to be ascertained prior to the tests, and acting to silence the Nigerian physicians critical of the company's test (III.6). However, the claimant's claim in the US courts ultimately failed on the basis of *forum non conveniens* as the NY District Court held that the Nigerian courts were a preferable forum in which to adjudicate the claim, notwithstanding the claimant's allegations of judicial and official corruption in Nigeria, a claim backed up by a UN report. After the claimant's case was adjourned 14 times in the Nigerian courts,[28] the US Court of Appeals for the Second Circuit vacated the 2002 NY District Court

---

24 Eg, Médecins sans Frontières (MSF) were treating children with chloramphenicol, a drug recommended by the WHO to treat bacterial meningitis in epidemic situations.

25 At II.4.

26 See for instance *Bigio v Coca-Cola Co* 239 F 3d 440, 451–53 (2d Cir 2000).

27 'When the relationship between the State and private actor is so close, so that the action of the (private actor) may be fairly treated as that of the State itself.'

28 Nigeria's Kano Federal High Court: *Zango & Others v Pfizer* (FHC/K/CS/204/2001).

decision on the motion to dismiss and remanded the matter to the District Court to determine whether it was corruption or delay of the sort alleged by the claimants that precipitated the dismissal or withdrawal of the Nigerian action, and to evaluate whether this impacted on the District Court's analysis of the proper forum.[29]

Pfizer thus illustrates the limitations of the Declaration of Helsinki as regards legal status and enforcement. Even when the principles contained in the Declaration are given judicial recognition in domestic courts, the *Pfizer* ruling shows that gross breaches of Helsinki principles and (international) standards are not by themselves sufficient to found liability when the breach is committed by corporations or companies in a private legal capacity because of the difficulties in satisfying the very high standard required to show that the conduct is of 'universal concern'. Neither can a remedy be readily obtained in the unlikely circumstance where there is sufficient evidence of collusion between the State and the corporation, as the claimants still have to be granted access to a domestic court where their claim can at least stand a reasonable chance of being impartially heard. Hence, from a strictly legal perspective, the Declaration offers limited assistance and protection to individuals and patients who have suffered at the hands of members of the medical profession who have acted in breach of its principles.[30]

More generally, the Declaration of Helsinki, like other ethical codes and forms of 'soft law', suffers from the absence of procedures for enforcement and penalties for breach. From the perspective of those who have been the victims of a breach of the Declaration's rules, Helsinki is an important but weak source. It may provide a point of reference or guidance for domestic courts which have jurisdiction over the claims complained of, but it lacks 'direct' legal authority and weight.

1.2   THE GROWTH OF BIOETHICS AND 'PRINCIPLE' DRIVEN REGULATION

The principles and 'medical ethics' ethos which permeate the original Declaration of Helsinki are symptomatic of the language and culture of the post-Second World War era, which saw the growth of a movement to 'humanise' medical education and practice in the West.[31] In the 1960s, the ideal of the 'humanistically responsive' physician led to the development of medical ethics programmes across medical

---

29   *Abdullahi v Pfizer Inc* [2003] (02-9223) (2d Cir 8 October 2003).

30   For an excellent analysis of the considerable substantive and procedural hurdles facing claimants on transnational access to justice see Ford and Tomossy, 2004. See also Fidler, 2001; Orlowski, 2003.

31   Pellegrino, 1999. See also Jonsen, 1998; Rothman, 1991. More generally, see Lovejoy, 1961; Jonsen, 1998.

schools in the US.[32] The intellectual elaboration of the core concepts and principles of the medical ethics, or bioethics movement as it was to become known, began in the next decade when the pace of advance of clinical medicine and new technologies forced a challenge of the old benevolent paternalistic ethics.[33]

In the US, the exposure of the abuses conducted in the experiments on the Tuskegee refugees was a turning point in prompting the establishment in 1974 of the National Commission for the Protection of Human Subjects.[34] The Commission produced the Belmont Report (1979) which identified a set of key ethical principles which should underpin all experimentation on human subjects. The 'principlism' implicit in the report was developed into a moral theory by Tom Beauchamp and James Childress in their seminal book *Principles of Biomedical Ethics*.[35] Their theory is deceptively simple and attractive. They claim that it is possible to identify a core set of fundamental principles which can gain assent irrespective of the theoretical perspectives of the parties. The principles are non-maleficence, beneficence, autonomy and justice. Beauchamp and Childress contend that the principles represent a mid-level point of convergence around which a consensus can be found between otherwise disparate theories such as virtue theory and utilitarianism.

The attraction of the theory lies in its alleged capacity to produce convergence and consensus around a core set of fundamental principles or values. The aspiration to bring about convergence and consensus in turn explains the spectacular success of the theory in shaping public debate and public policy on biomedical research not only in the US but across the world with the creation of national bioethics committees or multidisciplinary expert bodies, with an advisory function on bioethical matters.

1.2.1 The role of principles in bioethics committees

The creation of national bioethics committees began in technologically advanced countries in Europe, the US and Australia during the 1990s.[36] In Europe, there are

---

32 Eg, the Institute on Human Values in Medicine (IHVM), whose focus was the development of teachers and teaching programmes under the broad rubrics of Humanities, Human Values, and Medical Ethics. Over the decade which followed the creation of the IHVM, the Institute offered advice, consultation and training to 77 medical schools. See Pellegrino, 1999.

33 Jonsen, 1998; Rothman, 1991.

34 For a concise account of the history of regulation of medical research in the US, see ACHRE, 1996.

35 Beauchamp and Childress, 1979.

36 In the Netherlands, the Standing Committee on Medical Ethics was set up in 1977 and has since 1983 been designated as the Standing Committee on Medical Ethics and Health Law. It is part of the Health Council of the Netherlands (www.gr.nl). It consists of experts in the fields of medicine, medical ethics and health law. In Belgium Le Comité Consultatif de Bioethique was created by law in 1995 (www.health.fgov.be/bioeth/fr/presentation/composition-mission-fonctionnement.htm). Other national bioethics committees have similarly been created in the past decade in Greece (www.bioethics.gr/index.php), Italy (www.palazzochigi.it/bioetica), Portugal (www.cnecv.gov.pt), Spain (www.comiteetica.org) and Sweden (www.smer.gov.se). In Australia, the Australia Health and Ethics Committee (www.health.gov.au/nhmrc/issues/index.htm) was established in 1992.

currently more than 10 national bioethics committees which meet on a yearly basis under the umbrella of the European Conference of National Ethics Committees (ECNEC). The ECNEC was created in 1999 to promote co-operation between national bioethics committees and promote public debate on a pluralistic basis.[37] Most national bioethics committees across the world have been created either by executive decree/order or on a legislative basis with an advisory function to the executive. The members of the committees are usually experts appointed by the executive and drawn from a range of disciplines. For instance, the French Consultative Ethics Committee for Health and Life Sciences[38] was established by presidential decree in February 1983 but given a legislative basis in 1994[39] with a mission to 'give opinions on ethical problems raised by progress in the fields of biology, medicine and health, and to publish recommendations on this subject' (Art 23).[40]

The search for consensus around ethical principles is often perceived as central to the work of these committees. Sometimes the committee is explicitly mandated in the mission statements to identify ethical principles. For instance, the US National Bioethics Advisory Commission which was established by President Clinton in 1995[41] to provide advice to the government on bioethical issues arising from research on human biology is expressly mandated in s 4(c) of the executive order through which it was created: 'to identify broad principles to govern the ethical conduct of research, citing specific projects only as illustrations for such principles.'

Similarly, in Finland the National Advisory Board on Health Care Ethics (ETENE)[42] was created in 1998[43] with a mission statement expressly requiring it 'deal with ethical issues related to health care and the status and rights of patients *from the point of view of principle*' (emphasis added).

However, even when the committee is not expressly mandated to find a consensus around principles, the influence of 'principlism' in bioethical thinking and culture has been such that the reports or recommendations issued by national bioethics committees are often framed in terms of ethical principles. For instance, in the UK, the reports of the independent Nuffield Council on Bioethics[44] typically

---

37 Articles 2(a) and 2(b) of Resolution 1 of the European Conference of National Ethics Committees (COMETH), February 1999: www.legal.coe.int/bioethics/gb/pdf/resol_cometh.pdf. The conference has met six times since its creation: www.coe.int/T/E/Legal_Affairs/Legal_co-operation/Bioethics/COMETH/Presentation.asp.

38 www.ccne-ethique.fr/english/start.htm.

39 Law No 94-654 of 29 July 1994.

40 Similarly, in Germany, the National Ethics council was created by executive decree in April 2001 to provide a forum for dialogue and express views on ethical issues in the life sciences (Arts 1 and 2): www.ethikrat.org/_english/about_us/decree.html.

41 Executive Order 12975 of 3 October 1995: see www.georgetown.edu/research/nrcbl/nbac/general.html for general information.

42 www.etene.org/e/index.shtml.

43 Under the Act on the Status and Rights of Patients (785/1992, amendment 333/1998).

44 The Nuffield Council is an independent organisation, partly funded by the UK Medical Research Council. It was created which in 1991 to consider the ethical issues arising in medicine and biology: www.nuffieldbioethics.org.

rely on the identification of fundamental ethical principles which are used to 'evaluate the actions of individuals and bodies such as companies, non-governmental organisations (NGOs), international organisations and agencies'.[45] Their report, *The Ethics of Research Related to Healthcare in Developing Countries*, identifies four principles or duties: alleviation of suffering, respect for persons, sensitivity to cultural differences and non-exploitation of the vulnerable (2001, p 133).

Other supranational, regional and international initiatives include the creation of the European Group on Ethics in Science and New Technologies (EGE)[46] and UNESCO's International Bioethics Committee (IBC). The EGE was created under the Directive on Biotechnological Inventions adopted by the European Union in 1998. The function of the EGE is to advise the President of the European Commission on ethical issues arising from the application of new biotechnologies.[47] Since its inception, the EGE has issued a series of opinions or reports on controversial issues such as stem cell patents[48] and research in developing countries. Although not expressly mandated to do so in its opinions, the EGE has expressed adherence to a set of 'fundamental ethical principles' which include: the principle of respect for human dignity, the principle of individual autonomy, the principle of justice, the principle of beneficence and non-maleficence and the principle of proportionality.[49]

However, the uniformity of adoption of an ethical 'principled' approach in the search for convergence and agreement implicitly relies on the possibility of disengaging the principles from their theoretical foundations, as is sometimes explicitly acknowledged in the reports themselves:

> We do not present these principles as part of a more general ethical theory. This does not mean that the principles are drawn from nowhere: they are widely discussed in works on ethics and political theory. [Nuffield Bioethics Council, 2001, pp 49–50]

Whether such disengagement from background moral frameworks and theories is possible in reality is becoming increasingly doubtful in the light of the diversity of cultures and moral perspectives in pluralist democratic societies and against the fast increasing globalisation of biomedical practice (see below).

1.2.2 Philosophical and political limits

Principles are by their very nature general in their formulation. Agreement may well exist about the 'core' meaning of a principle, but the boundaries of the

---

45 Nuffield Council on Bioethics, 2001, p 49. The reports may be accessed on www.nuffieldbioethics.org.

46 http://europa.eu.int/comm/european_group_ethics/index_en.htm.

47 *Ibid*.

48 See, for instance, Opinion No 16, *Ethical Aspects of Patenting Inventions Involving Human Stem Cells* (7 May 2002) and Opinion No 17, *Ethical Aspects of Clinical Research in Developing Countries* (4 February 2003), available at http://europa.eu.int/comm/european_group_ethics/avis3_en.htm.

49 See Opinion No 17, *Ethical Aspects of Clinical Research in Developing Countries* (4 February 2003), p 12.

principle will usually be uncertain. Indeterminacy and openness normally characterise the meaning and application of a principle at its boundaries.[50] A general ethical principle such as the principle of non-maleficence can admit of an agreed determinate interpretation of its 'core' meaning without this indicating any agreement over its boundaries. For instance, there is undoubted agreement that the principle prohibits the deliberate inflection of cruelty and torture on persons and therefore rules out the kind of experimentation conducted on human beings by the Nazis in concentration camps. But does the principle also prohibit experimentation or even the destruction of frozen human embryos? Pro-life supporters clearly believe that it does. According to the professor of genetics who appeared as an expert witness in *Davis v Davis*, the frozen embryos which were the subject of a custody dispute between the divorced parents were 'tiny human beings' which ought to be freed from their 'concentration cans'.[51] By contrast, a minority of members of the President's Council on Bioethics set up by President Bush to advise on stem cell research took the view that the human embryo has no special moral status and 'should be treated essentially like all other human cells'.[52] The Executive Summary noted that: 'The Council reflecting the differences of opinion in American society is divided regarding the ethics of research involving (cloned) embryos.' The outcome of the report was a call for a four-year moratorium on embryonic stem cell research justified on the grounds that:

> It calls for and provides time for further democratic deliberation about cloning for biomedical research, a subject about which the nation is divided and where there remains great uncertainty. A national discourse on this subject has not yet taken place in full, and a moratorium, by making it impossible for either side to cling to the status quo, would force both to make their full case before the public. By banning all cloning for a time, it allows us to seek moral consensus on whether or not we should cross a major moral boundary (creating nascent cloned human life solely for research) and prevents our crossing it without deliberate decision.[53]

Similar difficulties regarding interpretation, meaning and scope of key concepts arise in relation to all the other bioethical principles usually invoked. What the principle of beneficence requires could be strikingly different depending on the background moral framework to which one is committed. As 'principlists' themselves acknowledge, even convergence on the core meaning of principle need not connote agreement about its theoretical basis and application in disputed contexts. For a utilitarian, beneficence may well require individuals to be compelled to sacrifice their own good for the good of others and be entered into research programmes either by deception or against their will, for example, the radiation experiments secretly conducted in the US and publicly uncovered in the

50   The view I am defending here derives from Wittgenstein, 1984. For an application of Wittgenstein's view to a political context see Waldron, 1999.

51   *Davis v Davis*, 842 SW 2d 588 Tenn 1992.

52   *Human Cloning and Human Dignity: An Ethical Inquiry*, 2002.

53   *Ibid*, Executive Summary.

ACHRE report.[54] By contrast, it is not even clear that Kantian theory recognises a moral *obligation* to act for the good of others as against a less demanding moral obligation not to cause harm (Kantian theory arguably construes acts of beneficence as morally commendable rather than obligatory). The principle of respect for human dignity, which figures so prominently in modern bioethics thinking, is essentially underdetermined,[55] as is the principle of justice and its application in global contexts where there is inequality of wealth and resources, vulnerability and the potential for exploitation, as the AIDS epidemic in Africa has made clear.[56]

Principles may have a fairly determinate and undisputed meaning in core areas, but the precise interpretation and scope of application of the principles at the boundaries or in disputed contexts may be indeterminate and uncertain, particularly when the principle is divorced from its theoretical origins. When the theoretical background justifying the principle is made explicit, controversies regarding the interpretation and scope of application of ethical principles may not admit of a logical resolution because background moral theoretical frameworks are typically founded on different and incommensurable assumptions regarding basic moral goods or values.[57] The interpretation and application of the principle may also depend on underlying political aspirations and ideals. Where the overarching political ideal is social solidarity and communitarianism,[58] the ethical principles of justice and beneficence will yield different practical imperatives from liberalism. Thus the role of ethical principles in policy formation may well be considerably more limited than some of the mission statements or reports from bioethics committees imply, particularly in their ability to reflect real consensus and agreement.

Hence, the danger with recourse to fundamental ethical principles in bioethical policy is that it can create an illusion of consensus and at its worst act as a poor substitute for democratic procedures and processes to find agreement and practical compromises between different moral cultures in pluralist societies. In liberal democracies, the search for ethical agreement must ultimately be congruent with respect for a plurality of moral perspectives. Where there exist profound and real differences in moral cultures about, for instance, the value of human life at the beginning and the end, so called fundamental ethical principles cannot magically dispel ethical differences.

The identification of and reliance on fundamental ethical principles by bioethics committees cannot ultimately displace the need for resolution of moral differences in pluralist societies through democratic procedures and processes.[59]

---

54 See Chapter 2 discussing the role of principles in recommendations on human radiation experiments in the US.
55 See Chapters 4 and 5.
56 See Gostin and Lazzarini, 1998; Kahn, Mastroianni and Sugarman, 1998.
57 Contrast Aristotle, 1954; Kant, 1984; and Mill, 1984.
58 Contrast Jonas, 1984; Rawls, 1972; Ter Meulen, Arts and Muffels, 2001.
59 See Waldron, 1999.

Indeed, regulation by means of ethical principles, particularly those elaborated and adopted by a profession in a code of practice, potentially suffers from a democratic deficit. The ethical principles elaborated and adopted by a profession or a group of non-elected members may have little democratic legitimacy and their elaboration or implementation will not usually afford much opportunity for public scrutiny and accountability. Consequently, the ethical norms or principles adopted may fail adequately to represent and protect the interests of all affected parties.[60]

1.2.3 New directions for bioethics committees

The tension between the search for fundamental ethical principles in policy formation on biomedical research and the need to respect the plurality and diversity of moral perspectives in liberal societies is becoming increasingly evident. In the US, the National Bioethics Advisory Committee (NBAC) appointed by President Clinton did not have its charter renewed by President Bush when it ran out in 2001. Instead, the NABC was replaced by the President's Council on Bioethics,[61] a body with a wider mission including advisory functions relating to bioethical issues.[62] Unlike its predecessor, the new Council is not mandated to identify guiding principles. Instead, the Executive Order provides that:

> The Council shall strive to develop a deep and comprehensive understanding of the issues that it considers. In pursuit of this goal, the Council shall be guided by the need to articulate fully the complex and often competing moral positions on any given issue, *rather than by an overriding concern to find consensus*. The Council may therefore choose to proceed by offering a variety of views on a particular issue, rather than attempt to reach a single consensus position. [at 4(c), emphasis added]

In Europe, after two reports from the EGE voicing qualified support for embryonic stem cell research within a limiting principled framework, the Commission is now acknowledging that the differences between those opposed to research and those in favour may be irreconcilable and that the funding policy of the European Union will ultimately have to comply with principles of subsidiarity and the need to respect the plurality of moral perspectives (see Chapter 4).

The evolution of the IBC points to similar difficulties in reconciling the search for universal principles with respect for pluralism and difference in ethics and bioethics. The IBC was created in September 1993 and established as a permanent committee of UNESCO in 1998[63] following the adoption of the Universal

---

60 For a defence of bioethics committees see Friele, 2003. For a wider discussion, see Held, 1996.
61 www.bioethics.gov/reports/executive.html.
62 Specifically, s 2(a) of Executive Order 13237 provides that the Council is mandated: (a) to undertake fundamental inquiry into the human and moral significance of developments in biomedical and behavioral science and technology; (b) to explore specific ethical and policy questions related to these developments; (c) to provide a forum for a national discussion of bioethical issues; (d) to facilitate a greater understanding of bioethical issues; and (e) to explore possibilities for useful international collaboration on bioethical issues.
63 UNESCO, 1998. See Kutukdjian, 1999.

Declaration on the Human Genome and Human Rights in 1997. It has 36 members from a distinguished multidisciplinary background who are appointed by UNESCO's Director-General for a four-year term. Its reports have focused mainly on genetic testing and screening, gene therapy, genetic counselling, neurosciences and population genetics. Its mission is 'to promote reflection on the ethical and legal issues raised by research in the life sciences and their applications'[64] and to contribute to the dissemination of the principles contained in the Declaration.[65] The IBC is also mandated to co-operate with international governmental and non-governmental organisations concerned with issues in bioethics.[66]

Having celebrated its 10th anniversary in May 2003, the IBC has begun to signal the challenge to bioethics posed by globalisation and multiculturalism. The IBC's current chairperson, Michèle Jean (from Canada) said:

> Although the IBC is like all ethical committees in being independent and pluridisciplinary, it differs in that ethics cannot be viewed in the same way at an international level as it is at the national or regional level. For example, the way in which different cultures see the beginning of life and the status attributed to the embryo, influence the direction and different lines of thinking that will be developed [...]. The challenge for such a committee resides in the need to balance the quest for a consensus that will advance the recognition of a common core of human values and the sensitivity that is required to understand the limits of a consensus that must respect diversity, without tipping over into cultural relativism.[67]

The chair of the IBC illustrated the approach of the Committee in a contested area where a consensus proved impossible. The report on *The Use of Embryonic Stem Cells in Therapeutic Research* (2001) 'did not take sides but provided the necessary clarifications – by outlining the different ethical arguments and listing ethically acceptable forms of research according to various points of view – to national authorities seeking to legislate in this domain'.[68]

1.3   ETHICAL v LEGAL REGULATION

The International Bioethics Committee has produced a draft report on the possibility of elaborating a Universal Instrument on Bioethics 'to contribute and support international efforts being made to provide ethical guidelines in matters related to recent scientific developments'.[69] The report gives a qualified support to the elaboration of an international instrument in the light of potential difficulties regarding its geographical and temporal application: 'when we try to elaborate

---

64   UNESCO, 1998, Art 2.1(a).
65   *Ibid*, Art 2.1(d)(i).
66   *Ibid*, Art 2.1(c).
67   UNESCO, 2003.
68   UNESCO, 2001.
69   Report of the IBC on the Possibility of Elaborating a Universal Instrument on Bioethics, 13 June 2003, Paris: IBC.

universal ethical principles we have to recognise the existence of many different ethics in general and bioethics in particular.'[70] The report suggests that use of the term 'universal' should be avoided because the extraordinary and rapid development of science and technology would in any event require the instrument to be revised at regular intervals. The report also draws a distinction between moral rules and legal rules and expresses a preference for an international instrument which would fall into the former category. The instrument should be a declaration (a statement of moral ideals) rather than a treaty (a legally enforceable instrument) to facilitate 'the broadest possible acceptance'. Other factors also include philosophical considerations on the nature of moral and legal rules and an underlying preference for liberal values and the primacy of individual autonomy:

> Moral and legal rules correspond to two distinct but interconnected orientations. Moral rules which are set in a cultural, philosophical and religious background of the various human communities, can develop by enrichment and consensus and thus contribute to common universal values. Legal rules cannot pretend to encompass all fields and cases of bioethics nor to judge or interfere in every moment of the lives and individual choices of persons. At any level, laws accompanied by effective control should be adopted in order to facilitate personal choices, and only a few substantial issues should be regulated through international rules. In other words, the aim should be to maximise moral evolution and to minimise the need for legislation. [para 40]

Undoubtedly legal *rules* do not as commonly understood have the same breadth of scope as legal *principles*.[71] Arguably, however, the limitation arises from their being rules rather than *legal* rules.[72] Like ethical principles, fundamental legal principles including those contained in international legal instruments such as the UN Declaration on Human Rights, share an aspiration to universality which is reflected in agreement over the 'core' or central meaning of the principles.[73] Like ethical principles, legal principles might admit of a variety of interpretations over issues beyond their 'core' meaning. However, unlike ethical principles, legal principles enshrined in local or international bills of rights or treaties are a form of 'negotiated moral order', the product of political negotiation and compromise between political actors and States which undertake to be legally bound by the texts. Hence, where there is a plurality of norms in morally contested areas, the wording of the legal instrument has to be sufficiently open-ended to both capture an agreed general value and allow for judicial interpretation to accommodate a plurality of moral (or legal) perspectives. A good example of textual openness is the use of the words 'all' or 'everyone' in treaties such as the European Convention on Human Rights (ECHR) or the CHRB, which deliberately refrained from specifying who could be the subject of rights.[74] Other legal devices include the use of derogation or qualifications of the specified rights allowing a margin of appreciation to signatories as to the scope of application of the right in question (for example, Art 8, right to family life, of the ECHR).

---

70   *Ibid*, para 39.
71   See Hart, 1994; Dworkin, 1986.
72   See Sunstein, 1966.
73   See Henkin, 1990.
74   See Chapter 4.

1.4   THE IMPORTANCE OF HUMAN RIGHTS

Fundamental ethical and legal principles both carry the potential for indeterminacy and controversy over their scope of application. In the case of legal principles, however, the controversy admits of a resolution through a legal forum such as a court, which is itself bound to follow agreed procedures and canons of interpretation. The outcome is legally binding on the parties and the court has the power to order remedies to be awarded to applicants whose rights have been breached. The adoption of a human rights instrument in an area where the prevailing mode of regulation had hitherto been ethics driven self-regulation or soft regulation is therefore a highly significant development. It marks the introduction of an external set of standards and procedures by which the biomedical profession's own standards may be judged, against which it may be held legally accountable by victims seeking redress. Because of their historical origins in 17th and 18th century resistance to religious and political oppression, human rights instruments have also focused traditionally on the protection of the individual against abuse and oppression.[75] Human rights instruments thus carry the potential to offer enhanced protection against professional abuse because they have traditionally been concerned with the protection of individual rights.

1.4.1   The Convention on Human Rights & Biomedicine (CHRB)

The Council of Europe's CHRB[76] is an important step towards European and international harmonisation of norms in the field of biomedicine. The Convention's aspiration to capture fundamental and universal values is clear from the preamble's resolve 'to take such measures as are necessary to safeguard human dignity and the fundamental rights and freedoms of the individual with regard to the application of biology and medicine'. The aspiration has to be reconciled with the reality of diversity of forms and norms of regulation of medical research across Europe and the rest of the world.[77]

The Convention begins with an acknowledgment of other international Treaties, including the UN's Universal Declaration of Human Rights (1948), the European Convention for the Protection of Human Rights and Fundamental Freedoms (ECHR) (1950), the European Social Charter (1961), the International Covenant on Civil and Political Rights (1966), the Convention for the Protection of Individuals with regard to Automatic Processing of Personal Data (1981) and the Convention on the Rights of the Child (1989). The preamble further adds the need to protect human dignity (mentioned three times) and safeguard the human individual and the human species from the 'misuse of biology' whilst ensuring that present and future generations enjoy the benefit of progress in biology and medicine. The purpose of the CHRB is as stated in Chapter I, Art 1:

---

75   Hobbes, 1988; Locke, 1975.
76   On the history of the drafting of the Convention see Zilgalvis, 2001.
77   See Sprumont, 1999, pp 25–43; Plomer, 2000a, pp 1–24.

Parties to this Convention shall protect the dignity and identity of all human beings and guarantee everyone, without discrimination, respect for their integrity and other rights and fundamental freedoms with regard to the application of biology and medicine.

Other general provisions in Chapter I include the primacy of the human being. The Convention expressly endorses the principle that the interests and welfare of the human being shall prevail over the sole interest of society or science (Art 2). Equality of access to health care is a separate requirement under Art 3 and is defined as follows: 'Parties, taking into account health needs and available resources, shall take appropriate measures with a view to providing, within their jurisdiction, equitable access to health care of appropriate quality.' Article 4 requires that any intervention in the health field should be carried out in accordance with relevant professional standards.

Overall, Chapter I provides a set of overarching principles against which to read the more detailed substantive provisions on discrete areas contained in Chapters II to VII. Chapter II contains rules on consent, Chapter III on privacy and right to information, Chapter IV on the human genome, Chapter V on scientific research, Chapter VI on organ and tissue removal from living donors for transplantation purposes and Chapter VII on prohibition of financial gain and disposal of a part of the human body. The Convention is to be followed by four Protocols and there is a provision to revise the Convention every five years. A Protocol on biomedical research has been adopted by the Committee of Ministers of the Council of Europe (Strasbourg, 30 June 2004) and will enter into force when four Member States have expressed their consent to be bound by the Protocol.

The rights detailed under the various articles may be limited or restricted by the State, but only as prescribed by law and necessary in a democratic society in the interest of public safety, for the prevention of crime, for the protection of public health or for the protection and freedoms of others (Chapter IX, Art 26) except for Arts 11 (human genome, non-discrimination), 13 (modification of the human genome), 14 (non-sex selection), 16 (research on the mentally competent), 17 (research on the mentally incompetent), 19 (general rule on organ and tissue removal), 20 (organ removal on the mentally incompetent) and 21 (prohibition of financial gain) which admit of no exception. However, the Convention allows reservations to be entered by States 'in respect of any particular provision of the Convention to the extent that any law then in force in its territory is not in conformity with the provision' (Art 36.1).

1.4.2 Legal force

The Council of Europe's CHRB was opened for signature and ratification in Oviedo in 1997.[78] The UK, along with other leading European States such as Germany, was a party to the negotiations which preceded the adoption of the Convention by the Council of Europe but has not yet signed and *a fortiori* ratified the Convention. What is more, even for States which have ratified the CHRB, its

---

78 See Zilgalvis, 2001.

practical impact appears to be considerably limited by the fact that the Convention does not confer on individuals a right of petition to the European Court of Human Rights (ECtHR). Instead, the ECtHR may give an *advisory* opinion on legal questions concerning the interpretation of the present CHRB, but only at the request of the *Government* of a party to the Convention (Art 29).[79] So, at first sight, the CHRB would appear to be of dubious practical interest to those who seek to rely on the text for a remedy against breach.

Notwithstanding this limitation, the rights protected by the CHRB could nevertheless be indirectly enforceable as follows. The CHRB could be invoked by individuals who are seeking to assert one or several of the rights contained in the main Treaty or the ECHR, such as the right to life (Art 2) or the right to respect for family life or privacy (Art 8). The Explanatory Report to the Convention on Human Rights and Biomedicine (Strasbourg, 1997) expressly canvasses such a possibility in a note to Art 29. Article 29 details the rules on interpretation of the CHRB:

> This Convention does not itself give individuals a right to bring proceedings before the European Court of Human Rights. However, facts which are an infringement of the rights contained in this Convention may be considered in proceedings under the European Convention on Human Rights, if they also constitute a violation of one of the rights contained in the latter Convention. [note 165][80]

For instance, an applicant could not bring an action against the UK in the ECtHR based directly on breach of Art 5 of the CHRB, which states that:

> An intervention in the health field may only be carried out after the person concerned has given free and informed consent to it. This person shall beforehand be given appropriate information as to the purpose and nature of the intervention as well as on its consequences and risks.

However, the applicant could allege instead breach of Art 8 of the ECHR (1950) which protects the individual's right to respect for his private and family life[81] and rely on the provisions on consent contained in the CHRB as a guide to the scope of application of Art 8 in a biomedical context.

The ECtHR followed precisely this approach in *Glass v UK*,[82] where the ECtHR for the first time relied on the Council of Europe's CHRB in its reading of Art 8. The applicants were respectively a mother and her severely disabled child. The child had been particularly unwell since July 1998 when he was admitted to St Mary's Hospital, one of two hospitals belonging to the Portsmouth Hospitals National Health Service (NHS) Trust ('the Trust'). He was operated on in order to

---

79 'The European Court of Human Rights may give, without direct reference to any specific proceedings pending in a court, advisory opinions on legal questions concerning the interpretation of the present Convention at the request of: The Government of a Party, after having informed the other parties; the Committee set up by Article 32, with membership restricted to the Representatives of the Parties to this Convention, by a decision adopted by a two-thirds majority of votes cast.'

80 Article 29 of the CHRB.

81 The ECtHR has held that the concept of 'private life' covers the physical and moral integrity of the person, including his or her sexual life: *X and Y v Netherlands* (1986) 8 EHRR 235.

82 *Glass v UK* [2004] 1 FLR 1019.

alleviate an upper respiratory tract obstruction and suffered post-operative complications, including infections which required him to be put on a ventilator since he had become critically ill. Discussions took place at the hospital between the mother and intensive care staff and paediatricians. The doctors were of the view that the child was dying and that further intensive care would be inappropriate. The mother and other family members disagreed. The hospital consulted its solicitors and advised the applicants to consult their solicitors.

The child's condition improved and on 31 July 1998 he was able to be returned from intensive care to the paediatric ward and then home. However, he had to be readmitted into hospital in September. From September to October the child suffered several episodes of respiratory failure. Doctors were of the opinion that the child was dying and should be administered morphine to alleviate distress. The mother and relatives opposed the administration of morphine which they considered would compromise the child's chances of recovery. The hospital went ahead with the administration of diamorphine and a 'Do Not Resuscitate' (DNR) order was put in the child's medical notes without consulting the child's mother. A dispute broke out between the doctors and the family members who believed that the child was being covertly euthanised and attempted to prevent the doctors from entering the first applicant's room. The hospital authorities called the security staff and threatened to exclude the family from the hospital by force. The child's condition deteriorated and the mother successfully revived the child whilst a fight broke between other members of the family and the doctors. The child survived and the mother brought a judicial review action in the domestic courts against the hospital.

In the High Court, Mr Justice Scott Baker said that judicial review was too blunt an instrument for the sensitive and on-going problems of the type raised by the case. In particular, he considered that it would be very difficult to frame any declaration in meaningful terms in a hypothetical situation so as not to restrict unnecessarily proper treatment by the doctors in an on-going and developing matter. He stressed in conclusion:

> Nothing, I would finally say, should be read into this judgment to infer that it is my view that the [Portsmouth Hospital] in this case acted either lawfully or unlawfully.

The Court of Appeal refused leave to appeal. Lord Woolf MR disagreed with Scott Baker J that the applicants had used the wrong procedure. He was of the view, however, that the considerations which might arise in relation to the child and other children who suffered from similar disabilities were almost infinite and for the courts to try to produce clarity would be a task fraught with danger. However, Lord Woolf stressed that in the event of the parents' views conflicting with that of the doctors, the matter must be brought before the courts who will decide which course of action is in the best interests of the patient.

The mother and child appealed to the ECtHR. They alleged, *inter alia*, that the decisions to administer diamorphine to the child against the mother's wishes and to place a DNR notice in his notes without the mother's knowledge interfered with the child's right to physical and moral integrity as well as with the mother's rights under Art 8. In their submission, the failure of the hospital authority to involve the domestic courts in the decision to intervene without the second applicant's consent resulted in a situation in which there was an interference with the child's right which was not in accordance with the law.

The ECtHR determined that the hospital's failure to refer the disagreement to the court and its decision to proceed with treatment in defiance of the child's legal representative's refusal amounted to a breach of the child's right to respect for his private life. An interference with rights under Art 8 may be legitimate if it is compatible with Art 8(2), namely that it is 'in accordance with the law', has an aim or aims that is or are legitimate under that paragraph and is 'necessary in a democratic society' for the aforesaid aim or aims. The applicants contended that the interference was not legitimate because it was not in accordance with law, which they claimed was loose and conferred too much discretion on doctors. The Court decided that it did not have to address this point, but noted that it did not consider that the regulatory framework in place in the UK is in any way inconsistent with the standards laid down in the Council of Europe's CHRB in the area of consent; nor did it accept the view that the many sources from which the rules, regulations and standards are derived only contribute to unpredictability and an excess of discretion in this area at the level of application. On the other hand, the Court considered that the issue here was whether the administration of the diamorphine without the mother's consent and without the authorisation of a court fulfilled the 'necessity' requirement under Art 8(2). In the Court's view it did not. The decision of the authorities to override the mother's objection to the proposed treatment in the absence of authorisation by a court resulted in a breach of Art 8 of the ECHR.

The CHRB was referred to twice in the course of the judgment. First, the provisions on consent were invoked by the Court in its review of the relevant international and domestic instruments and, secondly, in its application of Art 8(2) to the facts of the case. Significantly, the UK did not object. At the same time, the Court did not explain the basis on which the CHRB could legitimately be invoked. Arguably, the justification is as follows.

The rights protected by the ECHR are very general and broad. Their precise scope of application is left to be determined by the ECtHR. The ECtHR has considerable discretion to determine the specific nature and scope of the rights protected.[83] The principles of interpretation applied by the Court follow the general rules of international law on the interpretation of treaties contained in Arts 31–33 of the Vienna Convention on the Law of Treaties of 23 May 1969.[84] Article 31(1) of the Vienna Convention directs the court to interpret a treaty in its context and in the light of its object and purpose. Article 31(3) specifies that there shall be taken into account, together with the context:

(3) (a) any subsequent agreement between the parties regarding the interpretation of the treaty or the application of its provisions; and

83 Van Dijk and Van Hoof, 1998.
84 The Court endorsed these principles in the *Golder v UK* case, (1979–80) 1 EHRR 524, notwithstanding that the Vienna Convention was not yet in force at the time.

(b)   any subsequent practice in the application of the treaty which establishes
      the agreement of the parties regarding its interpretation.

The CHRB is not strictly an agreement regarding the interpretation or application
of the ECHR under 3(a). But the object of the CHRB, as indicated by its preamble,
is to give a specific application in the field of biomedicine to the general rights
contained in the ECHR. On this basis, once a majority of members of the Council
of Europe has signed and/or ratified the Convention, the ECtHR could
conceivably construe such widespread and formal endorsement as a practice
which establishes the agreement of the parties on the interpretation of the main
Treaty in the field of biomedicine. In this manner, the specific rules contained in
the CHRB to protect patients' rights on matters such as consent, research, genetic
information, etc, could in due course guide the interpretation of the ECtHR in
cases where the Court has to determine the specific application in a biomedical
context of one the Articles in the ECHR.

A majority of members of the Council of Europe have signed the CHRB,
although a majority has yet to ratify it. However, since the procedure for
ratification varies under domestic law and tends to be lengthy and drawn out, it
should only be a matter of time before a majority of members completes the
process of ratification. There might therefore come a point when the UK, and any
other member State of the Council of Europe which has not signed or ratified the
Convention, could nevertheless in theory find itself indirectly in breach of the
provisions contained in the CHRB. There is a parallel here between the scenario
just explored under Art 31(3)(b) of the Vienna Convention and the ECtHR's
application of Art 31(3)(a) in cases where the individual applicant has alleged a
violation of a Protocol which had not been ratified by the offending State. In such
cases, the State often seeks to argue that the whole matter is governed by the
Protocol. However, in the *Abdulaziz* case,[85] the applicant was able to rely on Art 8
on an issue concerning the UK immigration legislation, even though the UK is not
a party to the Fourth Protocol. On this basis, it seems that the potential legal
impact of the CHRB on the jurisprudence of the ECtHR could be considerably
greater than anticipated. In the UK, the Human Rights Act 1998 directs UK courts
to determine cases in the light of the jurisprudence of the ECtHR. The CHRB
might thus gradually reshape domestic law both in the UK and in other member
States which have not ratified the CHRB. *A fortiori*, the legal impact could be
equally momentous in other European States which grant higher legal status to
treaties than domestic law in their constitution.[86]

---

85   *Abdulaziz, Cabales and Balkandali v UK*, Judgment of 28 May 1985, Series A, No 94; (1985) 7
     EHRR 471. In the *Rasmussen* case, the applicant was able to rely on Art 8 in a case concerning
     paternity issues even though Denmark was not a party to the Seventh Protocol which sets out
     the rights of parents in relation to their children (*Rasmussen v Denmark*, Judgment of 28
     November 1984, Series A, No 87; (1985) 7 EHRR 372). Similarly in the *Guzzardi* case, the
     applicant was able to rely on Art 5 in a matter concerning the rights of free movement
     contained in the Fourth Protocol which had not been recognized by Italy (*Guzzardi v Italy*
     (7367/76 [1980] ECHR 5)).
86   Eg, France.

CHAPTER 2

HUMAN RIGHTS AND UNIVERSAL PRINCIPLES[1]

There is wide variation in norms and laws regulating biomedical research both within and outside Europe.[2] Some countries have statutory regimes, whilst others rely on softer forms of regulation including administrative or professional ethical rules.[3] In the case of research involving adults and children, the procurement of consent prior to medical interventions is usually a legal requirement, but there is no uniform norm on the level of information that patients should be given to ensure that consent is adequate or informed.[4] Neither is there a clear consensus on the circumstances in which consent can be dispensed with.[5] Forms and procedures for obtaining consent vary. So do other control mechanisms, such as the legal status, role and composition of Research Ethics Committees.[6] In the fast developing field of research involving the application of new biotechnologies such as stem cell research or research on human tissue, the law tends to lag behind the science. There is often a legal vacuum as policy makers strive to reach a consensus on guiding principles for regulation. The conduct of clinical trials by pharmaceutical corporations in the developing world, resulting in drugs which are then out of reach of the local populations, has also raised the question of whether universal standards of research can be formulated irrespective of inequality of health resources and wealth. In the light of geographical variations in the regulation of medical research, the adoption of a legally binding treaty which aspires to capture fundamental values as well as bringing 'greater unity between its members' is therefore an important step toward European and international harmonisation of norms in the field of biomedicine. The Convention on Human Rights & Biomedicine's (CHRB's) aspiration to capture fundamental universal values is clear from the preamble's resolve to 'take such measures as are necessary to safeguard human dignity and the fundamental rights and freedoms of the individual with regard to the application of biology and medicine'. However, the aspiration has to be reconciled with the reality of the diversity of forms and norms of regulation of medical research across Europe and the rest of the world.

It has therefore been suggested that harmonisation has the effect of driving down ethical standards to the lowest common denominator, and diluting the rights of individuals affected by the fields of biology and medicine.[7] This chapter seeks to explore the question of whether the rights contained in the CHRB reflect

---

1   An earlier version of this chapter appeared in a collection of edited papers on consent to the inclusion of neonates in clinical trials (Mason and Megone, 2001).
2   See Sprumont, 1999; Plomer, 2000.
3   Examples of countries which have introduced specific legislation to regulate medical research include France, Spain, Germany, Denmark and the Republic of Ireland.
4   Dalla-Vorgia, Plomer *et al*, 2001.
5   See Plomer, 2001b.
6   See Byk and Memeteau, 1996; Glasa, 2000.
7   Eg, by States such as Germany and the Republic of Ireland which have refused to sign the Convention.

universal ethical principles against which to judge domestic legal regimes on medical research. In the year before the CHRB was adopted, the US Advisory Committee on Human Radiation Experiments (ACHRE, 1996) independently claimed to have identified fundamental ethical principles which are valid across all cultures and at all times, and which can be used to judge the ethical soundness of experimentation with humans retroactively, if required. The report prompted a protracted exchange through the pages of the *Kennedy Institute of Ethics Journal* about the philosophical basis of the claim to universality of moral principles. Both the debate about the nature of moral principles and the principles on experimentation involving mentally competent and incompetent human beings identified by the ACHRE highlight some of the strengths and weaknesses of the Council of Europe's CHRB, and the extent to which it has the capacity to realise the aspiration to universality.

2.1   ETHICAL DIVIDES: THE BACKGROUND TO THE CONVENTION

The Council of Europe's CHRB was adopted on 4 April 1997, almost 10 years after the drafters were entrusted with the task of formulating a text which would command universal assent.[8] From the onset in 1992, the Steering Bioethics Committee of the Council of Europe agreed by a majority on a drafting strategy which left the determination of more specific definitions and rules to protocols which would be added to the Convention in due course.[9] In particular, the Committee decided to avoid specific definitions of pivotal but also highly disputed concepts. The Committee agreed:

- to specify that the term 'human being' should be understood in its widest sense and to avoid, at the present stage, the inclusion in the framework Convention of a definition of the human being;

- not to specify whether the framework Convention applies to the human being only after birth or also before;

- not to specify whether the framework Convention also applies to gametes and genetic engineering;

- not to include a definition of bioethics, the difference between the latter and medical deontology being sufficiently well established. Nevertheless, the Explanatory Report should give some details on the concept of bioethics.[10]

By opting for general definitions and deferring the specification of key concepts to later protocols, the Bioethics Committee was also undoubtedly aiming to

---

8 On the history of the drafting of the Convention see Zilgalvis, 2001, pp 31–47. On the legal status and legal scope of the Convention see Plomer, 2001a, pp 313–30.

9 Council of Europe Steering Committee on Bioethics (CDBI), 2000.

10 *Ibid.*

maximise the chances of avoiding outright divisions and reaching a consensus on broad, overarching principles which allowed States which were reluctant to sign up to common European legislation a wide margin of appreciation when implementing the Convention's provisions. But in so doing, the drafters also opened themselves to the charge that the Convention would either be an empty text, devoid of substantive meaning, or a 'conceptual muddle' glossing over sharp ethical divisions.[11]

To date, the CHRB has been ratified by 18 member States, whilst ratification is still awaiting from 13 member States who have signed but not ratified.[12] A few States from Northern Europe have ratified the Convention (Sweden, Finland, Iceland and Denmark), but the majority of ratifications comes from States in Southern and Eastern Europe. Notorious absentees which have neither signed nor ratified include States which consider the Convention either too restrictive or too permissive, particularly on the ethically divided issues of embryo research and research on the mentally incapacitated. Morally 'liberal' States include the UK and Belgium, whilst morally 'conservative' States include Germany, Austria and the Republic of Ireland. In Germany, by the summer of 1999 over two million people had petitioned against accession to the Convention.[13]

2.1.1 Embryos and genes

From the outset, the divide between the moral conservatives and liberals on the use of human gene technology beset the negotiators of the Convention.[14] Germany's morally conservative stance was partly based on the haunting memory of the brutalisation and dehumanisation of human life in the Holocaust. However, it was also ideologically sustained by the neo-conservatism of Hans Jonas's works on the moral dangers inherent in the application of new technologies to human embryos and germ cell lines. In line with this thinking, Germany sought a total prohibition of embryo and genetic research, irrespective of the potential health benefits of such research to existing or future populations. At the other end of the moral and political spectrum were countries such as the UK, which already had liberal legislation in place, and were not prepared to sacrifice the potential social and economic benefits of research to entrenched positions on the moral status of the human embryo or genetic material which did not reflect the diversity of moral opinions in modern, multicultural Britain. Unsurprisingly, as will be seen in Chapter 4, far from codifying universal principles, the text of the Convention is compatible with a variety of moral positions on the status of the human embryo and the permissibility of research.

---

11 See Delkeskamp-Hayes, 2000; Schmidt, 2000.
12 Council of Europe, 2004.
13 Schiermeier, 1999.
14 Riedel, 1997.

2.1.2 Non-therapeutic research

As far as research involving existing human subjects (either children or adults) is concerned, there had hitherto been an international consensus that the aim of scientific research should be to benefit the individual participating in the research as well as yielding knowledge which could benefit others in society by uncovering the causes of ill health or discovering new ways of treating or alleviating pain or illness.[15] This consensus was disturbed by the CHRB through the adoption of controversial clauses permitting non-therapeutic research on those unable to consent. The report of the Bioethics Committee on the drafting of the Convention shows repeated attempts by the drafters to come up with a wording which would facilitate consensus in the face of numerous representations by delegations querying the moral legitimacy of such research and asking for stronger protection of persons unable to consent.[16] But whether the text finally adopted can live up to the aspiration of laying down fundamental universal principles is doubtful. An analysis of the international principles preceding the Convention and a comparison with the principles adopted in the US by the ACHRE highlights the strengths and weaknesses of the Convention.

2.2   BEFORE THE CONVENTION: HELSINKI

Early modern theories envisaged medical research to be conducted only on human subjects who could directly or personally derive a benefit from the research. Any benefits conferred on others were justified on the grounds that they were incidental to the benefit conferred on the participating individual:

> The principle of medical and surgical morality, therefore, consists in never performing on man an experiment which might be harmful to him to any extent, even though the result might be highly advantageous to science, for instance, to the health of others. But performing experiments and operations exclusively from the point of view of the patient's own advantage does not prevent their turning out profitably to science.[17]

By the time the Declaration of Helsinki was revised in 1975, the climate of opinion had changed and non-therapeutic biomedical research involving human subjects was considered acceptable providing that the subject was a volunteer who had consented.[18] Paradoxically the 1975 revision of the Declaration also expressly stipulated that the experimental design should not be related to the patient's illness.[19] The practical impact was to exclude the possibility that a volunteer who

---

15 'The main purpose of medical research is "to improve diagnostic, therapeutic and prophylactic procedures and the understanding of the aetiology and pathogenesis of disease".' *Declaration of Helsinki* (revised 2000), Introduction.

16 *Op cit* 13.

17 Bernard, 1977.

18 *Declaration of Helsinki* (revised 1975), III.2.

19 'The subjects should be volunteers – either healthy persons or patients for whom the experimental design is not related to the patient's illness' *Declaration of Helsinki*, III.2.

consented to participate in non-therapeutic research could do so in contemplation of deriving a potential benefit at some unspecified time in the future, presumably to avoid exploitation or abuse of vulnerable patients by raising unfounded hopes. In the case of persons lacking the capacity to consent, the 1975 revision of the Declaration was ambiguous. Whilst not expressly prohibiting non-therapeutic research on those lacking the capacity to consent, the Declaration was nevertheless silent on the conditions, if any, under which such participants could be volunteered by others. Indeed, it is possible to interpret the omission as a tacit assumption that non-therapeutic research on the mentally incapacitated was considered unacceptable. Since such research cannot directly benefit the participating subject and in addition may expose him or her to risks of harm, it is plain that the purpose of the research is to benefit society rather than the individual participant. The Declaration of Helsinki makes clear that the guiding principle in the conduct of non-therapeutic research should be that 'the interest of science and society should never take precedence over considerations related to the well being of the subject'.[20]

2.2.1   The moral and political challenge

The Declaration's early ambiguity, if not contradiction, highlights the moral and political dilemmas besetting the drafters of the Convention. On the one hand, it may be argued that individuals have a moral duty to act for the benefit of others. The obligation to benefit, it is said, is based on reciprocity: 'All our obligations to do good to society seem to imply something reciprocal. I receive the benefits of society, and therefore ought to promote its interests.'[21] In practical terms, adherence to the view that individuals are under a moral obligation to act for the benefit of others may require that, in certain circumstances, social welfare should trump individual autonomy in recognition of other overreaching values such as social responsibility and solidarity.[22] An alternative view is that there is no moral duty to act so as to confer a benefit on others, or at any rate if there is such a duty, it is a weak moral duty. The contrast here is between the negative duty, captured in the Hippocratic oath 'at least do no harm', and a duty to take positive steps to benefit others.[23] According to the German philosopher Immanuel Kant, the latter may be morally laudable but only the former is morally obligatory. Kant's theory is founded on the primacy of respect for the individual's autonomy. In Kantian theory, autonomy is the basis of human dignity.[24] On this view, the deontological

---

20   *Declaration of Helsinki* (revised 1975), III.4. The principle has been retained in the 2000 revision (Introduction, 5).

21   Hume, 1985.

22   Jonas, 1984 and Jonas, 2003.

23   If the contrast is erased, the same degree of moral culpability would attach to acts and omissions. But whilst doing away with the distinction between positive and negative duties and acts may be plausible in some instances, it seems improbable in others. Although it has been argued that failure to make a donation to Oxfam is on a moral par with sending a poisoned food parcel, it is doubtful that many would agree. See Honderich, 1980.

24   Kant, 1969.

requirement that the individual's capacity to make autonomous (and rational) choices should be respected carries it with it the normative implication that collective and societal interests should be morally subordinate to the individual's exercise of his free and autonomous choices as reflective of human dignity.

From a political perspective, Kant's ethical and meta-ethical theory is conceptually most congruent with liberal rights-based political theories, which favour institutional arrangements which prioritise individual liberty over collective welfare. Such theories also typically favour negative over positive formulations of rights.[25] In political terms, the imposition of positive moral obligations on individuals to act for the benefit of others has the potential to translate into the exercise of State power to coerce the individual to participate in medical research intended to confer collective benefits on society but not on the individual himself. The potential for abuse is well documented, from medical experiments conducted by the Nazis to radiation experiments conducted for defence purposes, as late as the 1970s, in far less likely political regimes.[26] At the same time, the Kantian framework which underpins the traditional autonomy-centred liberal conception of rights has limited reach in the case of individuals who lack the capacity to make autonomous choices. The capacity to make autonomous choices may be limited by psychological or physiological factors, for example, in the case of children or the mentally incapacitated. In such cases a degree of benevolent paternalism is inevitable to ensure protection of non-autonomous individuals. Alternatively, the exercise of autonomy or free choice may be limited by the individual's socio-economic circumstances. Whether or not the latter is described as an attaint on autonomy largely depends on contrasting political conceptions of liberty.[27] On the classical liberal conception, liberty is essentially defined in negative terms as an absence or freedom from constraint, whereas in positive conceptions, true liberty or choice may only be exercised if the individual has the socio-economic means or resources to make a choice. In the context of medical research, negative conceptions of rights would prioritise the protection of individual autonomy and focus on consent, but have few intellectual resources to conceptualise the rights of those lacking autonomy. Positive conceptions rely on assumptions about the individual good and the common good[28] and may require positive steps to be taken to prevent exploitation or abuse of vulnerable individuals or populations.

The moral and political challenge for any guiding framework which aspires to capture universal or fundamental values in medical research is, therefore, to reconcile the legitimate aims of science to advance the interests of society with respect for the individual's right to autonomy and self-determination and the need to protect vulnerable individuals from exploitation in research. A comparative

25 Waldron, 1993.
26 See Advisory Committee on Human Radiation Experiments, 1996 and for further discussion see Plomer, 2001b.
27 See Berlin, 1969.
28 See for instance Hegel, 1949; Marx, 1977a; Marx, 1977b; Aristotle, 1954.

analysis of the principles and their moral basis identified by the ACHRE report and the Council of Europe's CHRB highlights the difficulties of the exercise.

2.3   US HUMAN RADIATION EXPERIMENTS: THE ACHRE REPORT[29]

Some of the most appalling evidence of abuse of human subjects in medical research to have come to light in the past decade has related to experiments conducted in liberal regimes such as the US and the UK. In the UK, a government investigation was launched in November 2000 after the Ministry of Defence admitted that 'potentially dangerous' tests had been conducted on thousands of servicemen since the end of the Second World War at a military base in Porton Down as late as 1983.[30] During the Cold War, the base became a centre for research into chemical weapons, although the tests remained secret until the 1960s. Thousands of servicemen at the base were asked to volunteer to take part in tests involving the use the deadly nerve gas sarin. Many participants claimed to have suffered long-term ill effects. The volunteers said that they been deceived about the nature of the experiments. One serviceman who died in 1953 thought that he was taking part in a programme to cure the common cold. An investigation into the allegations by Wiltshire Police led to a referral for prosecution to the Crown Prosecution Service (CPS). The CPS has decided not to prosecute for lack of evidence but a civil claim is still pending.[31]

In the US, evidence of deceit and abuse in human radiation experiments conducted during the Cold War up to the 1970s began to surface in the media in the early 1990s. The experiments, which had been sponsored by government departments, including the US Department of Defence, involved up to 4,000 human subjects whose health had been put at risk and whose consent had not been obtained, and/or who had been deceived about the nature and/or risks involved. They included hospitalised patients suffering from chronic or terminal illnesses who were injected with plutonium and uranium to obtain metabolic data related to the safety of those working on the production of nuclear weapons.[32] With only one exception, the records show that the subjects were not told of their involvement in the experiment, neither were they made aware that they would not derive any medical benefit but instead run an increased risk of developing cancer in 10 or 20 years' time. In the Cincinnati experiments,[33] which were conducted in the mid-1960s and early 1970s, cancer patients underwent total body irradiation (TBI). The experiments were sponsored by the Department of Defence,

---

29   Part of the discussion below originally appeared in Mason and Megone, 2001, pp 191–206.
30   Evans, 2000. The investigation was widely publicized in the media: http://news.bbc.co.uk/1/hi/uk/1463993.stm; www.bbc.co.uk/insideout/west/prog_08/index.shtml.
31   (2003) *The Independent*, 10 July.
32   ACHRE, Chapter 5.
33   ACHRE, Chapter 8.

which was interested in the study of the after-effects of radiation. The studies were not intended to benefit the patients and the patients were either not informed or not adequately informed about the nature of the experiment. Non-therapeutic experiments were carried out on institutionalised children, including some with mental impairment, at the Fernald School in the late 1940s and early 1950s. The experiments conducted by the Massachusetts Institute of Technology (MIT) involved feeding the children with food (Quaker oats) which had been irradiated with radioactive iron and calcium. Parental permission was sought, but the parents were told that the project was intended for the child's benefit, which was not true. Neither were the parents informed of the (minimal) risks to which the children were being exposed.

2.3.1 Six fundamental principles

In 1995 President Clinton appointed the ACHRE to investigate the allegations. Part of the brief of the Radiation Committee was to develop an ethical framework to evaluate, retroactively, the ethical soundness of the experiments under suspicion. In its report the ACHRE, claimed to have identified six basic ethical principles which are morally binding on medical researchers in all societies across time and space. The report grounded the validity of the principles on their acceptability to 'all morally serious individuals' and the fact that they are 'widely accepted and generally regarded as so fundamental as to be applicable to the past as well as the present'.[34]

The principles are:

(1) one ought not to treat people as mere means to the ends of others;

(2) one ought not to deceive others;

(3) one ought not to inflict harm or risk of harm;

(4) one ought to promote welfare and prevent harm;

(5) one ought to treat people fairly and with equal respect;

(6) one ought to respect the self-determination of others.

The ACHRE regarded these principles as 'basic' because 'any minimally acceptable ethical standpoint must include them'.[35] The principles are not hierarchically ordered and indeed 'all moral principles can justifiably be overridden by other basic principles in circumstances when they conflict'.[36] The ACHRE claimed that the principles reflect a social consensus about the validity of certain moral *norms* as opposed to moral theories. Moral theories may differ in their metaphysical or epistemological basis and provide different justifications for

---

34 ACHRE, Chapter 4, p 1.
35 ACHRE, Chapter 4, p 2.
36 ACHRE, Chapter 4, p 2.

a basic principle. However, theoretical divergence need not, and *de facto* does not, preclude convergence at the level of principles which in turn provide the grounding for more specific moral rules.

For instance, the requirement for informed consent may be based on the principle that one ought to promote welfare and prevent harm, which may in turn be grounded in the view that individuals are generally most interested in and knowledgeable about their own well-being. By contrast, an approach based on self-determination may assume that being able to make important decisions about one's own life and health is intrinsically valuable, independent of its contribution to promoting one's well-being.[37] Hence, cultural and ethical diversity need not preclude moral convergence on principles and particular moral rules such as the rule that 'competent individuals ought to be allowed to accept or refuse participation in experiments'.[38]

Applying the above ethical framework, the ACHRE drew a distinction between non-therapeutic experiments without the subject's consent and therapeutic experiments without the subject's consent. The former were held to be not only a violation of the basic principles listed above but also a violation of the Hippocratic principle that was the cornerstone of professional medical ethics at the time.[39] The ACHRE found that in 11 out of the 21 experiments conducted on children which it reviewed, the risks (of cancer) were in a range that would today be considered as more than minimal and thus as unacceptable in non-therapeutic research (although the Committee emphasised that often these non-therapeutic experiments on non-consenting patients constituted only minor wrongs because often there was little or no risk to patient-subjects and no inconvenience).

2.3.1.1 Non-therapeutic research without consent

Included in this category were experiments conducted on children who were sick or mentally handicapped, often confined to an institution such as a special needs school. The children were intentionally exposed to harmful radiation without adequate consent having been obtained from the parents or guardians. In these cases, the ACHRE argued, the children were being used as a *mere* means to the ends of the investigator conducting the experiment and the institutions sponsoring the experiment (breach of principle 1). The parents were not fully informed if informed at all (breach of principles 2 and 6). The infliction of harm was deliberate (breach of principle 3). Further, these children, the ACHRE argued, suffered the additional injustice of unfair and discriminatory treatment (breach of principle 5) as the evidence collected revealed that whilst there was a strong tradition of seeking consent with *healthy* subjects for research that generally offered no prospect of medical benefit to the participant, the same was not true in the case of subjects who were sick paediatric patients, especially those who were institutionalised and/or subjects whose mental capacities were impaired.

---

37   ACHRE, Chapter 4, p 4.
38   ACHRE, Chapter 4, p 5.
39   ACHRE, Chapter 4, p 8.

2.3.1.2 Therapeutic research without consent

The ACHRE argued that 'much the same can be said of experiments that were conducted on patient-subjects without their consent but that offered a prospect of medical benefit'.[40] To the extent that the physician's intention was to benefit the patient then 'the less blameworthy the physician was for failing to obtain consent. However, where the risks were great or where there were viable alternatives to participation in research, then the physician was more blameworthy for failing to obtain consent'.[41]

2.4   A MORALLY BANKRUPT FRAMEWORK?

In one of the most fascinating academic polemics to date, Robert Baker, a philosopher and historian of medicine, has argued that the search for universal moral principles is fundamentally misguided and charged the findings of the ACHRE report with moral bankruptcy. In the first of two articles published in the *Kennedy Institute of Ethics Journal* in 1998, Baker presents a powerful attack on what he described as the 'moral bankruptcy of fundamentalism', the thesis that cross-cultural moral judgments and international bioethical codes are justified by certain 'basic' or 'fundamental moral principles that are universally accepted in all cultures and eras'. The second article offers Baker's alternative model of a 'negotiated moral order'.[42]

The main gist of Baker's criticisms is this. Moral fundamentalism is essentially a rhetorical thesis with no social or historical basis. In the post-war era, the thesis has come under pressure from both multiculturalism and postmodernism. The former points to empirical evidence of the diversity of ethical norms in different cultures. The latter denies the possibility of normative convergence, as values or norms are seen as a reflection of the agents' perspective, gaze or narrative and their hegemony is a function of power not of principle. In order to justify cross-cultural and cross-temporal judgments, moral fundamentalists presume that a culture or era *accepts* or *agrees* to 'basic' or 'fundamental' principles of which its members are ignorant or which are inconsistent with the principles that the culture forthrightly avows.[43] But Baker contends that the thesis is historically untenable, as the ACHRE report itself shows. American researchers involved in the radiation experiments with humans in the post-war era did not at the time recognise the ethical centrality of the requirement to obtain consent. They were prevented by a form of 'cultural blindness' from recognising the moral blameworthiness of their wrongdoing. Baker argues that the report's failure to

---

40   ACHRE, Chapter 4, p 9.
41   ACHRE, Chapter 4, p 9.
42   Baker, 1998a, p 203.
43   Baker, 1998a, p 203.

attach moral blame to individual researchers, as opposed to government departments or regulatory agencies, shows the 'moral bankruptcy' of moral fundamentalism. On a postmodernist analysis, Baker claims, 'cultural blindness' could have equally excused the Nazi medical researchers indicted at the Nuremberg trial. If 'moral fundamentalism cannot justify the Nuremberg verdict, it has no *raison d'être* and moral fundamentalism is philosophically bankrupt'.[44]

In a separate article, Baker argues that moral fundamentalism must be abandoned and replaced by a contractarian theory, which he derives from the theories of Rawls and Nozick, in order to provide a theoretical framework for international bioethics which *can* bridge trans-cultural and trans-temporal moral judgments in a way that withstands the multicultural and postmodern critique.[45] International bioethics can be reconstructed as a 'negotiated moral order' which is consistent with traditional ideals about human rights, whilst respecting cultural difference but recognising defined areas of non-negotiability.

Baker's charges have been vigorously contested by Beauchamp and Macklin.[46] Both their responses contend that Baker has distorted the central postulates of moral fundamentalism and misrepresented the findings of the ACHRE report. Moral fundamentalism, they have argued, is not an empirical thesis. It does not postulate that universal principles find *de facto* acceptance across all cultures and times. It is a normative thesis. Further, Baker has seriously misrepresented the findings of the ACHRE report. The ACHRE did not find that American researchers who had conducted experiments found to be wrong could be excused on the grounds of cultural blindness. Quite the opposite. It was considerations of procedural justice, partial evidence, absence of individual representation and so forth which prevented the ACHRE from ascribing individual blame. The principles identified by the report remain intact. What is more, Baker's alternative theory is but a contractarian version of moral fundamentalism. Who is right?

Beauchamp and Macklin's rebuttal carries some force. Moral fundamentalism does certainly purport to be concerned with moral ideals rather than historically held values as suggested by Baker. Further, Baker does indeed appear to have misrepresented the finding of the ACHRE report. Individual researchers were not exonerated on the grounds of cultural blindness but ostensibly on procedural grounds. On the other hand, Baker's thesis that the legitimacy of international norms ultimately lies in *acceptance* by contracting parties of a negotiated moral order offers an attractive alternative reading of normative frameworks such as the Council of Europe's CHRB. Baker points out that the Convention is framed in terms of *rights* rather than principles and, in Baker's view, conceptualising international bioethics in terms of rights rather than principles has the attraction that rights are negotiable whereas universal principles are not.

---

44   Baker, 1998a, p 216.
45   Baker, 1998b.
46   Beauchamp, 1998; Macklin, 1998.

However, Baker's thesis is contestable on historical and epistemological grounds. Whilst it is undoubtedly true that the concept of rights has historically been associated with contractarian theories, it is also true that classical proponents of rights, most notably Locke[47] and Kant, aspired to capture through the concept of 'rights' what they perceived to be the universal dimension of morality. Neither Locke nor Kant contended that the epistemological grounding of rights is to be found in contingent, *de facto* social contracts or historical agreements between interested parties. To do so would have left them open to precisely the charge to which Baker's own thesis is open, namely that the resulting so called rights would necessarily lack the requisite dimension of trans-culturalism or universality, since a historical social contract would of necessity reflect and bind only the cultures or parties to it. The epistemological and metaphysical issues raised by Baker's thesis are therefore complex. Nevertheless, Baker needs to do more to establish that his thesis of a negotiated moral order of 'rights' rather than principles can retain a trans-cultural and trans-temporal dimension.

Notwithstanding this, since Baker contends that his contractarian theory is capable of yielding substantive norms and rights which do have a trans-temporal and trans-cultural dimension then, in practice, and in the context of a discussion regarding the ethics of medical research, it is the substantive principles or rights identified by the theory which will have to bear the burden of critical examination. In this respect, Beauchamp and Macklin's theories are more developed than Baker's, as the former have committed themselves to the six basic principles enunciated in the AHCRE report, whilst Baker offers some interesting but controversial views on examples of medical experiments which his theory would deem ethically acceptable (see below). How do the ACHRE principles stand up to critical scrutiny? To what extent do they coincide with or reflect the principles underlying the Council of Europe's CHRB?

2.4.1 Coherence, conflict and moral priorities

At first sight, most of the principles contained in the ACHRE report seem unremarkable and not contentious, at least as regards their 'core' meaning and possible application in areas which are not contested. Principles 1 and 6 which justify the moral obligation imposed on medical researchers to obtain informed consent have not always been clearly distinguished in deontological theories such as Kant's. The advantage of distinguishing the two principles is that the requirement not to treat individuals as a mere means to an end is broad enough to extend protection to individuals who lack the capacity to make choices for themselves, and who are therefore not caught by the classical Kantian requirement to respect autonomy and self-determination. On the other hand, it is not clear where the justificatory basis of the principle not to treat others as a means to an end lies when the principle is disengaged from its Kantian origins. This does not matter when the principle is applied, as the ACHRE report itself does, to condemn the radiation experiments conducted on institutionalised children who were

---

47   Locke, 1988; Kant, 1970; Kant, 1969.

mentally handicapped.[48] However, in other more contested contexts, for example, embryo research, the lack of a backing theoretical framework might render the interpretation and application of the principle more problematic.

The principle that one ought not to deceive others presumably requires qualification but otherwise provides a separate non-contentious justification for the requirement to obtain informed consent. Whether the principle is truly basic is perhaps more questionable. It could conceivably be argued that it may be derived from principles 1 and/or 6[49] which also happen to be the principles usually invoked in the ACHRE report to evaluate the radiation experiments.

The principle of fairness and equal respect is central to liberal theories derived from Kant. Liberal theories such as Rawls's have expressly situated themselves in opposition to welfare-based theories such as utilitarianism which they claim cannot consistently meet the requirements of fairness and justice.[50] But how fairness and justice are conceptualised depends largely on background moral and political theoretical frameworks.[51] The ACHRE report implicitly opted for a version of fairness as equal treatment and respect, in order to condemn trials which involved children or institutionalised mental incapacitated individuals, seriously ill and comatose patients.

The principle of non-maleficence is common to all ethical theories.[52] Notwithstanding this, the precise meaning and scope of application of the principle is uncertain and contested in some areas, for example, embryo research or research on the dead (see Chapter 4). In the context of scientific research involving live human beings who are already born, the principle arguably appears at first sight to have a settled 'core' meaning which prohibits the deliberate infliction of harm on others.[53] The principle would thus *prima facie* appear to have a major limiting effect on the conduct of scientific research on human participants, when the research brings no benefits to the individual concerned but instead carries with it a risk of harm, for instance, non-therapeutic research. However, the ACHRE opted instead for a weaker interpretation and application of the principle as non-maleficence was invoked to condemn only non-therapeutic research which carried risks which are more than minimal.

Finally, the ACHRE claims that the principle that one ought to promote welfare and prevent harm is a basic or fundamental principle for the conduct of research: the welfare principle. However, as stated the principle admits of several interpretations, some of which are controversial. The crucial ambiguity here rests on the absence of a clear indication of *whose* welfare medical researchers are supposedly under a moral obligation to promote: the individual's welfare or the welfare of society? The two are not necessarily compatible and, whilst the former may be non-contentious, the latter is not.

---

48 Advisory Committee on Human Radiation Experiments, Chapter 7.
49 As in Kant, 1969.
50 Rawls, 1972.
51 Eg, see Sandel, 1982. Also MacIntyre, 1981.
52 Beauchamp and Childress, 1979.
53 The question of what precisely constitutes harmful conduct is also open to argument: see Feinberg, 1988.

The report's ambiguity or evasion in the formulation of the 'welfare principle' is particularly problematic in the light of the further interpretation principle proposed by ACHRE which denies any hierarchical priority between the six stated principles and endorses the possibility of *any* principle overriding another in the event of conflict.[54] This opens the theoretical possibility of conferring moral legitimacy on medical experiments which are conducted primarily for the collective benefit of society rather than the benefit of the individual. In the hands of oppressive political regimes, individual rights could then be sacrificed to the interest of society and the State in biomedical research. Arguably, however, it is precisely such forms of abuse of individual rights which truly universal and basic principles should be able to condemn.

Examples of medical experiments prioritising collective over individual benefit can be found in the ACHRE report itself. In the great majority of cases the experiments reviewed were conducted to advance medical science or national interests in defence or space exploration.[55] The Committee also found that the human radiation experiments 'contributed significantly to advances in medicine and thus to the health of the public'. And yet the Committee not only found that some of the research subjects were exposed to unacceptable risks[56] but the Committee also found that during the 1944–74 period but especially through the early 1960s, physicians engaged in clinical research generally did not obtain consent for therapeutic research and, where the research was not therapeutic, *it was common* for physicians to conduct research on patients without their consent.[57] These practices on the part of the medical profession were condemned as morally wrong.[58] The Committee's recommendations also highlight the need to ensure that the individual's right to privacy and self-determination are protected in experiments conducted primarily for the purpose of promoting national security. However, it is not clear how the findings or recommendations are logically consistent with the Committee's expressed view that *any* of the six conflicts can override the others in the event of a conflict.

Another area where the application of the welfare principle could lead to abuse is in non-therapeutic experiments on individuals who lack the capacity to consent. ACHRE reported that it was 'ethically troubled' by the selection of subjects in many of the experiments reviewed, as these subjects were often drawn from relatively powerless, easily exploited groups and many of them were institutionalised or hospitalised patients.[59] The experiments were thus condemned as a breach of the principle of fairness and equal respect. Although this is unproblematic in itself, what is more difficult for ACHRE to show is why the pursuit of collective interests should not have prevailed over fairness since on its

---

54　Advisory Committee on Human Radiation Experiments, Chapter 4, p 2.
55　*Ibid*, Finding 1.
56　*Ibid*, Finding 2.
57　*Ibid*, Finding 10.
58　*Ibid*, Finding 11b. Note, however, that the Committee attributed moral fault to government agencies rather than individual medical researchers (Findings 4 and 5, 9, 11).
59　*Ibid*, Finding 9.

own system of hierarchical priority *any* principle can take priority over the others in the event of conflict.

The fundamental difficulty evaded by ACHRE is to provide an acceptable ethical justification for the conduct of medical experiments which are not intended to directly confer a benefit on the individual involved but when the primary purpose is to advance knowledge for the collective benefit of society instead. The difficulty is particularly acute in the case of human subjects who lack the capacity to consent. Such a justification would require two things. On the one hand, it is necessary to show why individuals are under a moral obligation to act for the benefit of others or the collective benefit, particularly when the individual himself does not stand to benefit and may even expose himself to risks of harm. Theoretical justifications for welfarist programmes or principles may certainly be found in utilitarian theories, but these theories do not command widespread acceptance; neither are they clearly consistent with political regimes committed to the protection of individual rights.[60] Secondly, even if an adequate elaboration and justification for the welfare principle was forthcoming, it is also necessary to show why in the event of a conflict between individual and collective welfare it is acceptable for the latter to prevail. The main weakness of the ethical framework advanced by ACHRE is that it does not adequately address either issue.

In conclusion, the ACHRE report does not conclusively settle the question of whether it is possible to identify fundamental moral principles which are universally valid across all cultures and all times. The difficulty lies in the absence of a systematic theoretical exploration and analysis of the scope, meaning and justification of the key principles identified in the report and the system of hierarchical priority proposed. The absence of articulation of the theoretical framework(s) underpinning the principles, particularly the welfare principle, paradoxically leaves open the possibility that the experiments condemned by ACHRE itself could after all be justified on the basis of ACHRE's own principles.

To what extent are the difficulties encountered by ACHRE avoided by the Council of Europe's CHRB? Is it possible to find any convergence between the alleged fundamental values uncovered by ACHRE and the aspiration to universality of the Convention?

2.5   THE CONVENTION ON HUMAN RIGHTS & BIOMEDICINE (CHRB)

The Council of Europe's CHRB aspires to capture fundamental or universal values in the field of biomedicine. The overarching fundamental values asserted in Chapter I of the Convention include the protection of dignity and identity of all human beings (Art 1), the primacy of the human being (Art 2), equitable access to health care (Art 3) and the requirement that any intervention in the health field should be carried out in accordance with relevant professional obligations and

---

60   See Rawls, 1972; Dworkin, 1977.

standards (Art 4). The specific rules on discrete areas including scientific research contained in other chapters have to be read consistently with the statement of general values and purpose of the Convention stated in Chapter I of the Convention.

In some respects the overarching values espoused in Chapter I of the Convention are broader and vaguer than the ACHRE principles. Where ACHRE talks of respect for self-determination, and the prohibition on treating human beings as mere means to an end, the Convention endorses instead the need to safeguard human dignity. According to the Explanatory Report: 'The concept of human dignity … constitutes the essential value to be upheld. It is the basis of most of the values in the Convention' (para 10).

However, the concept of human dignity, although central to international human rights instruments, is to a large extent underdetermined[61] and its interpretation and application uncertain and contested in some areas (see Chapters 4 and 5 of this book), although arguably less so in relation to its meaning in the context of research involving mentally competent adult human beings (see Chapter 3). It may, for instance, be presumed that the requirement for informed consent in Arts 5 and 16 of the Chapters on medical intervention and scientific research relates to the overarching requirement to respect human dignity, where human dignity could be understood in Kantian terms as a fundamental value originating in the individual's capacity to make autonomous choices.[62] This presumption is consistent with the explanation of Art 5 in the Explanatory Report, which states that:

> This Article deals with consent and affirms at the international level an already well-established rule, that is that no one may in principle be forced to undergo an intervention without his or her consent. Human beings must therefore be able freely to give or refuse their consent to any intervention involving their person. This rule makes clear patients' autonomy in their relationship with health care professionals and restrains the paternalist approaches which might ignore the wish of the patient. [para 34]

However, the Convention also contains what may be called a 'speciesist' slant, as it enjoins respect for the human being both as an individual and as a member of the human species. The Explanatory Report explains that, in the view of the drafters, many of the current advances of science, particularly genetics, pose a risk not only to the individual himself or society, but to the human species. Hence:

> The Convention sets up safeguards, starting with the preamble where reference is made to the benefits of future generations and to all humanity, while provision is made throughout the text for the necessary legal guarantees to protect the identity of the human being. [para 14]

In ascribing rights and dignity to the human species as a whole, the Council of Europe's CHRB stands apart from both first and second generation human rights

---

61   See Feldman, 1999a; Feldman, 1999b.
62   For a neo-Kantian view of human dignity see Beyleveld and Brownsword, 2001.

instruments which have traditionally sought to protect the negative and positive socio-economic rights of *individuals* and society respectively.[63] Instead, along with other third generation human rights instruments which seek to protect the rights not of individuals but of populations, or the environment, the CHRB asserts the need to protect the rights and dignity of the human species as a whole.[64] The focus on the human species, as opposed to the individual, as a source of dignity, moral value and rights is most definitely not Kantian and could potentially carry paternalistic requirements which would conflict with respect for autonomy and (the individual's) dignity.[65] There is no direct counterpart in the ACHRE report.

There could conceivably be an indirect link between the Convention's affirmation that 'progress in biology and medicine should be used for the benefit of present and future generations' and ACHRE's principle that one ought to promote welfare. In both cases there is a requirement that the common good be pursued. However, the emphasis is arguably different. First, where ACHRE uses the term 'welfare', the Convention talks instead of the 'benefits of present and future generations'. Admittedly, both expressions share a large degree of indeterminacy, but the formula adopted in the Convention suggests limits on the goals for which research may legitimately be pursued, namely the benefit of present and future generations (as against, for instance, the interest of commerce or private enterprise). This is quite different from the ACHRE principle which imposes on medical researchers a moral obligation to carry out research to promote welfare. In short, there is some clear divergence on the identification of basic or fundamental values or principles between ACHRE and the Convention as regards 'human dignity' and the bearers of rights (individuals and society in ACHRE) and the addition of the human species in the Convention.

Another crucial difference between ACHRE and the Convention is that the latter unequivocally asserts the moral priority of the interests of the individual over those of society whilst the former, as we saw earlier, does not. In the event of a conflict, as envisaged above, Art 2 of the Convention clearly asserts that the interests of the individual must prevail over those of society. The Explanatory Report unequivocally states:

> This Article affirms the primacy of the human being over the sole interest of science or society. Priority is given to the former, which must in principle take precedence over the latter in the event of a conflict between them. One of the important fields of application of this principle concerns research, as covered by the provisions of Chapter V of this Convention. [para 21]

In theory then, the general principles endorsed by the Convention should avert the problems of the ACHRE principles. Indeed, the Explanatory Report stresses that 'the whole Convention, the aim of which is to protect human rights and dignity, is inspired by the principle of the primacy of the human being, and all its

---

63 Eg, the International Covenant on Civil and Political Rights, the International Covenant on Economic, Social and Cultural Rights and the Convention on the Rights of the Child.
64 See Vasak, 1990. Also Byk, 1998; Lenoir and Mathieu, 1998.
65 See Beyleveld and Brownsword, 2001. Also Brownsword, 2003.

articles must be interpreted in this light'.[66] But as we shall see, in reality the specific rules on scientific research and the rights protected thereby appear to resolve the conflict with which ACHRE had wrestled in favour of societal over individual interests.

2.6   INDIVIDUAL v SOCIAL BENEFIT

The Convention contains a specific Chapter on scientific research (Chapter V). Article 15 asserts the freedom to carry out scientific research subject to limitations to ensure protection of the human being contained in Arts 16 and 17. Free and informed consent has to be given by the participant subject (or his legal representative) in advance (Art 5).[67] The participant has to be given appropriate information as to the purpose and nature of the intervention as well as on its consequences and risks (Art 5). The consent has to be given expressly, specifically and be documented (Art 16(v)). Article 16 also details limitations on research to ensure protection of human subjects. There is no alternative of comparable effectiveness to research on humans (Art 16(i)). The risks which may be incurred must not be disproportionate to the potential benefits of the research (Art 16(ii)) and the persons undergoing research must be informed of their rights and the safeguards prescribed by law for their protection (Art 16(iv)). The research must have been approved by a Research Ethics Committee (Art 16(iii)).

In the case of 'persons unable to consent', Art 17 draws a distinction between:

1   research which has the 'potential to produce real and direct benefit' to the individual (Art 17.19(ii)); and

2   research which has the 'aim of contributing ... to the ultimate attainment of results capable of conferring benefit to the person concerned or to other persons in the same age category or afflicted with the same disease or disorder or having the same condition'. (Art 17.2(i))

Although the terminology used is different, these two categories of research broadly map unto the traditional categories of therapeutic and non-therapeutic research. In addition to the general consent requirements imposed by Arts 5 and 6, both types of research are subject to the further (evidentiary) requirement that the authorisation of the legal representative be given specifically and in writing (Art 17.1(iv)). Non-therapeutic research must only carry *minimal* risk and burden for the individual concerned (Art 17.2(ii)).

---

66   Paragraph 22.

67   Article 5 specifically requires consent to be given prior to any medical intervention, but the meaning of the word 'intervention' in Art 5 is not restricted to 'medical treatment' and includes scientific research. The Explanatory Report stresses that 'one of the important fields of application of this principle concerns research' (para 21). However, the Convention contains additional specific rules on research.

2.7   CONVERGENCE ON FUNDAMENTAL AND UNIVERSAL VALUES?

Is it possible to discern any further convergence on fundamental and universal values between the Convention and the ACHRE report on the rights of human subjects in medical research?

Notwithstanding the absence of convergence on fundamental principles or values between ACHRE and the Convention, there is convergence on the importance of the rule for informed consent. Under either framework, medical researchers are under an obligation to obtain *informed* consent from a research subject (or the subject's proxy) in advance of the trial either on the basis of respect for individual autonomy (ACHRE) or respect for human dignity (CHRB). In the event of a conflict between the interests of the individual and those of society, the Convention, unlike ACHRE, unequivocally prioritises the interests of the individual over those of science and society (under the principle of the primacy of the human being): 'The whole Convention, the aim of which is to protect human rights and dignity, is inspired by the principle of the primacy of the human being, and all its articles must be interpreted in this light' (Explanatory Report, para 22).

Hence, under the Convention, mentally competent adults or children can simply decline to enter medical experiments for whatever reason and there is no question of their refusal being overridden for the greater good of society. By contrast, ACHRE implicitly leaves open the theoretical possibility that the interests of the individual and his autonomy may have to give way to the interests of science or society. ACHRE stops short of contemplating a scenario whereby human subjects may be compelled to enter research programs against their will. But in practical terms, the ACHRE rule requiring respect for the autonomy of others can be avoided or evaded by withholding information from the subject or misinforming the subject, albeit at the considerable cost of sacrificing the rule on non-deception and the rule on not treating others as a means to an end, providing that the value of the research in question is for the greater good of society and can justifiably be shown to take precedence over the need to respect individual autonomy. Such invasions or violations of the individual's body or liberty are admittedly less crude than those perpetuated by Nazi doctors. Nonetheless, deception sits ill at ease with respect for individual liberty. In short, in the case of individuals who are mentally competent, the primacy given to the interests of the individual in the Convention and the absence of qualification on the rule on informed consent ensures that informed consent acts as a political shield to protect the individual's liberty. By contrast, the political and legal implications of the ACHRE framework, which assigns no hierarchical priority to collective or individual welfare, are much more open and opaque.

Under either framework, the potential difficulties are compounded in the case of mentally incompetent children and adults, as consent is given by a proxy. More disturbingly, under the Convention, the shield provided by consent for mentally competent adults is weakened in the case of mentally incompetent adults or children. Whereas in the case of a mentally competent adult, the informed choice of the autonomous individual has to prevail over the interests of science and society, in the case of a mentally incompetent participant the Convention allows the legal representative to volunteer the subject even when the proposed research will not confer a benefit on the individual participant and may even carry risks, albeit of a minimal kind. Thus, in reality, the principle of the primacy of the human being in the Convention is displaced in the case of non-therapeutic research involving the mentally incompetent, since the Convention is prepared to allow the interests of science or society to prevail over those of an individual who is mentally incapacitated.

In conclusion, neither the ACHRE ethical principles nor the Convention offer a coherent system of principles or values or an adequate general ethical justification for prioritising the interests of society over those of individual participants, be they adults or children, mentally competent or incompetent. The difficulty is particularly acute in the case of non-therapeutic biomedical research, which offers no prospect of direct benefits to the individual. Ultimately, a legal or ethical framework purporting to identify fundamental and universal principles and rights in medical research has to provide adequate justifications for overriding individual autonomy and welfare for the sake of the common good. It is difficult to envisage how any proposed justification could not carry unsavoury political implications, and indirectly legitimise or open the way for State abuse of human subjects in scientific research programmes of the kind conducted under the auspices of government departments in the US and the UK to protect national security, which have led to such public outcry in those countries in the past decade. It is one thing to create an exception to a general principle to accommodate a particular set of circumstances which justify a departure from the general principle. It is another to turn the deviation itself into a general principle whose application in this case could logically encompass the kind of abuses which a human rights instrument should be seeking to avoid.

CHAPTER 3

NON-THERAPEUTIC RESEARCH: DOMESTIC REMEDIES AND CONVENTION RIGHTS

In Chapter 1 I suggested that whilst moral and legal principles may have a settled 'core' meaning, their interpretation and application at the boundaries may be uncertain, particularly in disputed contexts. Chapter 2 highlighted the theoretical difficulties in identifying universal principles on therapeutic and non-therapeutic research. At the same time, the specification of a principle need not necessarily be disputed and controverted. Often there is consensus and agreement on the specification of a substantive norm or right and its reach in a particular context,[1] in which case the question turns to whether the remedies offered by human rights instruments offer a higher degree of protection than domestic law to an applicant. This chapter focuses on this question in relation to the rules on 'consent' contained in the Council of Europe's Convention on Human Rights & Biomedicine (CHRB) and their application to non-therapeutic research, where arguably the 'core' meaning of the related underlying principles of respect for individual autonomy and bodily integrity are not in dispute, but where questions arise instead in respect of the degree of protection offered by the CHRB. By comparing Convention principles with domestic UK, Canadian and US civil law on the protection of participants in non-therapeutic research, it is possible to determine whether the Convention offers a higher or lower level of protection. The analysis specifically focuses on the Porton Down experiments in the UK and compares the civil remedies available under domestic law with the litigation surrounding the radiation experiments in the US. I highlight the weaknesses of the tort system as against judicial acknowledgment of the fundamental nature of the rights to autonomy and bodily integrity and their constitutional protection in the US. I conclude with an examination of the strengths and weaknesses of European Human Rights law, and highlight some significant differences between the European Convention on Human Rights (ECHR) (1950) and the CHRB (1997).

3.1 THE CENTRALITY OF CONSENT IN HUMAN RIGHTS INSTRUMENTS

There is widespread consensus in international ethical codes and human rights instruments that medical researchers must obtain the free and informed consent of the research participant in advance of a trial. The rule on consent has been present in all the versions of the Declaration of Helsinki since its original adoption in 1964. The 2000 version states that:

> In any research on human beings, each potential subject must be adequately informed of the aims, methods, sources of funding, any possible conflicts of interest, institutional affiliations of the researcher, the anticipated benefits and potential risks of

---

1   For instance, the absolute prohibition on torture in Art 3 of the ECHR.

the study and the discomfort it may entail. The subject should be informed of the right to abstain from participation in the study or to withdraw consent to participate at any time without reprisal. After ensuring that the subject has understood the information, the physician should then obtain the subject's freely given informed consent, preferably in writing. If the consent cannot be obtained in writing, the non-written consent must be formally documented and witnessed.[2]

It has also been endorsed by the International Covenant on Civil and Political Rights (ICCPR) (1966) which states that: 'No one shall be subjected to torture or to cruel, inhuman or degrading treatment or punishment. In particular, no one shall be subjected without his free consent to medical or scientific experimentation.'[3]

Thus, Art 5 of the CHRB, which requires that any intervention in the health field 'may only be carried out after the person concerned has given free and informed consent to it', simply affirms a well-established international rule.[4]

The purpose of the rule is to ensure respect for autonomy and the right of the individual to choose whether or not to participate in research.[5] According to the Explanatory Report, Art 5 affirms that:

... no one may in principle be forced to undergo an intervention without his or her consent. Human beings must therefore be able freely to give or refuse their consent to any intervention involving their person. This rule makes clear patients' autonomy in their relationship with health care professionals and restrains the paternalistic approaches which might ignore the wish of the patient.

Accordingly, a breach of Art 5 occurs whenever the individual's consent has been obtained by deceit or misinformation, irrespective of whether the individual has suffered harm or not. The right protected is in effect a right to freedom of choice in respect of participation in a research project. There is an attaint on the right when the individual has been illegitimately denied the opportunity to make an informed choice, even in circumstances where the individual stood to derive some health benefit from participation in the experiment.

Where the individual has also suffered harm as a result of participation in an experiment, then additional separate breaches of the Convention may be involved if the experiment failed to comply with the requirements listed in Arts 16 and 17 regarding the legitimacy of the purpose of the experiment, whether it was approved by an independent multidisciplinary ethics committee, whether the

---

2   Paragraph 22.

3   Article 7.

4   As the Explanatory Report itself acknowledges (para 34). Similar consent rules may be found in other international and regional instruments adopted after the Convention, including the EU Charter on Human Rights and the Clinical Trials Directive.

5   If anything, the consent rule is strengthened by the added detailed rules in the Council of Europe's Draft Additional Protocol to the Convention on Human Rights and Biomedicine, on Biomedical Research (2001). The Draft Protocol has yet to be adopted but nevertheless gives a clear indication of the intentions of the drafters of the CHRB. Article 16 of the Draft Protocol states that: 'The persons being asked to participate in a research project shall be given adequate information in a documented and comprehensible form on the purpose, overall plan and methods to be applied in the research project, including the opinion of the ethics committee, according to national law.' This information has to include the nature and extent of procedures and, in particular, details of any burden imposed, the risks involved, rights and safeguards prescribed by law.

risks were proportionate to the benefits and whether procedures regarding the procurement of consent have been complied with.

On this basis, the CHRB *prima facie* appears to outrule the kind of deception perpetrated on both civil and military participants in the human radiation experiments in the US, and the nerve gas experiments and the biochemical warfare agents in the UK respectively. Does it?

3.2   THE UK PORTON DOWN EXPERIMENTS

In the UK experiments, at the Porton Down biological weapons military base in Wiltshire, the volunteers were servicemen. The Ministry of Defence (MoD) admitted that the toxic nerve gas sarin had been tested at Porton Down between the 1950s and 1980s. One of the volunteers, Mr Maddison, aged 20, had died in 1953 after a few drops of liquid sarin were dropped onto his arm. Notwithstanding this, tests of toxic gases continued until the early 1980s. By the end of the 1990s, there were allegations from several hundred servicemen that they had been deceived into participating in the tests and had consequently suffered ill health effects. Mr Maddison's family claimed that he was under the impression that he was taking part in a test to research the common cold.

Another serviceman, Mr Bell, who was at the Porton Down base in the 1950s, told the BBC that he had no idea what they were doing. He too thought that he was volunteering for research into the common cold. In an interview given to the BBC Radio 4's *Today* programme, he said: 'They put us in the gas chambers. We tested CS gas, some of these tests are horrendous ...'[6]

According to Mr Bell, some substances were dropped onto his skin. He has suffered from skin problems ever since but still does not know what substances he was exposed to.

Mr Foulkes, a former soldier, volunteered to take part in tests in 1983. He was aware that he was taking part in a test for sarin, but he claimed to have been deceived by government scientists about the risks involved and not told about Mr Maddison's death in 1953 following exposure to sarin: 'I specifically asked them what the long-term implications of taking part in the tests were because I was not happy about it. Of course, if they had mentioned what happened to Ronald Maddison I would not have taken part.'[7]

Mr Foulkes had volunteered to take part in the tests, without an antidote, because he thought this would advance his chances of promotion. He also received £140 on top of his £400 monthly wage.[8] The test involved him being locked into a chamber while the gas was administered. In the test chamber he developed tunnel vision, was sick and felt his chest constricted. When the test was over he was let out of the chamber by scientists wearing respirators and overalls.

---

6   24 August 2001.
7   Syal, 2002.
8   *Ibid.*

He was told to 'go home and wash your uniform'. Mr Foulkes claims that his health has deteriorated since the tests and that he suffers from respiratory problems which prevent him from obtaining well-paid work.

A criminal investigation named 'Operation Antler' was opened by Wiltshire Police in 2000 to investigate claims by several hundred servicemen that they had been used as guinea pigs at Porton Down. After two years of investigations the police concluded that three of the scientists may have committed criminal offences under s 24 of the Offences Against the Person Act 1861. A file was sent to the Crown Prosecution Service which decided that there was insufficient evidence for a prosecution.[9] Meanwhile, in 2002 the High Court ordered the inquest into Maddison's death reopened. The original inquest had taken place behind closed doors 10 years after the death and resulted in a finding of 'death by misadventure'. A civil claim is also pending from more than 300 ex-servicemen who claim to have suffered from respiratory to kidney problems since taking part in the tests. The burden of proof in English civil law is lower than in criminal law (on the balance of probabilities, as against beyond reasonable doubt for criminal cases). How does the protection in domestic law compare to that offered by the Convention?

3.3 DEFINITIONS OF MEDICAL RESEARCH

Medical research on human subjects in the UK is currently regulated through a combination of administrative and professional rules rather than by statute.[10] There is no case law directly on medical research.[11] Thus, the potential liability of medical researchers has to be surmised from general principles of law and rules in related areas such as medical treatment with the proviso that existing principles and rules may require modification or adjustment to reflect any significant difference in the level of legal protection required in medical treatment and medical research.

There is no legal definition of medical research in the UK. The Declaration of Helsinki does not define medical research either but instead states the legitimate purposes for which research may be conducted:

> The primary purpose of medical research involving human subjects is to improve prophylactic, diagnostic and therapeutic procedures and the understanding of the aetiology and pathogenesis of disease. Even the best proven prophylactic, diagnostic, and therapeutic methods must be continuously be challenged through research for their effectiveness, efficiency, accessibility and quality.[12]

An implicit distinction is nevertheless drawn between medical research and medical care in para 28 of the Declaration, which allows a physician to combine

---

9 See Mason, McCall Smith and Laurie, 2001.
10 See Kennedy and Grubb, 2000; Brazier, 2003.
11 As opposed to 'experimental treatment'. See *Simms v Simms* [2003] 2 WLR 1465 where the untested innovative procedure was described in court as 'experimental treatment'.
12 Paragraph 6.

the two 'only to the extent that the research is justified by its potential prophylactic, diagnostic or therapeutic value'. A further distinction is drawn in para 32 between unproven or new prophylactic, diagnostic and therapeutic measures which Helsinki allows a physician to use in the treatment of a patient, when no proven therapeutic methods exist. Paragraph 32 states that 'where possible, these measures should be made the object of research, designed to evaluate their safety and efficacy'.

3.3.1   Experimental treatment v research

The distinction between experimental treatment and research is particularly significant in respect of the specification of the legal obligations imposed on researchers, with the risk that the categorisation of an intervention or procedure as innovative or experimental 'treatment', 'therapy' or 'practice' could be used to justify a lower level of legal protection on levels of information and disclosure of risks than those appropriate for research, notwithstanding the fact that the effects and risks of an innovative or experimental procedure by definition are yet to be proven. Undoubtedly, the recipient of an innovative or experimental treatment or therapy, like a participant in a therapeutic medical research program, potentially stands to derive a health benefit from the intervention *if* the anticipated, unproven health benefits materialise. For instance, in *Simms v Simms*[13] the High Court authorised the hospital to conduct invasive brain surgery, or 'experimental treatment', on a young adult in the terminal stages of CJD – notwithstanding the fact that the procedure had never been tested on humans and its effects and risks were not known – on the basis of what appeared to be promising results in experiments conducted on mice. At the same time, what made the procedure *experimental* was the fact that the anticipated benefits and risks had not been tested or proven and, unlike a research programme, the intervention did not involve the systematic investigation and collection of data in order to evaluate the scientific validity of the supposed 'treatment'.

In the case of pharmaceutical products, there is a clear legal demarcation in the UK between a product which is being tested in a trial and a product whose efficacy and benefits have already been proven. Tests on the former have to be part of a clinical trial which itself has to comply with the EU Clinical Trials Directive,[14] which requires the trial to be part of a protocol which has to conform with prescribed scientific and ethical standards. The protocol has to be approved by an independent research ethics committee. Compliance with the Directive is required to obtain a licence from the Medicines Evaluation Agency to market the product for treatment. By contrast, there are no equivalent legal controls on other types of medical research, such as novel experimental surgery, or the testing of substances such as sarin which are neither a medicinal product nor a medical device.

---

13   [2003] 2 WLR 1465.
14   Directive 2001/20/EC, implemented in the UK by the Medicines for Human Use (Clinical Trials) Regulations 2004.

Thus, the categorisation of an intervention or procedure as innovative or experimental treatment or therapy, as opposed to research, potentially carries important implications as to the applicable legal or regulatory regime, including procedures and nature of consent requirements. At the same time, from the perspective of the patient or subject, and the protection of his right to autonomy and bodily integrity, there is every reason to require full disclosure of the nature of the intervention and the anticipated risks, whether the intervention falls into the category of experimental/innovative treatment/practice or research, since in all the cases the anticipated benefits and risks have yet to be scientifically proven.

3.3.2 Judicial approaches in the US

Notwithstanding this, there are indications from litigation in the US that the categorisation of a procedure as innovative or experimental treatment or practice is being used to justify a lower level of protection for autonomy. In *Adams v Arthur*[15] the Supreme Court of Arkansas held that liability for failure to disclose the innovative nature of a procedure or intervention lay in negligence and was subject to the two-year limitation rules of the State statute. In a subsequent case where the claimants claimed that the defendant surgeon had used a novel product in their spinal surgeries without obtaining informed consent, Judge Andree Laiton Roaf lamented that he was bound by the decision of the higher court which he said 'recognised no distinction between the garden variety of informed consent cases and the situation in which, as in the instant case, a medical provider, without the knowledge or consent of a patient, in effect conducts an experiment on the patient'. Other cases showing a narrow judicial approach to the definition of medical research include *Ancheff v Hartford Hospital*.[16] In 2002, the Supreme Court of Connecticut rejected the claimant's claim that he had been involved in a research program without his consent. The claimant had developed a potentially fatal bone infection following a back operation. He suffered damage to his inner ear after being injected once a day with a high dose of gentamicin, a powerful antibiotic known to have toxic effects. The hospital's 'once-a-day' dosage had never been tested on humans and, by the hospital's own admission, represented a 'radical' departure from US Food and Drug Administration (FDA) approved dosage and method of administration (7 mg/kg once a day, as against FDA approved 3 mg/kg three times a day). The programme was implemented systematically in the hospital on a group of patients from whom data was collected. The results were published and communicated in lectures to the medical community. Notwithstanding this, the Supreme Court of Connecticut accepted the defendant hospital's claim that the program did not constitute medical research but constituted instead the implementation of a program or practice of medical therapy which, in turn, was aimed not at validating an untested theory or

15   333 Ark 53, 969 SW 2d 598 (1998).
16   260 Comm 785 799 A 2d 1067 (2002).

hypothesis but at using the available literature, including prior research and clinical data, for the improvement of patient care and safety.[17]

Notwithstanding judicial trends in the US to conflate liability for innovative or experimental medical treatment with liability for standard medical treatment, there are, as Dieter Giesen argues, compelling reasons to distinguish the two: 'the individual doctor trying out new techniques is undeniably engaged in medical experimentation. It is unacceptable ... to place the burden of this experimentation upon the patient by confining his right of recovery in relation to consent to the tort of negligence.'[18]

3.4   CIVIL REMEDIES IN ENGLISH LAW

As far as the rules on medical treatment are concerned, English law has been notoriously slow at acknowledging the right of a patient to consent to treatment.[19] It is only in the past decade that the Court of Appeal has expressly acknowledged that the doctor's legal duty to obtain consent for treatment is based on the fundamental principle of respect for the individual's right to self-determination and autonomy. In *Re T*,[20] Lord Donaldson said that the individual has a right 'to live his own life how he wishes, even if it will damage his health or lead to his premature death'.[21] From this it follows that every adult person who is mentally competent has an 'absolute right to choose whether to consent to medical treatment, to refuse it or to choose one rather than another of the treatments being offered, whether the reason is rational, irrational or there is no reason at all'.[22] This right has since been re-affirmed by the Court of Appeal in a number of cases. *Re MB (Medical Treatment)* (1997)[23] involved a refusal of treatment by a pregnant woman when the refusal endangered both her life and that of her baby. *Re W (Adult: Refusal of Treatment)*[24] involved a prisoner who refused treatment to a leg wound in full knowledge that septicaemia might result and lead to his death. In *Mrs B v An NHS Hospital Trust*[25] the Court of Appeal affirmed the right of a severely disabled but mentally competent woman to refuse life-saving treatment.

---

17 The question of whether the programme constituted research was litigated as a matter of fact. Both the trial judge and the appeal court rejected the claimant's submission that he should be allowed to present to the jury the Belmont report. Both courts agreed that the references to the Second World War experiments and the Tuskegee refugee experiments were likely to prejudice the jury!

18 Giesen, 1995.

19 See Kennedy and Grubb, 2000.

20 [1992] 4 All ER 649.

21 [1992] 4 All ER 649 at 661d–f.

22 *Ibid.*

23 [1997] 2 FLR 426.

24 *The Independent*, June 17, 2002; *Lawtel* 2/7/2002.

25 [2002] 2 All ER 449.

3.4.1 Battery

Autonomy and self-determination are protected in English civil law by the tort of battery: 'The essence of the wrong of battery is the unpermitted contact.'[26] The tort is committed when the individual's body is touched or invaded without the individual's consent or authorisation, irrespective of whether harm was intended or suffered.[27]

The tort of battery is therefore essentially concerned with the protection of a person's civil liberty or right to self-determination. In *Mrs B v An NHS Hospital Trust*[28] the patient had suffered an illness which had caused her to develop tetraplegia and become severely disabled. Surgery only improved her condition slightly. She was put on an artificial ventilator and hospital staff subsequently refused to disconnect the ventilator despite repeated requests. The hospital was found to have committed a battery and Mrs B was awarded damages.[29]

Consent is a defence to battery.[30] Thus, treatment involving bodily contact is lawful only if it has been permitted or authorised by the patient:

> The law requires that an adult patient who is mentally and physically capable of exercising a choice must consent if medical treatment of him is to be lawful ... Treating him without his consent or despite a refusal of consent will constitute the civil wrong of trespass to the person and may constitute a crime.[31]

To be effective in law the patient's consent must be valid. The Court of Appeal has held that consent will not be valid if it has been obtained by fraud or misrepresentation: 'misinforming a patient, whether or not innocently, and the withholding of information which is expressly or impliedly sought by the patient may well vitiate either a consent or a refusal.'[32]

The misinformation must relate to the nature of the procedure or the identity of the person carrying out the procedure.[33] Thus, consent was not vitiated in *R v Richardson (Diane)*,[34] where patients had been treated by a dentist who had been suspended by the General Dental Council without their knowledge.

---

26 Brazier, 2003.

27 *Colins v Wilcock* [1984] 3 All ER 374, but see *Wilson v Pringle* [1986] 2 All ER 440.

28 [2002] 2 All ER 449.

29 The refusal is only valid if the patient is mentally competent. In *Re AK* [2001] 1 FLR 129 the court held that a hospital had to respect the anticipatory wish of a patient who was suffering from motor neurone disease that his ventilator should be disconnected and other life-saving measures discontinued when his condition deteriorated to the point that he became unable to communicate.

30 *Re T* [1992] 4 All ER 649.

31 In *Devi v West Midlands Regional Health Authority* (1980) SCLY 687, a 29 year old woman was admitted to hospital for a minor gynaecological operation. In the course of the operation, the surgeon discovered that the woman's womb was ruptured and decided to sterilise her there and then. The woman had not agreed to the sterilisation. It was held that the operation constituted a battery.

32 663 f–g.

33 Contrast *R v Tabassum* [2000] 2 Cr App R 328; [2000] Crim LR 686, CA, where the defendant, who claimed to have trained as a cancer specialist, was convicted of indecent assault after examining women's breasts. The women had consented but the Court of Appeal held that the consent related to the nature of his acts, not their quality which was sexual rather than medical.

34 [1999] QB 444.

Undue influence or pressure may also invalidate consent. In the case of *Re T* the Court of Appeal was not satisfied about the validity of a refusal to consent to a blood transfusion by T, a young pregnant woman who had suffered severe injuries in a car crash. T had been under heavy sedation and considerable pain at the time. Her mother, who was a fervent Jehovah's Witness, had been alone with her before the hospital sought consent for the transfusion. Contrary to what was stated on the signed consent form, the hospital personnel had failed to explain adequately to T the gravity of the consequences of the refusal.[35]

On the basis of the principles stated in *Re T*, there are two possible legal grounds on which the MoD may be liable in battery to the volunteers in the sarin experiments. First, a battery would have been committed if, as alleged by some of the volunteers, the participants in the tests were misled as to the nature of the experiments; for example, they were misinformed and told that the aim of the experiments was to research the common cold when the true aim instead was to test the toxicity of a noxious gas under tightly controlled conditions. The deception or misinformation must also have been intentional, although not necessarily activated by malice.[36] The contrast here is between someone who inadvertently or carelessly misleads another and someone who deliberately chooses to conceal the truth or pass on inaccurate information. In the latter case, the defendants could also be liable for the separate torts of deceit[37] and misrepresentation, including fraudulent misrepresentation.[38] In order to prove fraud, the claimant must prove that a false representation was made knowingly, or without belief in its truth or recklessly whether it be true or false.[39] The most serious charge would include fraudulent misrepresentation which might give rise to criminal liability, an option which the Crown Prosecution Service decided was not viable for lack of evidence.

In the case of the volunteers who were aware that they were taking part in tests of sarin, there was no deception as to the nature of the experiments (as opposed to possibly the risks attached, see below) but it may be that the substantial payments that were offered and the raised expectations of career enhancement could constitute inducements liable to exercise 'undue' pressure or

---

35 Lord Donaldson MR said, *inter alia*, that he was surprised to find that hospitals used standard forms of refusal to accept a blood transfusion and that he was dismayed at the layout of the form. He said that it is clear that such forms are designed primarily to protect the hospital from legal action. But they 'will be wholly ineffective for this purpose if the patient is incapable of understanding them, they are not explained to him and there is no good evidence (apart from the patient's signature) that he had that understanding and fully appreciated the significance of signing it' at 663 c–e.

36 *Letang v Cooper* [1965] 232 1 QB.

37 *Derry v Peek* [1886–90] All ER Rep 1.

38 Misrepresentation Act 1967.

39 *Per* Lord Hershell in *Derry v Peek*. Unlike the claimant in the US case of *Whitlock v Duke University* 637 F Supp 1463 the claimant's claim failed because he was unable to establish that even if representation had been fraudulent, it would not have been reasonable for him to rely on it. The claimant, Mr Whitlock, had suffered brain damage after participating in simulated deep dives. Mr Whitlock was an experienced diver with a degree in oceanographic studies. The court concluded that even if risks had been understated or concealed, it would not have been reasonable for him to rely on statements.

'influence' of a sufficient weight to 'vitiate' and invalidate consent.[40] In either case, the damages recoverable are potentially substantial and could include a deterrent element in addition to compensation for any harm suffered.

3.4.2 Negligence

If there was no deceit, fraud or misrepresentation as to the nature of the tests and the individual was informed in broad terms and simple language of the nature and purpose of the intervention, then liability for failure to disclose risks cannot lie in battery.[41] Instead, liability would lie in negligence if the omission to disclose risks fell below professional standards:

> The purpose of the rule requiring doctors to give appropriate information to their patients is to enable the patient to exercise her right to choose whether or not to have the particular operation to which she is asked to give her consent. English law has rejected the proposition that a failure to give adequate warning vitiates the patient's consent, thus turning the operation into an assault: see *Chatterton v Gerson* [1981] QB 432. Liability lies in negligence rather than trespass. But the patient does still have the right to choose what will and will not be done with her body and the doctor must take the care expected of a reasonable doctor in the circumstances in giving her the information relevant to that choice.[42]

The legal standard of negligence for professional occupations was laid down in the celebrated case of *Bolam*,[43] where in his direction to the jury, McNair J said that the test for negligence is the standard of the ordinary skilled man exercising and professing to have that special skill: '... in the case of a medical man negligence means failure to act in accordance with the standards of reasonably competent medical men at the time.'[44]

McNair J said that reasonable professionals may differ in opinion and that a doctor cannot be held liable in negligence merely because he has a difference of opinion with another reasonable or responsible doctor. Hence, a doctor will not be liable in negligence for failure to disclose risks as long as the doctor acted in accordance with a practice accepted by a responsible body of medical opinion.[45] It matters not either if the responsible body in question represents a minority opinion,[46] although it is possible that the court may find a failure to disclose risks negligent if there was no logical basis for the practice, and if the principle applied to diagnosis and treatment in *Bolitho* is extended to disclosure of risks.[47] *Bolam*

---

40   See also Brazier's report on surrogacy recommending that payments for egg donation should not be permitted to avoid undue influence (Brazier *et al*, 1998).
41   *Chatterton v Gerson* [1981] QB 432.
42   *Per* Sir Denis Henry in *Chester v Afshar* [2002] 3 All ER 552 at para 47.
43   *Bolam v Friern Management Committee* [1957] 1 WLR 582.
44   117-F.
45   118-E.
46   *De Freitas v O'Brian* (1995) 6 Med LR 108.
47   *Bolitho (Deceased) v City and Hackney Health Authority* [1998] AC 232; see Brazier and Miola (2000) and Kennedy and Grubb (2000).

was approved by the House of Lords in *Sidaway*[48] where it was held that a failure by a neurosurgeon to disclose a 1% risk of injury to the spinal cord in a neck operation was not negligent. But Lord Bridge of Harwich said that a doctor could be liable if questioned by a patient about risks involved in a particular treatment proposed, as the doctor's duty must be to answer both as truthfully and as fully as the questioner requires (898b, c). Lord Templeman said that if Ms Sidaway had asked questions about this operation, 'she could and should have been informed that there was an aggregate risk of between 1% and 2% risk of some damage either to the spinal cord or to a nerve root resulting in some injury which might vary from irritation to paralysis'. On the basis of both these *obiter dicta*, the Court of Appeal held in *Chester v Afshar*[49] that a consultant had been negligent in failing to advise of a 1% to 2% risk of nerve damage when asked by a patient who was left paralysed after a back operation. Sir Denis Henry said that in the light of the *dicta* in *Sidaway* and the patient's questions: 'she should have been fully told what the risk was.'

On this basis, volunteers at Porton Down who claim to have been misled about the risks involved in the sarin tests may have a claim in negligence against the MoD, if the failure to disclose risks at the time was not supported by a responsible body of scientific opinion. Even if a responsible body of medical opinion would have supported non-disclosure of risks at the time, the MoD may still be liable if the court is satisfied that the risks were of such magnitude that no prudent scientist should have failed to disclose the risks,[50] or that there was no logical basis for the failure to disclose the risks,[51] and/or the participants had expressly asked about risks.

However, even if it could be satisfactorily established that there was in law a breach of duty to disclose risks, the victims would still have to establish that they suffered ill health or harm as a result of the breach, that the harm was caused by or could be legally attributed to the breach[52] and that had they been aware of the risks they would have chosen not to participate in the tests.[53] In the Canadian case

---

48 *Sidaway v Board of Governors of the Bethlem Royal and the Maudsley Hospital* [1985] 2 WLR 871, AC.

49 [2002] 3 All ER 552.

50 Eg, 10% risk of a stroke, *per* Lord Bridge in *Sidaway*.

51 For contrasting views on the effect of *Bolitho* on consent see Brazier and Miola, 2000 and Plomer, 2000.

52 The leading case is *Hotson v East Berkshire AHA* [1987] AC 750. The claimant must prove that the defendant's negligence was more likely than not to have caused his injury. The difficulty for the claimant arises when the 'guilty conduct' is one of several possible causes as in *Wilsher v Essex AHA* [1988] 1 All ER 871; but contrast *McGhee v National Coal Board* [1973] 1 WLR 1. See also *Christopher David Hossack v Ministry of Defence, Lawtel* 19/4/2000.

53 *Smith v Barking, Havering and Brentwood Health Authority* (1994) 5 Med LR 285. The patient was not adequately warned of risks of tetraplegia following an operation but the hospital was not liable because the judge found that the patient would still have had the operation if warned. The same principle was applied in *McAllister v Lewisham and North Southwark Health Authority* [1994] 5 Med LR 343, but the judge reached the opposite conclusion on finding that the patient would have declined the operation had she been warned of the risks. Compare the ruling of the Australian High Court in *Chapel v Hart* (1998) 195 CLR 1232, approved by the Court of Appeal in *Chester v Afshar* [2002] 3 All ER 552. For a discussion of the majority and minority views in *Chapel v Hart* see Cane, 1999; and Stauch, 2000.

of *Zimmer v Ringrose* (1981) the defendant obstetrician had used an innovative and untested surgical procedure to sterilise the claimant patient. She suffered extended injuries but was unable to recover any damages. The court found that the surgeon had been negligent in failing to disclose the risks attending the experimental treatment, but the patient failed in her claim as the court determined that she would still have undergone the operation had she been adequately informed of the risks. The rule adopted by the English Court of Appeal in *Chester v Afshar* is the most favourable to the claimant, as it attributes liability to the defendant when the defendant was under a legal duty to warn of certain risks, failed to do so and the very risks against which he should have warned materialise. According to Sir Denis Henry:

> The law is designed to require doctors properly to inform their patients of the risks attendant on their treatment and to answer questions put to them as to that treatment and its dangers, such answers to be judged in the context of good professional practice, which has tended to a greater degree of frankness over the years, with more respect being given to patient autonomy. The object is to enable the patient to decide whether or not to run the risks of having that operation at that time. If the doctor's failure to take that care results in her consenting to an operation to which she would not otherwise have given her consent, the purpose of that rule would be thwarted if he were not to be held responsible when the very risk about which he failed to warn her materialises and causes her an injury which she would not have suffered then and there. [at 47]

However, leave to appeal to the House of Lords has been granted and the Court of Appeal ruling is yet to be affirmed by the House of Lords.

The other main source of difficulty is the issue of causation. The claimant has to show that his injuries were caused by the defendant's negligence. The nature of the potential evidential difficulties facing the Porton Down victims to establish that any ill health effects that they have suffered were *caused* by exposure to risks attached to the noxious substances tested may be surmised from the fact that a study into the effects of the experiments on the health of the participants was only commissioned by the Government in 2001. This raises the question of what was scientifically known about risks of exposure at the time. The answer is crucial to the claimants as they would have to establish that, at the time they agreed to participate in the research programme, there existed clear scientific evidence as to risks, unlike *Roe v Ministry of Health* where the claimants were children who had been inoculated with vaccines which had been contaminated through invisible cracks in the containers whose existence was not discovered until several years later. The defendants were not liable.

To conclude, if the standard English rules on consent to treatment and liability in negligence were simply extended to scientific research without modification, the volunteers at Porton Down might find it difficult to succeed in a negligence claim because:

- it might be difficult to ascertain what was demonstrably known about risks *at the time*;
- the degree of latitude on disclosure of risks allowed to the professions by the *Bolam* rule is fairly wide;

- it may be difficult to establish on the balance of probabilities that any harm suffered by the participants was caused by exposure to the risks attending the tests (rather than something else);

- it may be difficult to establish that participants would have opted not to take part in the tests had they been warned of the risks;

- even when participants can prove that they would not have participated in the tests had they known about the risks, there is some uncertainty as to the circumstances under which English law is prepared to treat a failure to warn of risks as the cause of any harm suffered by the claimant.

Hence, in spite of evidence of a judicial retreat in recent years from the dominant judicial deferential attitude to the medical profession in the past,[54] the difficulties attached to establishing liability in negligence for failure to obtain informed consent remain substantial. Negligence rules provide an uncertain basis on which to remedy the wrong suffered by research participants who were deceived as to the nature of the risks attached to the tests (as opposed to the nature of the tests).

Arguably, the standard legal rules on liability in negligence for medical treatment should be distinguished and strengthened in the case of scientific research. Negligent failure to obtain informed consent may leave the patient exposed to the risks inherent in the treatment but the balance of risks to benefits should still in theory be such that the patient potentially stands to benefit from the treatment. By contrast, participants in a non-therapeutic research program cannot, by definition, stand to derive any health benefits. In the Porton Down experiments, the participants could only suffer harm if the anticipated (or unknown) risks materialised. Since participation in a non-therapeutic research programme can only potentially harm the volunteer's health, there is a compelling argument that the legal standard of disclosure should be higher than for medical treatment. The few court rulings in Canada and the US on the doctor's duty of disclosure in medical research programmes all concur that the nature of the subject's interests and rights affected in non-therapeutic experiments require stricter legal standards and remedies than the general remedies of the law of negligence.

3.5 CANADA AND THE US

In *Halushka v University of Saskatchewan*[55] the Canadian Court of Saskatchewan stated that:

> In order for a consent to be effective, it must be an informed consent, freely given and it is the duty of the doctor to give a fair and reasonable explanation of the proposed treatment including the probable effect thereof and any special unusual risks. Such being the duty owed by a physician to his patient in ordinary medical practice, the duty to inform is at least as great, if not greater in the case of those engaged in medical

---

54 Lord Woolf, 2001.
55 *Halushka v University of Saskatchewan* (1965) 53 DLR 2d 436.

research to persons who offer themselves as subjects for experimentation because in the latter case, there can be no exception to the requirements of full disclosure whereas it may be necessary to keep certain things from the patient, in the interest of the peace of mind, when a medical operation is being performed.[56]

Similarly, in *Weiss v Solomon*[57] the Superior Court of Quebec held that: 'The Court must thus conclude that in a purely experimental research programme, the doctor must disclose all known risks, including those which are very rare or remote and *a fortiori* those whose consequences would be grave.'[58]

The US cases point to an even stricter standard of disclosure for non-therapeutic experiments.[59] In *Whitlock v Duke University*[60] the claimant had suffered brain damage after taking part in the Atlantis Series of dives conducted by the FG Hall Laboratory of Duke University. The purpose of the experimental simulated deep dives was to research high pressure nervous syndrome. The District Court of North Carolina rejected the claimant's claim that the defendants had concealed risks and failed to obtain informed consent. The court distinguished the standard for informed consent in a medical therapeutic context[61] from that in a research, non-therapeutic context where 'the policy considerations and balance of interests are different'. In a research context, the court said that the standard should be the 'Nuremberg' standard adopted by the US Military Tribunal in the Nuremberg Trials:

1   The voluntary consent of the human subject is absolutely essential. This means that the person involved should have legal capacity to give consent: should be so situated as to be able to exercise free power of choice without the intervention of

---

56 (1965) 52 WWR 608 at 616–17, 53 DLR 2d 436 (Sask CA): applying the Supreme Court cases of *Hopp v Lepp* (1980) 112 DLR 3d 67 and *Reibl v Hughes* (1980) 114 DLR (3d) 1. In *Zimmer v Ringrose* (1981) 124 DLR 3d 215, the Alberta Court of Appeal refused to extend the higher standard of disclosure in *Halushka* to innovative but untested medical treatment: 'In the case of a truly "experimental" procedure, like the one conducted in *Halushka v Univ of Sask, supra*, no therapeutic benefit is intended to accrue to the participant. The subject is simply part of a scientific investigation designed to enhance human knowledge. By contrast, the sterilization procedure performed by the appellant in this case was directed towards achieving a therapeutic end. By means of a successful sterilization, the respondent could avoid the occurrence of an unwanted pregnancy and the adverse health problems associated with it. In my opinion, the silver nitrate method was experimental only in the sense that it represented an innovation in sterilization techniques which were relatively untried. According to the testimony of the respondent's expert witness, the procedure itself could not be dismissed out of hand as being medically untenable. Indeed, his primary criticism of the method appears to have been the absence of adequate clinical evaluation. To hold that every new development in medical methodology was "experimental" in the sense outlined in of Sask *Halushka v Univ* would be to discourage advances in the field of medicine. In view of these considerations, the application of the standard of disclosure stated in the *Halushka* case 'would be inappropriate in this instance' (at para 18). For a criticisms of the distinction between 'innovative' treatment and medical experiment see Giesen, 1995: 'The individual doctor trying out new techniques is undeniably engaged in medical experimentation. It is unacceptable ... to place the burden of this experimentation upon the patient by confining his right of recovery in relation to consent to the tort of negligence.'
57 (1989) Carswell Que 72.
58 At 109.
59 Eg, *Whitlock v Duke University* (NC 1986) 637 F Supp 1463, affd 829 F 2d 1340 (1987). For a discussion see Mason, McCall Smith and Laurie, 2001 and Morin, 1998.
60 637 F Supp 1463 (NC, 1986).
61 Regulated by statute 90-21.13.

any element of force, fraud, deceit, duress, over reaching, or other ulterior form of constraint or coercion and should have sufficient knowledge and comprehension of the elements of the subject matter involved as to enable him to make an understanding and enlightened decision. This latter element requires that before the acceptance of an affirmative decision by the experimental subject there should be made known to him the nature, duration, and purpose of the experiment; the method and means by which it is to be conducted; *all* inconveniences and hazards *reasonably* to be expected; and the effects upon his health or person which may possibly come from his participation in the experiment.

2   The duty and responsibility for ascertaining the quality of the consent rests upon each individual who initiates, directs, or engages in the experiment. It is a personal duty and responsibility which may not be delegated to another with impunity. [emphasis added]

The Court noted with approval that the 'Nuremberg' standard is stricter than the medical standard of informed consent, in that the experimenter is put under a duty to disclose *all* risks which may reasonably be anticipated and not just the 'usual and most frequent' risks. In addition, the standard of disclosure in the Nuremberg Code is subjective and puts the doctor or experimenter under an obligation to disclose to the subject all the risks which may have an adverse effect which the subject may personally suffer, as against the risks that a reasonable subject may suffer.[62] The Court thus concluded that 'the degree of required disclosure of risks is higher in the non-therapeutic context than required under §90-20.13 (in the therapeutic context)' (p 1471).

In *Wright v The Fred Hutchinson Cancer Research Centre*[63] the participants in a cancer research program were informed of the nature of the experiment but alleged that they had not been informed about all the risks. The District Court of Washington rejected the relatives of the deceased participants' claim that the

---

62   But note that US courts have since consistently rejected a private right of action under either the Nuremberg Code or Helsinki. In *Robertson v McGee* (2002) WL 5350-45, the Oklahoma District Court rejected the claimants' claim that their participation in a cancer research program to which they had consented but which had been conducted in violation of FDA regulations, gave rise to a violation of their constitutional right to privacy and dignity: 'Although somewhat unclear, apparently, the claimants are contending that by the defendants conducting the melanoma study in violation of federal regulations for the protection of human subjects, such conduct gives rise to an independent private cause of action by incorporating the Declaration of Helsinki and the Nuremberg Code. The claimants contend that these international laws are the "minimum international standards of conduct governing biomedical research on human subjects into which all the citizens of all nations are subject". This Court agrees with other jurisdictions which have found that there is no private right of action for an alleged violation of international law for the protection of human research subjects under the Declaration of Helsinki and the Nuremberg Code. See, eg, *White v Paulsen* 997 F Supp 1380, 1383 (ED Wash) (1998) and *Hoover v West Virginia Department of Health and Human Services* 984 F Supp 978 (1997 SDWVr) affd 129 F 3d 1259 (11 superth Cir 1997). Moreover, the standard in the US for conducting research on human subjects is contained in the Code of Federal Regulations and, thus, there is no need for the courts to resort to international law to impute a standard.'

63   206 FRD 679 (2002).

doctors' failure to disclose risks amounted to a violation of the participants fundamental and constitutionally protected right to life and liberty. The Court said that the therapeutic nature of the trial rendered a remedy in negligence more appropriate:

> ... the Court finds that the type of wrongful conduct alleged in claimants' Second Amended Complaint, namely defendants' failure to make disclosures necessary to the informed consent process in a therapeutic, experimental setting, does not implicate rights that are so rooted in the tradition and conscience of our people as to be ranked as fundamental. A doctor's tortious failure to obtain informed consent is not a threat to our citizens' enjoyment of ordered liberty, even when the doctor is employed by the state. Although the failure to obtain informed consent necessarily throws some doubt on the voluntariness of the patient's participation in a research study, such a failure does not raise the spectre of the type of involuntary, non-therapeutic experimentation which shocked the nation after World War II and gave rise to the Nuremberg Code.[64]

On the other hand, the Court noted that 'the judiciary has not hesitated to find that, where the human research subjects were not told that they were participating in an experiment and/or the government conducted the experiments knowing they had no therapeutic value, the subject's constitutionally protected right to life and/or liberty had been violated'.[65]

3.6   AUTONOMY AND BODILY INTEGRITY AS CONSTITUTIONALLY PROTECTED FUNDAMENTAL RIGHTS

In the cases arising from the human radiation experiments,[66] several State courts in the US have accepted the claimants' claims that their participation in experiments whose true nature and risks had been concealed from them was so serious as to constitute a violation of their fundamental right to life and liberty constitutional protected by the due process clause in the Fourteenth Amendment. In the *Cincinnati* case[67] the claimants were patients suffering from cancer who had life expectancies of up to two years. They were predominantly African-Americans who were primarily poorly educated and of lower than average intelligence. They were told that they were receiving radiation as a treatment for their cancer when the radiation tests were in fact designed to test the psychological and physiological effect of radiation on humans for the Department of Defense:

> Radiation exposure either led to the patients' death, seriously shortened the patients' life expectancy and/or led to radiation injury resulting in bone marrow failure or suppression, nausea, vomiting, burns on the patients' bodies, severe and permanent pain, and/or suffering and emotional distress.[68]

---

64   At p 7.
65   *Ibid*, p 7.
66   See Chapter 2.
67   *In Re Cincinnati Radiation Litig* 874 F Supp 796 (SD Ohio 1995).
68   *Ibid* at p 8.

The claimants alleged that their participation in the experiments without informed consent resulted *inter alia* in a violation of their right to equal protection under the law, including the right to be free of state-sponsored invasion of their bodily integrity protected by the Due Process clause of the Fourteenth Amendment of the US Constitution, which provides that no state shall 'deprive a person of life, liberty, or property without due process of law'. The court agreed with the claimants,[69] stating that:

> If the Constitution protects 'personal autonomy in making certain types of important decision' *Whalen v Roe* 429 US 589, 97 S Ct 869 (1977), the decision whether to participate in the Human Radiation Experiments was one that each individual claimant was entitled to make freely and with full knowledge of the purpose and attendant circumstances involved. [p 15]

The claimants succeeded in establishing that their right to make an informed decision on whether to participate in the human radiation experiments was an aspect of a constitutionally protected fundamental liberty under the Due Process Clause. A fundamental right may be abridged or curtailed by the State if the aims are legitimate and the means are necessary and proportionate, but in the court's view none of these requirements were satisfied. If the allegations were true, they amounted to a claim that the defendants, who were government officials, had lied to the claimants and exposed them to drastic doses of radiation without procedural safeguards. In the court's view, the bodily invasions also had the character of needless severity[70] which was sufficient to trigger Fifth Amendment protection. The defendants' alleged conduct thus amounted to an unconstitutional arbitrary deprivation of the subject's liberty and life.

The court rejected the defendants' attempt to frame the claim as one of 'simple medical malpractice' or 'an ordinary tort case'. In the court's view, the distinction between this case and an ordinary tort case is not one of degree but rather of kind:

> Government actors in cases such as this violate a different kind of duty from that owed by a private tort defendant. Individuals in our society are largely left free to

---

69 Reviewing the jurisprudence of the Supreme Court, the Ohio District Court noted that although the literal wording of the clause might suggest that it governs only the procedures by which a State might deprive persons of liberty, the clause has been understood to contain a substantive component as well, which included the subject's right to be free of state-sponsored invasion of bodily integrity. At p 14, citing Chief Justice Rehnquist that 'the protections of substantive due process have for the most part been accorded to matters relating to marriage, family, procreation, *and the right to bodily integrity*' in *Albright v Oliver* 510 US 266, 114 S Ct 807 (1994).

70 Crucial factors are presence of physical pain, permanence of any disfigurement or ensuing complication, risk of irreversible injury to health and danger to life itself: *Schmerber v California* 384 US 757 (1966) at p 772. (The Supreme Court held that blood tests for alcohol content of a car accident victim in hospital were reasonable because of minimal intrusion involved and lack of permanent effect.) But forcibly extracting narcotics from individual's stomach 'shocks conscience': *Rochin v California* 342 US 165 (1952). Compulsory vaccination for smallpox legitimate because of need to prevent epidemic and invasion was minimal: *Jacobson v Massachusetts* 197 US 11 (1905) at p 29. An intrusion which may otherwise be sufficiently minimal to pass the test would be beyond the boundaries of due process if less severe means could be used to achieve the same purpose. For instance, the Supreme Court unanimously held that compelling a suspect to submit to surgical removal under general anesthesia of a bullet which the authorities believed would link suspect to crime violated the Constitution if the State already possessed substantial, independent evidence of the origin of the bullet.

pursue their own ends without regard for others, save a general duty not to harm others by negligent conduct. This is the 'ordinary' tort case. The relationship between government is neither an autonomous actor nor a master to whom the people must acquiesce. The function of government is to serve the people and to enhance the quality of life. The broad purpose of all constitutional limits on government power is to ensure that government does not stray from that role or abuse its power. [p 20]

The defendants' attempt to frame the claim in tort thus revealed an interpretation of the Constitution which would vitiate the fundamental Constitutional principles of autonomy and liberty, which are deeply rooted in American constitutional history and tradition and the concern to protect individual liberty from coercive government.

The Massachusetts Supreme Court and the New York District Court subsequently followed the same reasoning in *Heinrich v Sweet* where the government used false pretences to lure claimants into participating in radiation experiments which the government knew had no therapeutic value and in *Stadt v University of Rochester* where the claimant, who thought she was receiving medical treatment for scleroderma, was injected with plutonium without her knowledge or consent.

The US judicial analysis of informed consent in a non-therapeutic research context as an aspect of a fundamental, constitutionally protected right evinces a more robust legal position than the traditional analysis of consent as a subset of negligence. In the English context, the closest common law counterpart would be to treat a failure to disclose risks in a non-therapeutic research programmes as having the legal effect of invalidating or vitiating consent. In such contexts, the rule in *Chatterton v Gerson* would no longer provide a shield against an action in battery, thus avoiding the weaknesses of negligence rules which have been claimed by human rights scholars to constitute '... a dangerous threat to their [the patient's] autonomy, and sometimes, to their lives'.[71] Does the CHRB provide stronger protection?

3.7   CONVENTION RIGHTS

As explained in Chapter 1, the CHRB could be relied upon indirectly by a claimant who brought a claim under the ECHR. The most likely vehicles under which the provisions on consent in Arts 5, 16 and 17 of the CHRB could be invoked would be Arts 3 and 8 of the ECHR.

3.8   ARTICLE 3

Article 3 of the ECHR provides that: 'No one shall be subjected to torture or to inhuman or degrading treatment or punishment.'

---

71 Feldman, 2002, p 279.

The Article imposes an absolute prohibition on torture or inhuman or degrading treatment or punishment.[72] It has been described by the European Court of Human Rights (ECtHR) as 'one of the most fundamental provisions of the Convention and as enshrining core values of the democratic societies making up the Council of Europe'.[73] Because of the absolute nature of the prohibition, the ECtHR has stressed that '"treatment" should not be given an unrestricted or extravagant meaning'.[74] However, it is likely that the word 'treatment' would include scientific or medical experiments. Such a reading of Art 3 of the ECHR would be consistent with the later ICCPR (1966) which includes a specific prohibition on medical or scientific experimentation without consent as a particular example of the general prohibition on torture, cruel, inhuman or degrading treatment in Art 7. However, it is unclear whether the absence of consent would, in itself, be sufficient to render participation in the experiment 'inhuman' or 'degrading' as required by Art 3 of the ECHR.

The ECtHR's interpretation of what constitutes 'inhuman' or 'degrading' treatment is very much linked to the particular factual situation of each claim.[75] Inhuman or degrading treatment may include conduct which constitutes an attaint on the individual's right to physical integrity and human dignity.[76] In general, however, the threshold of pain or degree of humiliation has to be fairly high or severe in order to come within the sphere of application of Art 3. In the case of *Kudla v Poland*[77] the Grand Chamber of the ECtHR stated that:

> … ill-treatment must attain a minimum level of severity if it is to fall within the scope of Article 3. The assessment of this minimum is, in the nature of things, relative; it depends on all the circumstances of the case, such as the nature and context of the treatment, the manner and method of its execution, its duration, its physical or mental effects and, in some instances, the sex, age and state of health of the victim … The Court has considered the treatment to be 'inhuman' because, *inter alia*, it was premeditated, was applied for hours at a stretch and caused either actual bodily injury or intense mental suffering. It has deemed treatment to be 'degrading' because it was such as to arouse in the victim feelings of fear, anguish and inferiority capable of humiliating and debasing them. On the other hand, the Court has consistently stressed that the suffering and humiliation must in any event go beyond that inevitable element of suffering or humiliation connected with a legitimate form of legitimate treatment or punishment …

---

72 At its minimum, the prohibition on inhuman or degrading treatment imposes on member States a negative obligation to refrain from inflicting serious harm on persons within their jurisdiction. However, a positive obligation on State authorities to protect the health of persons deprived of liberty or to take steps to protect individuals from being subjected to inhuman or degrading treatment has also been said to arise in *Z v UK* [2001] 2 FCR 246, and *Keenan v UK* (2001) 10 BHRC 319.

73 *Soering v UK* (1989) 11 EHRR 439 at 467, and *Kelly v UK* (2002) 2 FCR 97 at para 13. On Art 3 generally see Duffy, 1983, pp 316–46 and Feldman, 2002.

74 *Kelly v UK* at para 13.

75 The terms 'inhuman' and 'degrading' are not synonymous. For instance, in *A v UK* (1998) 27 EHRR 611, the ECtHR held that repeated and painful beating of a nine year old boy with a cane was degrading but not inhuman. See Feldman, 2002.

76 *X v Germany* (1985) 7 EHRR 152 where the applicant had been force-fed by prison authorities whilst being on hunger strike. The ECtHR held that force-feeding did constitute an attaint to the individual's dignity, but no violation because the aim was to preserve life which the State had an obligation do under Art 2.

77 App No 30210/96, Judgment of 26 October 2000 (Grand Chamber), at paras 91–92.

On this basis, it would seem that absence of consent would not in itself necessarily render medical or scientific experimentation 'inhuman' or 'degrading' unless some fairly severe degree of pain, suffering and humiliation was attached. If so, only the experiments which exposed volunteers to highly unpleasant conditions (for example, chamber gas) at Porton Down might found a claim under Art 3. It is a moot point whether prior knowledge and consent to the risks would allow the MoD to avoid liability for breach of Art 3. The ECtHR has held in *Laskey v UK* that restrictions imposed by the State on conduct between consenting adults which goes beyond posing a potential risk and carries a sufficient degree of seriousness of harm could not possibly amount to a breach of Art 8.[78] However, by contrast to Art 8 to which limitations apply, the obligation imposed by Art 3 is absolute. The question which would arise would thus be whether prior knowledge and consent divested the experiments of any degrading or inhuman quality.

3.9   ARTICLE 8

The fundamental importance of the principle of self-determination has recently been acknowledged by the ECtHR in *Pretty v UK* (2002) 35 EHRR 1 where it was said at para 61 that:

> The concept of 'private life' is a broad term not susceptible to exhaustive definition. The notion of personal autonomy is an important principle underlying the interpretation of the guarantees in Article 8.

And that:

> Although no previous case has established as such any right to self-determination as being contained in Article 8 of the Convention, the court considers that the notion of personal autonomy is an important principle underlying the interpretation of its guarantees... It covers the physical and psychological integrity of a person.

The Court explicitly said that the right protected by Art 8 extended to the right to consent to treatment:

> ... the imposition of medical treatment, without the consent of a mentally competent adult patient, would interfere with a person's physical integrity in a manner capable of engaging the rights protected under Article 8(1) of the Convention. [para 63]

Diane Pretty had argued that she had a right to determine whether or not to remain alive and to receive assistance in ending her own life. She argued that the criminal prohibitions on assisted suicide constituted a violation of her right which was protected by Arts 2, 3, 8 and 9. The ECtHR rejected her claim that the prohibition on assisted suicide forced her into an undignified and cruel death (Art 3) but held, *contra* the UK court, that Ms Pretty could found a claim under Art 8 as she had a right to self-determination, which extended to choosing the manner and time of her death. However, the right protected by Art 8 may be

---

78 In *R v Brown* [1994] AC 212, the House of Lords held that the nature and degree of the sado-masochistic acts engaged in by the defendants were such as to invalidate consent. The ECtHR has also tolerated greater interferences with conscripts' rights/liberties than with those of civilians, eg, the right to liberty under Art 5 in *Engel v Netherlands* (1976).

restricted or limited by the State under the conditions specified in Art 8(2), namely if the interference is 'in accordance with the law', has an aim or aims that is or are legitimate and is 'necessary in a democratic society' for the aforesaid aim or aims.

Since Art 8 was engaged, the question was whether the UK's criminalisation of assisted suicide constituted a necessary and proportionate limitation on Ms Pretty's right. The ECtHR held that the interference was necessary and proportionate, since the aim of the criminal prohibition was to protect vulnerable people who could be put at risk of having their life ended, a risk widely acknowledged across the international community. The reasoning in *Pretty* gives a fairly clear indication of how Art 8 may apply to a claim regarding participation in experiments without consent.

There is no doubt after *Pretty v UK* that Art 8 of the ECHR includes protection for the individual's right to self-determination. A more detailed elaboration of what the right entails in the case of biomedical interventions may be imported from Arts 5, 16 and 17 of the Council of Europe's CHRB. Article 8 is thus clearly engaged in the Porton Down experiments.

3.10 LIMITATIONS: NATIONAL SECURITY

Nevertheless, as was made clear in *Pretty*, the right protected by Art 8 is not absolute. A State may lawfully interfere with and limit the right if the interference is necessary in order to fulfil aims which comply with the legitimacy and proportionality requirements in a democratic society. In particular, Art 8(2) states that: 'There shall be no interference by a public authority with the exercise of this right except such as is in accordance with the law and is necessary in a democratic society in the interests of national security ...'

In the event that the participants in the Porton Down experiments were kept in the dark about the nature of the experiments or risks, could the MoD successfully plead that the individual's right to self-determination could justifiably give way to the interests of national security? Article 8 expressly allows for the rights of the individual to be trumped by the interests of society in specified compelling circumstances, including national security, providing the requirements of legitimacy, proportionality and subsidiarity are satisfied. In theory, it is not therefore possible to rule out, *a priori*, factual circumstances which may justify an encroachment on the individual's right to self-determination in experiments conducted in the interests of national security. Whether the experiments conducted at Porton Down satisfy these requirements is far from clear.[79]

By contrast, the expanded provisions on the right to self-determination and its application in a biomedical context which are contained in the Council of Europe's CHRB point to a different answer on the balance to be struck between the

---

79 Although in *Smith and Grady v UK* (1999) 29 EHRR 493, the ECtHR rejected the government's reliance on national security arguments under Art 8(2).

protection of fundamental rights and the interests of society. Article 26 of the CHRB on restrictions on the exercise of rights states that:

No restrictions shall be placed on the exercise of the rights and protective provisions contained in this Convention other than such as are prescribed by law and are necessary in a democratic society in the interest of public safety, for the prevention of crime, for the protection of public health or for the protection of the rights and freedoms of others.

There are clear similarities in the wording of Art 26 of the CHRB and Art 8 of the ECHR. However, unlike Art 8, Art 26 does not include a reference to national security. According to the Explanatory Report the omission is deliberate, as the drafters of the CHRB expressly sought to avoid encroachments on fundamental rights in the interests of national security:

Moreover, defending the economic well-being of the country, public order or morals and national security are not included amongst the general exceptions referred to in the first paragraph of this Article (26), unlike Article 8 of the European Convention on Human Rights. It did not appear desirable, in the context of this Convention, to make the exercise of fundamental rights chiefly concerned with the protection of a person's rights in the health sphere subject to the economic well-being of the country, to public order, to morals or to national security. [para 156]

In strict legal terms there is therefore an inconsistency between Art 8 of the ECHR and Art 26 of the CHRB which purports to expand upon the earlier and more general Convention. The CHRB indicates a social evolution in favour of a higher degree of protection for fundamental individual rights, particularly autonomy and self-determination. Technically, however, it is the earlier and more general Convention which provides the framework of rights and principles whose breach is actionable in the ECtHR. How the inconsistency may be resolved by the ECtHR is a moot point.

The potential difficulties facing claimants may be gleaned from a decision of the US Supreme Court in 1987 in *United States v Stanley* where the Army administered LSD to an unwitting enlisted man. The Supreme Court ruled by a majority (Justice O'Connor dissenting) that Mr Stanley could not obtain a financial remedy for his involvement in the experiments. Justice Scalia, delivering the majority judgment, expressed concern that to permit an enlisted man to sue the Army 'would call into serious question military discipline and decision-making'. Justice O'Connor's forceful dissent was relied upon in the *Cincinnati* and other human radiation cases:

... the US military played an instrumental role in the criminal prosecution of Nazi officials who experimented with human beings during the Second World War ... and the standards that the Nuremberg Military Tribunals developed to judge the behaviour of the defendants stated that the voluntary consent of the human subject is absolutely essential ... to satisfy moral, ethical, and legal concepts ... If this principle is violated, the very least society can do is to see that the victims are compensated, as best they can be, by the perpetrators. I am prepared to say that our Constitution's promise of due process of law guarantees this much.

Thus, the claimants in the human radiation experiments were only able to succeed in the *Cincinnati* and subsequent cases because, unlike Mr Stanley, they were not military enlisted personnel. In short, the Supreme Court in *Stanley* reasoned that the subject's fundamental right to bodily integrity and self-determination were outweighed by the public interest in maintaining military discipline.

CHAPTER 4

EMBRYONIC STEM CELL RESEARCH: HUMAN DIGNITY AND THE RIGHT TO LIFE

It is becoming increasingly clear that the ethical controversy over the legitimacy of stem cell research, and embryonic cloning in particular, is proving difficult to resolve. In the US, the President's Council on Bioethics has called for a moratorium on embryonic cloning, pending further public debate.[1] In September 2003 the European Commission adopted a temporary moratorium on the funding of stem cell research under the Framework 6 programme, also pending further discussion by EU organs. In the meantime, the Commission issued a report, *Commission Staff Working Paper Report on Human Embryonic Stem Cell Research*,[2] to provide background factual information on scientific, legal and social aspects of embryonic stem cell research. The report notes that, in its Opinion No 15 on ethical aspects of human stem cell research and use, the European Group on Ethics (EGE)[3] recommended a precautionary approach, condemning the creation of embryos for the sole purpose of research as this 'represents a further step in the instrumentalisation of human life', and a moratorium on the creation of embryos by somatic cell nuclear transfer for therapeutic purposes. The opinion of the EGE rested on the identification of a set of 'fundamental ethical principles' which were said to be applicable to embryonic stem cell research and included, *inter alia*, the principle of respect for human dignity, the principle of individual autonomy, justice and beneficence, freedom of research and proportionality. Notwithstanding this, the Commission found that 'opinions on the legitimacy of experiments using human embryos are divided according to the different ethical, philosophical, and religious traditions in which they are rooted'.[4] EU Member States have taken very different positions regarding the regulation of human embryonic stem cell research with the Commission's report confirming that 'there exists different views exist throughout the European Union concerning what is and what is not ethically defensible'.[5] Furthermore, it is becoming increasingly evident that the ethical differences are irreconcilable. At the inter-institutional seminar of 24 April 2003, the Commission concluded that 'despite all attempts to reduce the scope of the ethical debate, on the crucial issue of research using spare human embryos created for *in vitro* fertilisation purposes, the fundamentally incompatible moral positions of different Member States could not be reconciled'.[6] The proposed

---

1 President's Council on Bioethics, 2002. Professor Leon Kass was chairman and had previously expressed his opposition to cloning in Kass, 2000.

2 European Commission, 2003 (Report of 3 April).

3 The EGE was set up in December 1997 by the European Commission set to advise the European Commission on ethical aspects of science and new technologies in connection with the preparation and implementation of Community legislation or policies: see http://europa.eu.int/comm/european_group_ethics/index_en.htm. For Opinion, see EGE, 2000.

4 Note 2, p 8.

5 Note 2, p 8.

6 Cordis, *Beyond 2002, Inter-institutional Debate on Stem Cell Research Reveals Extent of Ethical Split Within Europe* 2003-04-25.

guidelines drawn by the Commission in June 2003 to limit funding for research to ethically derived stem cell lines were considered too restrictive by the European Parliament in November 2003. On 3 December 2003 the Council of Ministers was then unable to reach an agreement before the deadline for the moratorium on research funding expired at the end of December 2003.[7] Opponents of embryonic stem cell research had argued that such research was both unethical and illegal under Art 6(1) of the Treaty of the European Union which asserts that the Union is founded, *inter alia*, on the principles of 'respect for human rights and fundamental freedom' and that:

> The Union shall respect fundamental rights, as guaranteed by the European Convention for the protection of Human Rights and Fundamental Freedoms signed in Rome on 4 November 2003 and as they result from the constitutional traditions common to the Member States, as general principles of community law. [Art 6(2)]

At the same time, Art 6 also states that the EU has no competence to legislate on ethical matters and that each Member State retains its full prerogative to legislate on ethical matters.[8] The question thus remains of whether research on embryonic stem cells constitutes a violation of fundamental human rights, in particular the principle of respect for human dignity and the right to life. This chapter reviews the scope of international human rights instruments to determine whether human embryonic stem cell research does indeed involve a violation of fundamental human rights. I suggest that both the ethical and legal concept of human dignity is underdetermined and encompasses a plurality of ethical perspectives which are in turn compatible with a diversity of legal perspectives on the human embryo's right to life.

4.1 MORAL PERSPECTIVES ON HUMAN DIGNITY

Opponents of embryonic stem cell research allege that research on human embryos constitutes an affront to human dignity[9] and a violation of the human embryo's right to life.[10] In so far as the objections are intended to reflect the critics' understanding of what *ethical* principles of respect for human dignity and the right to life entail, then it is clear that there is considerable disagreement about the precise nature and scope of these ethical principles, as is in fact acknowledged by the critics themselves. For instance, at the first reading of a draft directive on human tissues and cells PROV (2003)0182 (A5-01/03/2003) in the European Parliament, opponents of stem cell research introduced an amendment which asserts that:

---

7 'Europe dithers over regulations for stem-cell research', *Nature*, 2003.

8 See European Commission, 2003, p 12 and Open Address by President Busquin at Inter-Institutional Seminar on Stem Cell Research, Brussels, *op cit*, fn 6.

9 See, for instance, debates of European Parliament. Resolution 2000 against UK and amendments to first reading of Directive on Human Tissue. Also, debates of German Bundestag.

10 See, for instance, speeches from the Austrian and German representatives at the Inter-Institutional Seminar on Stem Cell Research, Brussels, 24–25 April 2003; see fn 6.

(7a) There is no consensus within the European Union as to whether, and in what circumstances, embryonic stem cells may be processed. The processing of stem cells, and in particular the creation of stem cells in cases in which the embryo from which they originate has to be destroyed, is scientifically and *ethically* controversial and illegal in many Member States. [Amendment 9] [emphasis added]

Disagreements over the ethical nature and scope of the principle of respect for human dignity and the right to life in respect of the possible use of human embryos reflect deeper theoretical disagreements over philosophical and religious perspectives. For instance, Aristotelian, utilitarian and deontological theories are premised on fundamentally different philosophical perspectives and consequently yield different ethical principles or guides for conduct on matters of life and death.[11]

The principle of human dignity is a relatively modern 18th century western concept which has no direct translation in Aristotelian theory.[12] It could be adapted in modern virtue theories to yield guides of good conduct in relation to human foetuses or embryos.[13] However, since the essence of Aristotelianism is a conception of ethical life as a manifestation of virtuous character or conduct which requires the application of qualities of wisdom, knowledge and goodness to each particular factual situation, even neo-Aristotelian theories would not and could not ultimately justify an absolute prohibition on research on human embryos.[14] Aristotle himself, relying partly on 'scientific' understanding of foetal development at the time, did not think that human foetuses were worthy of protection until the point of 'quickening'. *A fortiori*, there would have been no reason in his view to protect the life of an embryo at a considerably less advanced stage of development. In short, from an Aristotelian or neo-Aristotelian perspective, neither the principle of respect for human dignity nor the right to life provide sufficient reasons to confer absolute protection on the life of early human embryos.

Similarly, the concept of human dignity has no distinct role to play in utilitarian or consequentialist theories, which by their very nature are committed to the hierarchical priority of aggregate and collective welfare over individual well-being, defined in the classical statement of the theory by John Stuart Mill as the 'greatest happiness of the greatest number'. Since the experience of happiness requires, at its minimum, sentience and ideally consciousness and/or the capacity to reason, it follows that the degree of protection to be afforded to human embryos and foetuses must of necessity vary depending on the embryo's actual capacity and potential at any point in time and must, in any event, be balanced against the totality of collective welfare or well-being.[15] The early embryo has neither

---

11 See Hursthouse, 1987.
12 See McIntyre, 1981; Crisp and Slote, 1997.
13 See Hursthouse, 1987.
14 *Ibid.*
15 See Singer and Kuhse, 2002; Harris, 1985; Harris, 1999.

sentience nor consciousness. It follows that its interests may only carry at most minimal weight in calculations of aggregate welfare against the potential therapeutic benefit to be derived by individuals who are already born and who are suffering from crippling or incurable diseases.[16]

Amongst classical moral theories, the only theory which expressly accords fundamental importance to the principle of respect for human dignity is Kantian theory. Kant is traditionally credited with the seminal principle that persons should never be treated as a means to an end only, but as an end in themselves. Kant reasoned that since persons have the capacity to reason and therefore make autonomous choices and determine their own ends, to treat persons as a means to an end only is to negate a person's very essence and dignity. On this view of human dignity, however, membership of the human species is not sufficient to confer dignity on an individual,[17] since it is the capacity to reason and make autonomous choices which is the source of human dignity. Since a human embryo lacks the capacity to reason, it follows that a human embryo may not necessarily be endowed with human dignity, at least as traditionally understood in the original classical version of the theory. Neither do neo-Kantian versions of human dignity provide any further reason to ascribe human dignity to early embryos. For instance, in Beyleveld and Brownsword's view: '(human) dignity as the basis of rights is *constituted* by the property of being an agent' (emphasis added).[18]

Beyleveld and Brownsword further add that it is the capacity for awareness that one's ability to pursue and achieve chosen purposes is not secure but can be threatened which 'constitutes the dignity that grounds the generic rights'.[19] Since, on this basis, agency is the basis of human dignity, 'human beings ostensibly only acquire rights ... at some point after birth'.[20] The human embryo is not an agent. It follows that 'to destroy an embryo or foetus cannot therefore be said to violate its dignity unequivocally'.[21]

To conclude, human dignity and the right to life are indeterminate concepts which admit of different interpretations and applications depending on one's moral theoretical perspective. When the concepts of human dignity and the right to life are explicated through the underlying background assumptions and fundamental values elaborated in different theoretical perspectives, divergence and disagreement over specific applications are likely to emerge. When the disagreement is not about facts (for instance, at what point in time a human foetus acquires the capacity for sentience) but about fundamental values (for instance, whether the human embryo has intrinsic value or worth) there may be no prospect of logical reconciliation.[22] Divergence at the level of fundamental

---

16 For different utilitarian approaches to the felicity calculus see Singer and Kuhse, 2002 and Singer, 1993; see also Hare, 1981 and Griffin, 1986. For a utilitarian defence of stem cell research see Harris, 2004.

17 Arguably, neither is it necessary, as Kant focuses on rationality as the basis for dignity.

18 Beyleveld and Brownsword, 2001, p 110. Their view explicitly adopts and elaborates upon Gewirth's view that only beings who are agents have dignity.

19 *Ibid*, p 111.

20 *Ibid*, p 157.

21 *Ibid*, p 158.

22 See Glover, 1977.

assumptions and premises in moral theories is not unlike divergence at the level of fundamental postulates and theorems in scientific theories. It renders the theories incommensurable.[23] Social convergence and agreement on the universal or fundamental character of *general* values such as human dignity or life need not therefore connote or reflect agreement on the particular interpretation or concrete application to be given to these concepts. The same is true of principles denoting general values such as autonomy, beneficence, non-maleficence and justice which were introduced and have been claimed by the American bioethicists, Childress and Beauchamp, to capture a mid-level point of agreement between otherwise divergent theories. To a classical utilitarian like Singer, or Harris, the principle of non-maleficence cannot justify a prohibition on the destruction of human embryos, since in their view an early embryo cannot strictly suffer harm. By contrast, to an orthodox catholic, embryo destruction is not just a harm to be prevented but an evil. In short, convergence on general ethical values or principles need not imply agreement, and indeed may obscure deep disagreement, in the determination and concrete application of the principles in particular cases.[24]

4.2 LEGAL CONCEPTS OF HUMAN DIGNITY AND THE RIGHT TO LIFE

The potential for divergence and disagreement over the understanding and application of general *ethical* principles or values such as human dignity or life is to some extent mirrored in *legal* contexts where the formulation and wording of human rights instruments has to be interpreted and applied by courts in particular cases. There are also separate additional reasons why legal rights instruments may admit of a variety of interpretations. By contrast to ethical or philosophical reasoning, legal reasoning has to follow conventions or prescribed rules of interpretation.[25] For instance, in its interpretation and application of the rights protected by the European Convention on Human Rights (ECHR), the European Court of Human Rights (ECtHR) aims to ascertain the intention of the drafters at the time, whilst taking into account changing social practices or values. The Court itself has repeatedly said that the instrument is a 'living text' which has to be adapted to changing social values.[26] What is more, it is clear from both the interpretative practice of the Court and the actual wording of some of the Articles in the Convention (for example, Art 8) that States retain a considerable margin of appreciation over 'ethical' matters. Finally, both the content and wording of the Convention or instrument are the outcome of an agreement between contracting

---

23 Kuhn, 1996.
24 Disagreement at the margins need not, however, preclude agreement on the core meaning of a concept. See Wittgenstein, 1984.
25 See Harris and Mowbray, 2001.
26 See *Tyrer v UK* (1978) ECHR 2 and subsequent case law.

States and as such constitute a form of 'negotiated moral order'[27] which is intended to accommodate a variety and plurality of accepted practices and values – albeit within prescribed common boundaries. For instance, the Explanatory Report to the Council of Europe's Convention on Human Rights & Biomedicine (CHRB) expressly acknowledges that whilst the purpose of the Convention as stated in Art 1 is to protect the dignity of every human being, the precise interpretation of who is the subject of such protection is left to the appreciation of member States:

> The Convention does not define the term 'everyone' (in French, 'toute personne'). These two terms are equivalent and found in the English and French versions of the ECHR which, however, does not define them. In the absence of a unanimous agreement on the definition of these terms among member States of the Council of Europe, it was decided to allow domestic law to define them for the purposes of the application of the present Convention. [para 18]

Against this background, as will be seen below, it is perhaps not surprising to find that neither the texts themselves nor the jurisprudence of the ECtHR provide support for an unequivocal interpretation of concepts such as human dignity and the right to life, and their possible application to early human embryos.

4.3 HUMAN DIGNITY IN INTERNATIONAL HUMAN RIGHTS INSTRUMENTS

References to the 'inherent dignity of the human person' in human rights instruments are usually found in the various preambles to each instrument.[28] Thus, the preamble to the Charter of the United Nations (1945) reaffirms faith in the dignity and worth of the human person. Each of the preambles to the UN Declaration of Human Rights (1948), the International Covenant on Civil and Political Rights (1966) and the International Covenant on Economic, Social and Cultural Rights (1966) begins with a 'recognition of the inherent dignity and of the equal and inalienable rights of all members of the human family' which is then further described as 'the foundation of freedom, justice and peace in the world'. The reference in the ECHR is more oblique as the Convention begins instead with an acknowledgment of the UN Declaration (1948). Hence, human dignity typically appears in international instruments as a background value or principle which underpins the protection of substantive rights, rather than a right itself. It has been suggested that:

> ... human dignity is the rock on which the superstructure of human rights is built. The logic of this conception of human dignity as the ground of human rights, however, is that the primary *practical* and *political* discourse is that of human rights rather than that of human dignity.[29]

---

27 The expression was first coined by Baker to draw a midway between what he calls 'fundamentalist' reasoning in ethics and relativism. I use the expression here in a more restricted way than Baker, and merely to describe the status of a human rights instrument with no implications as to universal or otherwise nature of moral principles.

28 Feldman, 1999a.

29 Beyleveld and Brownsword, 2001, p 13.

And that:

> ... instead of giving a right to dignity to every adult, international human-rights instruments require institutional (including legal) arrangements in states to respect peoples' rights.[30]

However, whether as a background value or a right, human dignity is essentially an underdetermined concept. The concept of human dignity has its origins in 18th century liberal thought where it implied absence of State interference and protection of individual liberty and equality of all. Divorced from its liberal origins, human dignity can potentially carry authoritarian overtones and function to constrain rather than promote and protect individual choice.

For instance, in relation to the protection of privacy, the ECtHR's interpretation of Art 8 in the recent case of *Pretty v UK*[31] is consistent with the liberal view of human dignity as implying respect for individual autonomy. The claimant had alleged that the criminalisation of assisted suicide prevented her from exercising her choice to receive help from her husband to terminate her life. The ECtHR concurred and stated:

> Although no previous case has established as such any right to self-determination as being contained in Art 8 of the Convention, the Court considers that the notion of personal autonomy is an important principle underlying the interpretation of its guarantees.

By contrast, where human dignity is thought to rest not on the individual's capacity to exercise autonomous choices but on some other attribute such as membership of the human species,[32] then human dignity could potentially operate so as to justify interference with the individual's choice. The example often cited to illustrate this point is the decision of the French *Conseil d'Etat* to ban a dwarf from taking part in a spectacle which involved him being catapulted from a cannon, on the grounds that such a spectacle constituted an affront to human dignity.[33] Strictly, on a classical, liberal neo-Kantian view of human dignity, such State interference with individual choice could only be justified if there were reasons to believe that the individual's choice was not genuinely autonomous (for example, if the individual was 'forced' into making such a choice by reason of his deprived socio-economic circumstances).[34]

---

30 Feldman, 1999a.

31 (2002) 35 EHRR 1.

32 The civil and political rights which had their origins in 18th and 19th century revolutions and which aimed to vindicate and secure individual liberty against the State have been described as 'first generation' rights. The largely 'negative' first generation rights have been contrasted to a second generation socio-economic rights imposing on the State an obligation to take positive steps to secure these rights (eg, right to education, right to housing or right to a minimum wage). The new rights in biomedicine have been described as 'third generation' rights which pertain not to individuals or social classes but to humanity as a whole and which are grounded on the idea of a common heritage or membership of the 'human family'. See Vasak, 1990. Also Byk, 1998.

33 CE, ass, 27 1995, *Cne de Morsang-sur-Orge*, Dalloz Jur 1995, p 257; CE ass, 27 octobre 1995, *Ville d'Aix-en-Provence, Rec* CE, p 372; *Dalloz Jur* 1996, p 177, with annotation by G Leberton.

34 Similarly, in the classical Kantian exposition of the concept, restraint or interference with the agent's choices may be justified if the choice is not genuinely autonomous or rational: eg, a rational agent could not will to sell their body or person since this would require their treating their person as a means to an end only rather than an end in itself. Rather than furthering respect for human dignity, such a choice would involve an affront to human dignity: only that which has dignity has value, other things have a price.

Much more difficult to reconcile with the classical liberal tradition in which classical international human rights instruments originate would be interferences which rely on some uniform or official view of what human dignity would supposedly entail in relation to the ascription and formulation of substantive rights in areas such as embryo research where there is no common understanding about the application of the concept of human dignity and where there is instead dispute and deep controversy. Since the concept of human dignity is indeterminate and its extension in some contexts is ethically contested, the imposition of an official or uniform view of human dignity in just those areas where there is no agreement or common view would be contrary to another fundamental principle which underpins international human rights instruments, namely respect for pluralism and democracy.[35] For instance, the ECHR reaffirms the profound beliefs of the State signatories in:

> ... those fundamental freedoms which are the foundation of justice and peace in the world and are best maintained on the one hand by *an effective political democracy* and on the other by a common understanding and observance of the human rights upon which they depend. [emphasis added]

The preamble to the European Union's Charter on Fundamental Rights is even more explicit in stating that the Union 'is based on the principles of democracy and the rule of law' whilst noting that 'the Union contributes to the preservation and to the development of these common values while respecting the diversity of the cultures and traditions of the peoples of Europe ...' and reaffirming the principle of subsidiarity.

As will be seen, the unprecedented and massive increase in references to human dignity in the new human rights instruments in biomedicine does not conclusively dispel the uncertainty and controversy regarding the scope of application of the concept; neither is it possible to discern a common view which would cut a wedge across the disputed field of embryo research and reconcile opposed perspectives.

4.4 HUMAN DIGNITY IN THE NEW HUMAN RIGHTS INSTRUMENTS IN BIOMEDICINE

4.4.1 Unesco's Universal Declaration on the Human Genome and Human Rights

References to human dignity in the new human rights instruments, particularly those in the field of biomedicine, have acquired an unprecedented and hitherto unknown prominence,[36] so much so that the words 'human dignity' have been described as the 'key' words in those instruments.[37] The UNESCO Universal Declaration on the Human Genome and Human Rights (1997) states that

---

35 See Brownsword, 2003; Brownsword, 2004.
36 See Andorno, 2001: 'Never before had the concept of human dignity acquired such a central role in human rights instruments.'
37 Lenoir and Mathieu, 1998, p 110.

'practices which are contrary to human dignity, such as reproductive cloning of human beings, shall not be permitted', in an instrument where the expression 'human dignity' is mentioned no less than 15 times.

4.4.2 Convention on Human Rights & Biomedicine (CHRB)

References to 'human dignity' also have a prominent role in the text of the Convention on Human Rights & Biomedicine (CHRB) (1997), the full title of which is the 'Convention for the Protection of Human Rights and Dignity of the Human Being with regard to the Application of Biology and Medicine: Convention on Human Rights and Biomedicine'. The preamble contains three separate references to human dignity, the parties to the Convention first recognising 'the importance of ensuring the dignity of the human being', secondly 'conscious that the misuse of biology and medicine may lead to acts endangering human dignity' and thirdly 'resolving to take such measures as are necessary to safeguard human dignity and the fundamental rights and freedoms of the individual with regard to the application of biology and medicine'. In addition, human dignity receives special mention in Art 1, which states that:

> Parties to this Convention shall protect the dignity and identity of all human beings and guarantee everyone, without discrimination, respect for their integrity and other rights and fundamental freedoms with regard to the application of biology and medicine. Each Party shall take in its internal law the necessary measures to give effect to the provisions of this Convention.

Here, human dignity appears almost as a distinct right rather than a background value as it does in the Charter on Fundamental Rights of the European Union (2000) which declares in its first Article that 'human dignity is inviolable and must be respected and protected'.

However, despite the unprecedented and prominent references to human dignity in the new human rights instruments, there remains considerable uncertainty about the precise meaning and scope of the concept and its role as a background value or a distinct right. For instance, in the Explanatory Report to the Charter on Fundamental Rights of the European Union, the right to dignity protected by Art 1 is expressly assigned only to the 'human person'. On this basis, human dignity could only be attributed to individuals who are already born and therefore not to foetuses, embryos or zygotes.

Similarly, Art 1 of the CHRB proclaims the need to 'protect the dignity and identity of all *human beings* and guarantee *everyone*, without discrimination, respect for their integrity and other rights and fundamental freedoms with regard to the application of biology and medicine' (emphasis added). The difficulty here lies in determining whether zygotes or human embryos come within the scope of definition of a 'human being' or 'everyone'. The Explanatory Report provides an ambivalent and seemingly contradictory answer by asserting on the one hand that:

> The Convention also uses the expression 'human being' to state the necessity to protect the dignity and identity of all human beings. It was acknowledged that it was a generally accepted principle that human dignity and the identity of the human being had to be respected as soon as life began. [para 19]

On the other hand, the Explanatory Report acknowledges that the Convention (like its predecessors) does not define the term 'everyone' and:

> In the absence of a unanimous agreement on the definition of these terms among member States of the Council of Europe, it was decided to allow domestic law to define them for the purposes of the application of the present Convention. [para 18]

Paragraphs 18 and 19 thus contains an apparent contradiction between the ascription of human dignity 'as soon as life begins' and the deferral to contracting parties to determine who should count as 'everyone'. What 'life' precisely is supposed to be referring to (for example, live unfertilised egg, fertilised egg, enucleated egg, zygote, unborn foetus, person already born) and when precisely 'life' is taken to begin (for example, conception, fertilisation, birth) are not defined. Further, para 19 makes sense only if it is assumed that a zygote is 'a human being' (as opposed perhaps to a form of human life). But if a zygote is a human being, then how could there be disagreement as to whether it could count as someone or 'everyone'? One can make sense of there being a disagreement as to whether 'everyone' covers every stage or form of human life but the same doubt cannot reasonably arise in relation to human beings. As commonly understood, 'everyone' includes 'every human being'. If it is accepted or assumed that a zygote or embryo is a human being, then there can be no doubt that a zygote or human embryo should be entitled to the same protection and rights as an individual who is already born, as argued by the German Federal Constitutional Court in the judgment of 25 February 1975.[38] But this line of reasoning presupposes precisely that which is in dispute, namely the precise status of the embryo.

One possible way to effect a reconciliation between the different parts of Art 1 and the seemingly inconclusive explanations given in the Explanatory Report is to read the reference to human dignity in the first part of Art 1 as representing the view that human dignity is a fundamental and background value which attaches to all 'human beings', whilst the second part of the Article, which imposes a requirement on States to 'guarantee everyone respect for their integrity and rights', would be reasserting the classical liberal position that rights which are based on or derived from human dignity should be secured for all and respected. However, this interpretation would produce the problematic implication that respect for human dignity need not necessarily result in the protection of substantive rights or, alternatively, that the enunciated rights could not be equally attributed to or claimed by all.

Ultimately, even if human dignity is extended to embryos under Art 1, in the absence of clearly specified rights or prohibitions in the rest of the text, it would still be unclear what specific rights may be entailed.[39] For instance, on the basis of

---

38 Cited in the case of *Brüggemann and Scheuten v Federal Republic of Germany* (1981) EHRR 244.

39 The Additional Protocol to the Council of Europe CHRB provides that 'any intervention seeking to create a human being genetically identical to another human being whether living or dead is prohibited'; and Art 3(2) of the Charter of Fundamental Rights of the European Union states that the prohibition of the reproductive cloning of human beings must be respected.

the expansive construction of human dignity suggested by para 19 of the Explanatory Report to the CHRB, whereby human dignity should be taken to accrue the moment life begins, one could reasonably infer that embryo research, particularly research which would result in ending the life of the embryo, should not be permitted as contrary to human dignity. However, this is not necessarily so, as Art 18 of the CHRB provides that:

1   Where the law allows research on embryos in vitro, it shall ensure adequate protection of the embryo.

2   The creation of human embryos for research purposes is prohibited.

But what precisely does 'adequate protection' entail? Paragraph 115 of the Explanatory Report merely reiterates that where national law allows research on embryos *in vitro* the law must ensure adequate protection of the embryo. No explanation is offered; neither is there any attempt to state the kind of limits stipulated in other parts of the Convention in respect of persons who are already born, namely that the research should only be conducted for the benefit of the individual him or herself or, if conducted for the benefit of others, should be subjected to a minimal risk requirement (see Arts 5 and 17). Paragraph 116 expressly notes that the Article does not take a stand on the admissibility of the principle of research on *in vitro* embryos, but that para 2 of the Article prohibits the creation of human embryos, with the aim of carrying out research on them. There is no allusion to prohibition of research which would result in ending the life of the embryo. Such research may therefore be permissible if conducted with 'adequate protection', whatever that may mean precisely? Hence, even if human dignity could conclusively be said to attach to an early human embryo under the CHRB, it would not necessarily follow that the early embryo has a right to life. Neither would the protection of such a right have to be *guaranteed* under Art 1, since the Explanatory Report acknowledges that there is disagreement as to who may be the subject of the rights grounded in human dignity.

Even if the text of the CHRB and the precise scope of the concept of human dignity were less ambiguous, there are separate considerations which dictate caution in the interpretation and application of this Convention. As the drafters of the CHRB acknowledge in the Explanatory Report, there were considerable disagreements at the time of the drafting of the Convention as to the range of individuals who should be brought within the sphere of its protection. Six years after the adoption of the Convention, a substantial number of States in Europe still have not signed or ratified the Convention, largely because of deep divisions over the legitimacy of embryo research. Thus, whilst countries such as Germany and Ireland will not ratify the Convention because they consider it too liberal in allowing research to be conducted on human embryos, countries such as the UK and Belgium hold the opposite view and have in fact adopted legislation which permits the creation of embryos for research purposes directly at odds with Art 18 of the CHRB.[40] Notwithstanding this, should the UK or indeed other States wish

---

40   It is also worth noting that the list of signatories to the Convention includes States, such as Italy, which have a not entered a reservation against Art 18 and until December 2003 through the absence of legislation permitted clinics to create embryos for research purposes, including cloned embryos.

to become a signatories at some point in the future, they could do so without having to repeal domestic law currently flouting Art 18 of the Convention which prohibits the creation of human embryos for research purposes. This is because Art 36 of the CHRB allows a prospective signatory to enter reservations in respect of any particular provision of the Convention 'to the extent that any law then in force in its territory is not in conformity with the provision'. The only requirement is that 'any reservation made under this Article shall contain a brief statement of the relevant law'.[41]

In short, despite its prominence in the new human rights instruments on biomedicine, human dignity as a background value remains an indeterminate guide from which to derive the nature and scope of rights in contested areas such as embryo research. Altogether, the diversity of opinions (and indeed laws) on the legitimacy of embryo research and the lack of a common agreed view should militate against any uniform view of human dignity from which categorical assertions about rights could be deduced.

4.5   THE RIGHT TO LIFE UNDER THE ECHR

Irrespective of the uncertainty regarding the precise scope of application of the concept of human dignity, and the question of whether a right to life could conclusively be assigned to human embryos under the CHRB, it is important to realise that the Convention itself is not directly actionable in the ECtHR. Unlike the ECHR, the CHRB does not confer on individuals a right to petition the ECtHR to obtain a remedy for a putative breach of their rights. Notwithstanding this important limitation, the ECtHR could undoubtedly refer to the CHRB in a claim arising under the ECHR (1950) if the alleged breach related to the sphere of application of the CHRB (for example, Art 2, attaint on right to life in a biomedical context)[42] since the CHRB constitutes a statement of ideals regarding the elaboration of fundamental rights in the field of biomedicine. The actionable rights which are juridically protected, however, are those contained in the ECHR. To what extent, then, does the right to life stated in Art 2 of the ECHR protect the life of the human embryo?

The ECHR does not contain any specific provisions relating to the protection and rights of human embryos. Art 2 states:

1   Everyone's right to life shall be protected by law. No one shall be deprived of his life intentionally save in the execution of a sentence of a court following his conviction of a crime for which this penalty is provided by law.

2   Deprivation of life shall not be regarded as inflicted in contravention of this Article when it results from the use of force which is no more than absolutely necessary:

---

41 This type of derogation procedure which allows a contracting party to waive its obligation to secure some of the rights expressly contained in the instrument has been traditionally described as highly contentious.

42 Plomer, 2001a.

    (a) in defence of any person from unlawful violence;

    (b) in order to effect a lawful arrest or to prevent the escape of a person lawfully detained;

    (c) in action lawfully taken for the purpose of quelling a riot or insurrection.

Whether the right in question is attributable to the embryo is far from clear. There is no indication in the Explanatory Report that the drafters of the Convention intended to extend the right to life to the unborn. Further, the jurisprudence on Art 2 and its possible application to the human embryo is scarce and consists of a handful of decisions relating to abortion, with only a couple of decisions from the ECtHR, the rest having been issued by the now defunct European Commission of Human Rights. Notwithstanding the paucity of legal sources, there is a clear interpretative approach in all the cases regarding the possible application of Art 2 to the unborn. Both the European Commission and the ECtHR have deliberately sought to avoid making any general and categorical statements regarding the possible extension of the right to life to the unborn foetus or embryo, largely in express recognition of the plurality of views on the moral and legal status of the embryo and foetus amongst parties to the Convention.

In *Brüggemann and Scheuten v Federal Republic of Germany*,[43] the European Commission of Human Rights dismissed a claim from the applicants that new restrictive legislation on abortion adopted by the German Bundestag, together with the judgment of the Federal Constitutional Court of 25 February 1975, violated the applicants' right to respect for their private life under Art 8 of the Convention. The Commission held, by a majority, that pregnancy cannot be said to pertain uniquely to the sphere of private life, since whenever a woman is pregnant her private life becomes closely connected with the developing foetus (para 59). However, the Commission did not find it necessary to decide, in this context, whether the unborn child is to be considered as 'life' in the sense of Art 2 of the Convention, or whether it could be regarded as an entity which under Art 8(2) could justify an interference 'for the protection of others' (para 60). Significantly, in reaching its decision the Commission had regard to the fact that:

> there is no evidence that it was the intention of the parties to the Convention to bind themselves in favour of any particular solution under discussion – eg, a solution of the kind set out in the Fifth Criminal Law Reform Act (setting time limits on abortion) which was not yet under public discussion at the time the Convention was drafted and adopted. [para 64]

In *Paton v UK*[44] the applicant was seeking to prevent the termination of his estranged wife's pregnancy. He submitted that the UK Abortion Act (1967), under which this abortion was authorised and eventually carried out, violated Arts 2 and/or 5, 6, 8 and 9 of the Convention.

The Commission dismissed the claim, noting that the question of whether the unborn child is covered by Art 2 was expressly left open in the *Brüggemann and*

Scheuten case and had not yet been considered by the Commission in any other case. The Commission also noted that constitutional courts had expressed different views on the question of what constitutes life, when life begins and whether the term 'everyone' in Art 2 includes the human embryo. For instance, the Commission cited the ruling of the Austrian Constitutional Court which had noted the different views expressed in legal writings, and found that Art 2(1), first sentence, interpreted in the context of Art 2, paras (1) and (2), does not cover the unborn life. On the other hand, the Commission also noted that the German Federal Constitutional Court had taken the view that the right to life is guaranteed to everyone who 'lives' or 'every living human being'. Hence, 'everyone' includes unborn human beings. The Commission itself noted that the term 'everyone' is not defined in the Convention and further that in all the instances the use of the word is such that it can apply only postnatally: 'None indicates clearly that it has any possible prenatal application, although such application in a rare case, for example, under Art 6(1), cannot be entirely excluded.'[45]

Furthermore in the view of the Commission, the express limitations[46] on the right to life contained in Art 2 'by their nature, concern persons already born and cannot be applied to the foetus. Together, these support the view that it does not include the unborn'.

Notwithstanding this, and because of the wide divergence of thinking on the question of where life begins and the fact that the term 'life' may be subject to different interpretations in different legal instruments, depending on the context in which it is used, in the instrument concerned the Commission sought to consider a range of possible interpretations of the scope of Art 2, including whether a foetus would have an absolute right to life, a qualified or limited right to life, or no right to life at all.

The Commission dismissed the view that Art 2 could be construed as recognising an 'absolute' right to life of the foetus as contrary to the object and purpose of Convention, noting that 'already at the time of signature of the Convention (4 November 1950) all High Contracting Parties, with one possible exception, permitted abortion when necessary to save the life of the mother and that, in the meanwhile, the national law on termination of pregnancy has shown a tendency towards further liberalisation'.[47] On the question of whether Art 2 could be construed as conferring a qualified right to life on the embryo or no right at all, the Commission considered that it did not have to decide either, since the

---

45 It appears in Art 1 and in Section I, apart from Art 2(1), in Arts 5, 6, 8–11 and 13.

46 As regards, more particularly, Art 2, it contains the following limitations of 'everyone's' right to life enounced in the first sentence of para (1): a clause permitting the death penalty in para (1), second sentence: 'No one shall be deprived of his life intentionally save in the execution of a sentence of a court following his conviction of a crime for which this penalty is provided by law'; and the provision, in para (2), that deprivation of life shall not be regarded as inflicted in contravention of Art 2 when it results from 'the use of force which is no more than absolutely necessary' in the following three cases: 'In defence of any person from unlawful violence'; 'in order to effect a lawful arrest or to prevent the escape of a person lawfully detained'; 'in action lawfully taken for the purpose of quelling a riot or insurrection.'

47 At 20.

termination in question was at the initial stage of the pregnancy and was authorised only to protect the life and health of the mother. The reasoning, however, is not so clear. The Commission's argument appears to be that, on the assumption that the life of the early embryo is protected by Art 2, then such a life could legitimately be construed as subject to an 'implied' limitation to protect the life and health of the pregnant woman. Such a construction, however, would be problematic and contentious, because it has the effect of widening the range of circumstances under which life may be curtailed beyond those defined in Art 2(2) to include other circumstances which are not expressly mentioned.[48] For this reason, it is difficult to extrapolate anything definite from this decision.

The only judgment of the ECtHR which until July 2004 touched on the possible application of Art 2 to the human embryo is the decision in *Open Door Counselling and Dublin Well Woman v Ireland*[49] where the applicants contended that their rights under Art 10 to impart and receive information concerning abortion abroad had been breached. The Irish Government had maintained that the injunction was necessary in a democratic society for the protection of the right to life of the unborn and that Art 10 should be interpreted, *inter alia*, against the background of Art 2 of the Convention which, it argued, also protected unborn life. The Court conceded that the view that abortion was morally wrong was the deeply held view of the majority of the people in Ireland and it was not the proper function of the ECtHR to seek to impose a different viewpoint.[50] However, the Court observed that in the present case it was not called upon to examine whether a right to abortion is guaranteed under the Convention or whether the foetus is encompassed by the right to life as contained in Art 2. Furthermore, the Court acknowledged that:

> ... the national authorities enjoy a wide margin of appreciation in matters of morals, particularly in an area such as the present which touches on matters of belief concerning the nature of human life. As the Court has observed before, it is not possible to find in the legal and social orders of the Contracting States a uniform European conception of morals, and the State authorities are, in principle, in a better position than the international judge to give an opinion on the exact content of the requirements of morals as well as on the 'necessity' of a 'restriction' or 'penalty' intended to meet them. [para 68]

However, the Court did not agree that the State's discretion in the field of the protection of morals is unfettered and unreviewable on information concerning activities such as abortion which, notwithstanding their moral implications, have been and continue to be tolerated by national authorities.[51] In the Court's view, restrictions imposed by national authorities in such circumstances 'call for careful scrutiny by the Convention institutions as to their conformity with the tenets of a democratic society'. In the instant case the Court decided that the restriction was disproportionate and unnecessary in a democratic society.

---

48 See Harris and Mowbray, 2001.
49 (1993) 15 EHRR 244.
50 At 66.
51 *Norris v Ireland* (1991) 13 EHRR 186.

In conclusion, in the few cases raising the question of whether the right to life protected by Art 2 of the ECHR extends to the unborn, the common interpretative approach of the (now defunct) European Commission and the ECtHR has been to acknowledge the diversity of views on the moral and legal status of the human embryo amongst Member States, whilst refraining from adopting any definite interpretation. Far from establishing a common view on the right to life of the embryo, the jurisprudence on Art 2 evidences the absence of agreement and the diversity and plurality of views amongst Member States. This analysis has just been confirmed by the judgment of the ECtHR in the case of *VO v France*.[52] A doctor had mistakenly terminated the pregnancy of the applicant. The applicant complained of the authorities' refusal to classify the taking of her unborn child's life as unintentional homicide. She argued that the absence of criminal legislation to prevent and punish such an act breached Art 2 of the Convention. The ECtHR disagreed and refused to 'answer in the abstract the question whether the unborn child is a person for the purposes of Art 2' (para 85). The Court's decision was based on the premise that:

> ... the issue of when the right to life begins comes within the margin of appreciation which the Court generally considers that States should enjoy in this sphere, notwithstanding an evolutive interpretation of the Convention ... The reasons for that conclusion are, firstly that the issue of such protection has not been resolved within the majority of the Contracting States themselves, in France in particular, where it is the subject of debate ... and, secondly, there is no European consensus on the scientific and legal definition of the beginning of life. [para 81]

The Court also specifically referred to the CHRB and the additional Protocol on the Prohibition of Cloning and reached precisely the same conclusion as suggested above (para 84). Although the ECtHR did not refer to the interpretation of the Convention by constitutional domestic courts in its judgment in *VO v France*, the same diversity of views may be found therein.

4.6   THE EMBRYO'S RIGHT TO LIFE IN CONSTITUTIONAL COURTS IN EUROPE

As alluded to in the Irish case, the diversity of views on the status and rights of the embryo is reflected both in the differences between constitutional courts in Europe and the different legislative approaches of the contracting parties. At the time the subject matter of those cases and legislation was abortion. However, the same diversity may be found in more recent decisions of constitutional courts and the legislation adopted by Member States on the application of new biotechnologies and in particular the use of frozen embryos.[53]

In a case which challenged the constitutionality of the 1994 French law on bioethics, the claimants had contended that the 1994 legislation violated the principle of respect for human dignity and the right to life of the embryo in

---

52 Application No 539244/00, 8 July 2004.
53 See European Commission, 2003.

permitting research on frozen human embryos which are no longer viable.[54] In the claimant's view, the violation arose because frozen embryos have all the attributes of a human being from the moment of conception. The French Conseil Constitutionel rejected the claim. The 1994 legislation affirmed the fundamental principle of respect for human dignity as well as other fundamental principles including the primacy of the human person, respect for human life from the beginning, the inviolability of the human body, the principle that the human body was not a commodity and the inviolability of the human species. Parliament had considered that research on embryos was not contrary to fundamental principles as it was permitted only on embryos which the legislator considered were no longer viable after a period of cryopreservation lasting five years. It was not within the power of the Conseil Constitutionel to review the content of legislation which had been enacted by an elected Parliament with regard to the state of scientific knowledge and technology at the time.

In 1998, the Portuguese Constitutional Court was asked to review the legality of a proposed referendum on the decriminalisation of abortion in the first 10 weeks of the pregnancy.[55] The claimants sought to challenge the constitutionality of the subject matter of the referendum, alleging that it involved a breach of Art 24 of the Portuguese Constitution, which states that human life is inviolable. The Court held that the issue of whether to decriminalise abortion may be regarded purely as a matter of criminal policy: the legislative authority may choose whether or not to make abortion a criminal offence because, while life *in utero* may constitute legal property (thus entailing potential conflict with other rights of the woman in question), *it is not protected by the right to life* enshrined in Art 24.1 of the Constitution. Notwithstanding this, Art 24.1 was held to extend protection to a life developing in a mother's womb (life *in utero*); there is thus a constitutional obligation to protect that life. However, the protection of the human embryo cannot be as substantial (nor can it be ensured by the same methods) as the protection of the subjective right to life inherent in every individual person from birth onwards.

The right to life of the embryo *in vitro* was considered by the Spanish Constitutional Court in 1999.[56] The Court held that Art 15 of the Constitution, which protects the right to life, affords not direct but only indirect constitutional to human embryos. The unborn human foetus did not have a fundamental right to life.

However, the life of the embryo was constitutionally protected and effective arrangements had to be made to protect life. Parliament could legitimately regulate research on human embryos. The aims pursued by the legislation were lawful, and the limits it sets and the arrangements for administrative supervision

---

54 Décision No 94-343/344 DC du 27 Juillet 1994, CODICES, FRA-1994-2-004.
55 Diário da Repúbblica (Official Gazette), 91 (Series I-A), 18/04/1998, 1714 (2) – 1714 (35) / (h), CODICES, POR-1998-1-001.
56 Judgment of the Spanish Constitutional Court, No 116/1999, 17/06/1999. Boletín oficial del Estado (Official Gazette), 08/07/1999, 67–80. CODICES digest ESP-1999-3-014.

were consistent with the Constitution since only research on 'pre-embryos' which are not viable was permitted. Such embryos did not qualify for constitutional protection of human life. The 1999 decision followed the decision of the same court in 1996 which challenged the constitutionality of the 1988 statute (42/1988 of 28 December) permitting donation of embryos for research purposes.[57] The claimants had alleged a violation of Art 15 of the Constitution affirming the right of every human being to life. The Spanish Constitutional Court held that the life of an unborn individual does not constitute a fundamental right whose protection requires enactments to be made in the form of organic as opposed to ordinary laws, but rather a legal interest which receives constitutional protection as part of the prescriptive content of Art 15. The Court determined that by definition human embryos and foetuses which are not viable could not be assigned the status of unborn individuals within the meaning of the expression since they are never to be born in the sense of never being able to lead lives of their own in complete independence from the mother.

Can a common view on the scope of application of the right to life be discerned from the rulings of these constitutional courts? All of the rulings unequivocally state that the fundamental right to life does not extend to the unborn foetus or embryo. From this it follows that States do not have to *guarantee* protection for the life of the unborn foetus or embryo. At the same time, the rulings also maintain that human life may be the subject of constitutional protection but that this protection does not extend to a prohibition on research on frozen embryos which are not viable. There are no rulings on the admissibility of research on frozen human embryos which are viable, or on the creation of human embryos *in vitro* for research purposes. On the other hand, permissive legislation on embryo research allowing for the creation of embryos for research purposes, including Cell Nuclear Replacement (CNR), has now been adopted in three States including the UK, Belgium and Sweden.[58] By contrast, Germany, Austria and others have legislated to prohibit all research on human embryos, including non-viable human embryos. In short, the decisions from constitutional courts in Europe, together with the range of legislative approaches on embryo research adopted by European States, confirm that there is no common juridical view on the legal status of the human embryo *in vitro* or on the degree of constitutional protection which may be claimed for its life. Further difficulties and uncertainties regarding the legal status of the embryo *in vitro* may be gleaned from decisions of US courts over the disposition of frozen embryos.

4.7 POLICY AND LAW IN THE US

The US currently has no federal law regulating cloning and stem cell research. Under President Clinton's presidency, the National Bioethics Advisory

---

57 Judgment of the Spanish Constitutional Court, No 212/1996, 19/12/1996. Boletín oficial del Estado (Official Gazette), 19, 22/01/1997, 32–43, CODICES Digest ESP-1996-3-031.
58 See European Commission, 2003.

Commission (NBAC)[59] had produced a report, *Ethical Issues in Human Stem Cell Research*, and concluded that whilst many of the issues remained contested on moral grounds, a consensus could nevertheless be constructed on the permissibility of embryonic research around the sources from which the stem cells originate. The NBAC report noted that many people, including President Clinton himself, opposed the creation of human embryos for research purposes. However, research on embryos surplus to IVF treatment or indeed research on cadaveric foetal tissue was considered less problematic. The report thus recommended that federal funding should be limited to research involving stem cells obtained from cadaveric foetal tissue and/or from stem cells obtained from surplus embryos remaining after infertility treatment.[60] President Bush succeeded President Clinton before the policy was implemented. Federal funding for stem cell research was frozen pending a review of the policy in the midst of conflicting lobbying and pressure from within the Republican Party to ban embryonic stem cell research.[61] The outcome in the summer of 2001 was a considerably more restrictive policy than the one advocated by the NBAC, namely to allow federal funding only for *existing* stem cell lines which had been ethically derived from surplus embryos.[62] At the same time, President Bush dismantled the National Bioethics Advisory Commission and replaced it with a new advisory body – the President's Council on Bioethics[63] – chaired by Leon Kass.[64] A report on stem cell research, *Human Cloning and Human Dignity: An Ethical Inquiry*, was issued in July 2002 calling for a complete ban on reproductive cloning. However, the Executive Summary noted that: 'The Council, reflecting the differences of opinion in American society, is divided regarding the ethics of research involving (cloned) embryos.' Ten members opposed embryonic stem cell research on the grounds, *inter alia*, that it diminished the 'special respect' owed to embryos. Amongst the seven members who supported cloning for biomedical research, the majority took a gradualist view of the moral worth of the embryo and on that basis called for a limit on research up to the first 14 days of the embryo's development (or appearance of the primitive streak). By contrast, a minority who accorded 'no special moral status to the early-stage cloned embryo' and 'believe it should be treated essentially like all other human cells' thought that there should no special restrictions on research. One member was undecided. The outcome was a call for a four-year moratorium on embryonic stem cell research, justified on the grounds that:

---

59 Established in October 1995 by Executive Order 12975, to advise the President on bioethical issues arising from research on human biology and behaviour.

60 National Bioethics Advisory Commission, 1999, Recommendations 1 and 2, pp 3–4.

61 For instance, lobbying in favour of stem cell research from anti-abortion groups/individuals like Nancy Reagan who continue to oppose Bush's restrictive policy: 'Nancy Reagan fights Bush over stem cells' (2002) *New York Times*, 29 September.

62 The President's Address to the Nation, 9 August 2001, www.nih.gov/news/stemcell. For a discussion of US policy on stem cell research, see Annas, Caplan and Elias, 1999, pp 1339–41 and Holden, p 1567.

63 www.bioethics.gov.

64 A bioethics professor opposed to cloning for whatever purpose. See Kass, 2001.

It calls for and provides time for further democratic deliberation about cloning-for-biomedical research, a subject about which the nation is divided and where there remains great uncertainty. A national discourse on this subject has not yet taken place in full, and a moratorium, by making it impossible for either side to cling to the status quo, would force both to make their full case before the public. By banning all cloning for a time, it allows us to seek moral consensus on whether or not we should cross a major moral boundary (creating nascent cloned human life solely for research) and prevents our crossing it without deliberate decision.[65]

A new Bill purporting to ban all forms of cloning, whether for reproductive or biomedical research purposes, has been introduced in the 108th Congress by the Florida Republican Dave Weldon. He believes that 'any attempt at human cloning, for whatever purpose, is a gross form of human experimentation that American people oppose'.[66] The Bill is virtually identical to the Bill approved by the House in 2001 and is therefore guaranteed to receive approval.[67] Meanwhile, a competing Bill outlawing reproductive cloning and permitting cloning for biomedical research under strict controls is also being introduced by Democrat Senator Feinstein. Although there is a possibility that Senate will follow the House, as the Republicans now have the majority in Senate too, the outcome is far from certain as the debate does not strictly follow political lines. Republicans themselves are divided on ideological lines, with the classical school favouring a 'hands-off' free market approach which facilitates investment in the biotech industry, whilst the new 'moral' Republicans seek State intervention to control investment and research. Altogether there are now five Bills on cloning awaiting hearing by the Senate.[68]

4.7.1 The status of the frozen embryo in US courts

The legal status of the frozen embryo in the US may be gleaned from a handful of rulings from the Supreme Courts of Tennessee, Massachusetts, New York, New Jersey and Washington. In all the cases, the litigation originates in a dispute or disagreement between a divorcing couple over disposal of unused frozen embryos originally created for implantation purposes. In the first case, *Davis v Davis*,[69] the Supreme Court of Tennessee laid out a framework which has since been followed by other State courts.

In *Davis v Davis* both parties were progenitors (the woman had provided the eggs and the man the sperm). The dispute concerned rights over disposition of the embryos following divorce. Initially, Mrs Davis wanted to retain the embryos for future use but she later decided she wanted to donate them to another couple. Mr Davis always sought to have the pre-embryos discarded. The trial court awarded 'custody' of the frozen embryos to Ms Davies. The Court of Appeals overturned the decision and the Supreme Court of Tennessee affirmed the Court of Appeals'

---

65 Executive Summary.
66 (2003) *Washington Times*, 13 January.
67 Bill HR 234/534 was approved by the House on 27 February 2003 by a vote of 241 to 155.
68 See legislative update on the website of the Office of Legislative Policy & Analysis, tracking the progress of five bills awaiting hearing by the Senate: http://olpa.od.nih.gov/legislation/108/pendinglegislation/cloning1.asp.
69 842 SW 2d 588 Tenn 1992.

ruling, after being asked by the American Fertility Society[70] to respond to this issue because of its far-reaching implications in other cases of this kind. The Supreme Court held that disputes involving disposition of pre-embryos produced by *in vitro* fertilisation (IVF) should be resolved, first, by looking to the preferences of progenitors. If their wishes cannot be ascertained, then their prior agreement or contract concerning disposition should be carried out. If no prior agreement exists, then the relative interests of the parties in using or not using the pre-embryos must be weighed.

The Supreme Court judgment contains several significant *dicta* on the legal status of the frozen embryo. First, the Supreme Court rejected the trial judge's finding that there is no distinction of significance to be drawn between the term 'embryo' and 'pre-embryo' and affirmed the legitimacy of using the term 'pre-embryo' to describe a human embryo up to an eight-cell stage of development, as proposed by the American Infertility Society. The term 'pre-embryo' rather than embryo has since become accepted usage in the rulings of other Supreme State Courts, although the precise boundaries of when the pre-embryo becomes an embryo vary from case to case and range from the eight-cell to the 16-cell stage of development and in one case the term is applied only to frozen embryos.[71] The Supreme Court of Tennessee further rejected the trial judge's description of pre-embryos as 'children *in vitro*' who have a legal right to be born. The trial judge had invoked the doctrine of *parens patriae* and held that it was 'in the best interest of the children' to be born rather than destroyed. Mrs Davis was willing to provide such an opportunity but Mr Davis was not. On this basis, the trial judge had awarded Mrs Davis 'custody' of the 'children *in vitro*'. The Court of Appeals had explicitly rejected the trial judge's reasoning, as well as the result, describing the expert evidence relied upon by the trial judge as revealing a profound confusion between science and religion. The argument that an eight-cell embryo was a 'human being' with a legal right to be born was abandoned by the appellants in the Court of Appeals, where the 'pre-embryos' were described instead as 'potential life'.

---

70 Joined by 19 other national organisations allied in this case as *amici curiae*.

71 In *Litowitz v Litowitz* (2002), the Washington Supreme Court adopted the following definition: 'The term "pre-embryo" denotes that stage in human development immediately after fertilisation occurs. The pre-embryo "comes into existence with the first cell division and lasts until the appearance of a single primitive streak, which is the first sign of organ differentiation. This [primitive streak] occurs at about 14 days of development".' Two years earlier the Massachusetts Supreme Court in *AZ v BZ* (2000) had used the term 'pre-embryo' to refer to the four- to-eight-cell stage of a developing fertilised egg, following the report of the Ethics Committee of the American Fertility Society, Ethical Considerations of Assisted Reproductive Technologies, Fertility and Sterility at 29S-30S (Supp 1 November 1994) (explaining terminology and transformation of single cell into multicellular newborn). The following year, the New Jersey Supreme Court in *JB v MB* (2001) adopted an altogether different definition: 'A pre-embryo is a fertilised ovum (egg cell) up to approximately 14 days old (the point when it implants in the uterus). *The American Heritage Stedman's Medical Dictionary*, 1995, p 667. Throughout this opinion, we use the term "pre-embryo" rather than "embryo" because "pre-embryo" is technically descriptive of the cells' stage of development when they are cryopreserved (frozen).' Sometimes the term 'zygote' is used interchangeably with 'pre-embryos' (see *Kass v Kass* below): 'Fertilisation takes several hours as the 24 chromosomes of each gamete (egg and sperm) fuse, yielding a zygote with a unique genome of 48 chromosomes. The zygote is then allowed to divide for about three days until it reaches the two-to-eight-cell stage. These pre-embryos consisting of a few undifferentiated cells are either implanted or cryopreserved for implantation at a later date. It is not until the cell mass proceeds beyond 16 cells and implants that it can give rise to an embryo.'

The Supreme Court noted that one of the fundamental issues posed by the case is the question of whether pre-embryos should be considered 'persons' or 'property' in law. The Supreme Court found that the Court of Appeals had held, correctly, that they cannot be considered 'persons' under Tennessee law. Neither do pre-embryos enjoy protection as 'persons' under federal law. In *Roe v Wade*,[72] the United States Supreme Court explicitly refused to hold that the foetus possesses independent rights, on the basis of a thorough examination of the federal constitution, relevant common law principles and the lack of scientific consensus as to when life begins. The Tennessee Supreme Court thus noted both the finding in *Roe v Wade* that 'the unborn have never been recognised in the law as persons in the whole sense. As a matter of constitutional law, this conclusion has never been seriously challenged' and Justice O'Connor's ruling in *Webster* that viability remains the 'critical point' and 'that stage of foetal development is far removed, both qualitatively and quantitatively, from that of the four- to-eight-cell pre-embryos in this case'.[73]

On this basis, the Supreme Court of Tennessee concluded that pre-embryos are not, strictly speaking, either 'persons' or 'property', but occupy an interim category that entitles them to special respect because of their potential for human life:

> It follows that any interest that Mary Sue Davis and Junior Davis have in the pre-embryos in this case is not a true property interest. However, they do have an interest in the nature of ownership, to the extent that they have decision-making authority concerning disposition of the pre-embryos, within the scope of policy set by law.[74]

In this case the parties had no agreement and the court determined that Mr Davis should be granted rights of disposal over the embryos. However, where agreement existed, it should generally be presumed to be valid and enforceable.

Kass v Kass[75] was another divorce dispute that involved the disposition of frozen pre-embryos. The former wife sought 'custody' of the frozen pre-embryos to use them for implantation. The husband wanted to have the embryos destroyed. The New York court agreed with the Tennessee Supreme Court in *Davis v Davis* that agreements should generally be presumed valid, binding and enforceable in any dispute between parties. The New York court also found that 'pre-zygotes[76] are not recognised as "persons" for constitutional purposes' and 'pre-embryos have never enjoyed protection as "persons" under the federal law'.[77] The language of the contract itself in this case suggested that disposal of embryos in the event of divorce was something that the parties understood raised issues of 'legal ownership of any stored pre-zygotes' which had to be determined in a 'property settlement' and will be released as directed by order of a court of competent jurisdiction.[78] In the instant case, the court determined that the clear

---

72   410 US 113, 93 S Ct 705; 35 L Ed 2d 147 (1973).

73   *Ibid* at 529, 109 S Ct at 3062; *Webster v Reproductive Health Services* 492 US 490 (1989) at 529.

74   *Davis v Davis* 842 SW 2d 588, 597 at para 63.

75   696 NE 2d 174, 179 (NY 1998)

76   The court defined 'pre-zygote' as 'eggs which have been penetrated by sperm but have not yet joined genetic material' (*Kass*, 91 NY 2d at 556 n 1, 673 NYS 2d 350, 696 NE2d 174).

77   *Ibid* (discussing *Roe v Wade*) 410 US 113, 35 L Ed 2d 147, 93 S Ct 705.

78   *Kass*, 673 NYS 2d 350, 696 NE 2d at 176.

and unambiguous intention of the parties was to donate the pre-zygotes for research to the clinic in the event that they no longer wished to initiate a pregnancy or if they were unable to make a decision regarding disposition of their frozen pre-zygotes.

In *AZ v BZ*[79] the Massachusetts Supreme Court had to consider the effect of a consent form between a married couple and an IVF clinic concerning disposition of frozen pre-embryos.[80] The Probate and Family Court had granted a permanent injunction in favour of the husband (AZ), prohibiting the former wife from 'utilising' the frozen pre-embryos held in cryopreservation. The former wife appealed and the Supreme Court of its own motion transferred the hearing from the Court of Appeals. The Supreme Court affirmed the judgment of the probate court. The probate judge had held that the agreement which the couple had signed with the clinic four years earlier, granting the wife use of the eggs for implantation in the event of a separation, was unenforceable because it no longer represented the true intention of the parties in the changed circumstances. Particular weight was given to the fact that since signing the forms, the wife's treatment with IVF had successfully resulted in the birth of twins. The husband had later filed a divorce claim and no longer wanted to have children.

The Supreme Court went further than the Probate Court in finding that even if the contract had been unambiguous, the Court would still have been unwilling to have enforced an agreement that would compel one donor to become a parent against his or her will on grounds of public policy: 'As a matter of public policy, we conclude that forced procreation is not an area amenable to judicial enforcement.'

In *JB v MB*,[81] a former wife and husband had sought infertility treatment together. Following IVF treatment, the woman JB had successfully borne a child either through IVF or natural means. When the marriage was dissolved she wished to discard the remaining seven pre-embryos. The man, MB, wished to have them implanted or donated to infertile couples. The New Jersey Supreme Court affirmed the decision of the court below which granted rights over disposition of the embryos to the woman. The Supreme Court agreed with the approach taken by the Massachusetts Supreme Court affirming the constitutionally protected right to procreate and not to procreate, and holding that even an unambiguously worded agreement over disposition of pre-embryos would not be enforceable if it compelled the party seeking to avoid procreation to become a parent against his will. In the instant case, the Court found that the agreement with the clinic did not disclose a clear intention from the parties as to disposal of the pre-embryos in the event of a separation or divorce. The husband's

---

79   431 Mass 725 NE 2d 1051 (2000) SJC-08098 (2000).

80   The Supreme Court defined its use the term 'pre-embryo' to refer to the four- to-eight-cell stage of a developing fertilised egg. See Ethics Committee of the American Fertility Society, 1994, at 29S–30S (explaining terminology and transformation of single cell into multicellular newborn).

81   170 NJ 9, 783 A 2d 707 NJ Aug 14, 2001.

constitutional right to procreate was unaffected as he was already a parent and would be able to father other children in future. By contrast, the wife's right not to procreate would be violated as she would be compelled to have genetic offspring.

Litowitz v Litowitz[82] is the last and most recent case heard by a US State Supreme Court and involves another dispute between a divorcing couple over frozen pre-embryos in which, unlike all the other cases where both parties were progenitors, the woman had not provided the eggs and had no biological connection to the frozen embryos, whilst the man had provided the sperm. Five embryos were created; three of them were implanted in a surrogate and produced a child. The couple separated before the child was born. The dispute concerned the disposition of the two remaining embryos which had been cryopreserved in the clinic. Mr Litowitz wanted to have them put up for 'adoption' whilst Mrs Litowitz wanted to have them implanted in a surrogate. The trial judge awarded the embryos to Mr Litowitz having determined that the embryos were children whose 'best interests' dictated that they should not be born to a divorced single parent. Mrs Litowitz appealed, claiming that the judge had erred in failing to implement the terms of the agreement with the clinic and that any right she may have to the pre-embryos must be based solely upon contract. The egg donor contract provided that:

> All eggs produced by the Egg Donor pursuant to this Agreement shall be deemed the property of the Intended Parents and as such, the Intended Parents shall have the sole right to determine the disposition of said egg(s). In no event may the Intended Parents allow any other party the use of said eggs without express written permission of the Egg Donor.

The Court of Appeals affirmed the judgment of the trial court on different grounds. The contracts signed by the couple and the clinic did not require the couple to continue with their family plan and Mr Litowitz's right not to procreate compelled the court to award the pre-embryos to him.

The Supreme Court reversed the Court of Appeals' judgment (Sanders J dissenting) and remanded for further proceedings. In the majority's view the trial judge's decision should have been based solely on the contract. Despite what the Supreme Court described as the 'questionable characterisation by the trial court of the pre-embryo as a "child"', the Supreme Court said that the question of 'whether a pre-embryo is a "child" is not a logical or relevant inquiry under the record now before the court'. The trial judge had said that: 'My decision on the pre-embryo has very little to do with property, very little to do with constitutional rights, everything to do with the benefit of the child.' The Supreme Court disagreed but considered that it was not necessary for the court to engage in a 'legal, medical or philosophical discussion whether the pre-embryos in this case are "children"'. The court was only concerned with the pre-embryo cryopreservation contract. Under that contract the couple had agreed to submit to the court the question of the disposition of the remaining embryos in the event of a dispute. The couple could not reach an agreement. The contract provided that the embryos should be thawed by the clinic after a period of five years, failing a request from the couple

---

82   48 P 3d 261 Wash 2002.

to undergo further development. The request did not take place, the embryos should have been thawed but the record did not indicate whether the embryos were still in existence. Bridgwater J concurred with the majority in the result, but differed slightly from the reasoning. He agreed that there was no contract in this case and that the trial judge had used an improper test when it considered the 'best interests' of the embryo. He also agreed with the majority that the husband had a constitutional right to privacy in procreative choice to dispose of the pre-embryos as he chose. However, in his view parental rights were not an issue in this case and would only become an issue where the embryo[83] had been implanted or the child had been born. He said: 'This case is not about termination of fertilised eggs ... This is a dispute between a divorcing couple over pre-embryos to which only one party contributed DNA – the husband ... I would decide this case based solely on the genetic connection to the husband and his fundamental right to reproductive autonomy.'

4.8   POINTS OF CONVERGENCE

There are undoubted differences between the various rulings of the Supreme Courts on the fate of the frozen pre-embryos/embryos in dispute, particularly over the status of any original agreement or contract and the effect of any subsequent change of mind. There are also differences in the construction and extent of procreative rights. Most of the commentaries on the cases have focused on these two central issues.[84] However, the fact that there is convergence in the Supreme Court rulings on the adoption of a dual legal approach combining contractual and constitutional rights to procreative autonomy is also indicative of the limited legal protection extended to the frozen embryo or pre-embryo. None of the Supreme Courts were prepared to assign rights or even legal interests to the frozen embryo. All agreed that the frozen embryo is not a person. It was said in *Davis v Davis* that the frozen embryo is not property either, but it can clearly form the subject matter of contractual rights, including rights of disposition leading to its destruction. Questions of viability or non-viability did not figure in the judgments, the only relevant type of viability mentioned being of an altogether different kind, namely the point at which the unborn foetus acquires the capacity to exist independently of the pregnant woman and the only point from which the United States Supreme Court has determined that the State acquires a compelling interest in the legal protection of the life of the foetus.[85] The reason for this can be found in the speech of Blackmun LJ:

---

83   Bridgwater J said he used the term 'embryo' to describe an implanted and developing embryo.

84   Coleman, 1999, pp 55, 80–88; Dehmel, 1995; Forster, 1998; Robertson, 1990b; Sheinbach, 1999; Steinberg, 1998; Walter, 1999.

85   'With respect to the State's important and legitimate interest in potential life, the "compelling" point is at viability. This is so because the fetus then presumably has the capability of meaningful life outside the mother's womb. State regulation protective of fetal life after viability thus has both logical and biological justifications.' *Per* Blackmun LJ in *Roe v Wade*.

Texas urges that, apart from the Fourteenth Amendment, life begins at conception and is present throughout pregnancy and that, therefore, the State has a compelling interest in protecting that life from and after conception. We need not resolve the difficult question of when life begins. When those trained in the respective disciplines of medicine, philosophy and theology are unable to arrive at any consensus, the judiciary, at this point in the development of man's knowledge, is not in a position to speculate as to the answer ... It should be sufficient to note briefly the wide divergence of thinking on this most sensitive and difficult question. The Constitution does not define 'person' in so many words. But in nearly all these instances, the use of the word is such that it has application only postnatally. None indicates, with any assurance, that it has any possible prenatal application.[86]

A quarter of a century later, the plurality and divergence of views over the moral status of the human embryo continue to haunt judges and legislators across the world. The increased emphasis on human dignity in the new human rights instruments on biomedicine should not obscure the difficulties in identifying a common position on the moral and legal rights of the human embryo and of the right to life in particular.

As this book goes into press, the English Court of Appeal ruling in *Evans v Amicus Healthcare Ltd*[87] shows the growing convergence between UK and US courts on the analysis and weighting of competing parental and embryo rights, albeit from a different legal perspective. The claimant was seeking to have embryos created with her own and former partner's gametes implanted after the couple had separated. The former partner refused, notwithstanding the fact that this would be the only chance for the woman to have her own genetic children. The Court of Appeal confirmed that the Human Fertilisation and Embryology Act 1990 conferred on either party the right to vary or withdraw consent to the storage and use of an embryo at any time (Sched 3, (v) and (vi)) and further held that the statutory provisions were compliant with Art 8 of the ECHR which protects the right to private life, including the right to procreate and not to procreate. The fate of the embryos was decided strictly by reference to the procreative rights of the parents, and in particular the right of any genetic parent not to become a parent (paras 109–11).

---

86 *Roe v Wade* 93 S Ct 705 US Tex 1973.
87 [2004] EWCA Civ 727.

CHAPTER 5

THE RIGHTS OF THE DEAD: RESEARCH ON HUMAN TISSUE AND BODY PARTS AFTER BRISTOL AND ALDER HEY

The scandals at the Alder Hey Children's Hospital in Liverpool and at Bristol Royal Infirmary[1] have prompted a major review of UK law on the removal and retention of human tissue and organs. The Bristol and Alder Hey inquiries found that thousands of human body parts and tissue samples had been removed from the dead, stored and used without consent. The practice of removing organs and tissue from corpses without consent was found by the official inquiries to be widespread and tacitly accepted by professional colleges, universities and hospital management. By contrast, the scandal caused considerable distress to the relatives of the dead and horrified the public, thereby exposing a troubling cultural and moral schism between the medical establishment and the rest of society.[2] Three years after the scandal was uncovered, a new Bill on Human Tissue was introduced in the House of Commons in December 2003. The Bill is unlikely to be passed in its original form, following accusations of poor drafting by the medical profession and concerns that the Bill would seriously hamper medical research.[3] This chapter reviews the background moral cultures and legal framework behind Bristol and Alder Hey. I suggest that normative practices vis à vis corpses are dependent on the social perspective of the onlooker. I begin by exploring the distinct meanings ascribed to the human corpse by science and by society to explain the different values and normative practices attached to the dead. I then suggest that the distinct value conferred by relatives and society on a human corpse explain why English common law has resisted pressure to construct the

---

1 *Interim Report: Removal and Retention of Human Material*, May 2000, Bristol Royal Infirmary Inquiry; *Report of the Royal Liverpool Children's (Alder Hey) Inquiry*, January 2001, HC (Redfern Report); *The Removal, Retention and Use of Human Organs and Tissue from Post-mortem Examination*, Advice from the Chief Medical Officer, 2001; *Report of a Census of Organs and Tissue Retained by Pathology Services in England*, Advice from the Chief Medical Officer, 2001; *Report of Content Analysis of NHS Trust Policies and Protocols on Consent to Organ and Tissue Retention at Post-mortem Examination and Disposal of Human Materials in the Chief Medical Officer's Census of NHS Pathology Services*, 2000, all accessible on www.doh.gov.uk. For Scotland, see *Report of the Independent Review Group on the Retention of Organs at Post-mortem*, January 2001 (McLean Report).

2 Families of children whose organs were wrongly kept by Liverpool's Alder Hey Hospital have accepted a £5 million out-of-court settlement. A judge ruled the cash offer of £5,000 for each dead child was a 'sensible and fair settlement'. But 13 of the 1,154 claimants have either rejected or not responded to the offer. They have been given leave to join a national group pursuing litigation over other organ scandals across the country. The deal was struck between lawyers representing the hospital, the University of Liverpool and the hundreds of families affected. The offer will be met by the National Health Service Litigation Authority. Mr Justice Gage, sitting at Nottingham Crown Court, approved the settlement. 'I am quite certain that that represents a sensible and fair settlement so far as they are concerned and I very much hope that these parties can adopt a closure in what has been a very distressing and serious event.'

3 See Parry, Zimmern, Hall and Liddell, 2004 and the Public Health Genetics Unit: www.cgkp.org.uk/topics/human_tissue/bill_critique.pdf. See also Wellcome Trust, 2004.

human body as property. In the last section, I explore how European human rights law could be extended to secure adequate legal protection of the dead whilst recognising the public interest and legitimacy in some forms of interference with human corpses in order to facilitate the conduct of scientific research.

5.1   THE MEANING OF HUMAN CORPSES

Scientific research on human tissue or body parts is needed to advance our knowledge of the causes of death and disease. However, the scientific community and the medical profession have to operate within the cultural and moral bounds of society. The Bristol and Alder Hey inquiries indicate that scientists had hitherto been operating within a normative framework which is *prima facie* at odds with that of the relatives and the rest of society. Why?

A human corpse is both an object of scientific investigation and the deceased's loved child, father, sister, etc. The meaning ascribed to a human corpse is therefore dependent on the social perspective of the onlooker.[4] From the perspective of science, a human corpse is primarily an object of enquiry. *Qua* object of scientific enquiry the human corpse is purely a compound of physical matter which, like other compounds of matter or physical objects, can be studied by applying the laws of physics, chemistry, biology, etc. To the grieving relatives, however, and to the rest of society, the body of the deceased is never merely a physical object or compound of matter. It is invested with a social meaning and emotional value which distinguishes it from other physical objects and which requires a different normative attitude from that appropriate to the handling of pure compounds of matter.[5] Relatives and society expect this unique social and affective relationship to the body of the dead to be reflected in the way human corpses are treated. Society expects human corpses to be handled with respect and 'dignity'. However, from science's perspective, no such expectations apply to mere physical objects. In short, the meaning ascribed to the human body implies distinct normative values and associated practices. The challenge for scientists is to adjust their practice to acknowledge society's different perspective on human corpses whilst retaining the scientific outlook in their research. How can the scientific and social perspectives be reconciled?

5.2   MORAL PERSPECTIVES

The social and scientific perspective on the human corpse imply distinct moral perspectives vis à vis the dead. However, a significant finding of the Scottish and

---

4   This analysis draws on the works of phenomenologists, particularly Husserl, 1970a; Husserl, 1970b; and Merleau-Ponty, 2002.
5   *Ibid.*

English inquiries was that the purportedly 'beneficent' or altruistic motives of the profession were not questioned by relatives. Most parents or relatives, when asked, said that they would have been happy to consent to the removal or use of body parts and tissue for altruistic purposes, for example, for research intended to benefit others. For instance, the Scottish Executive report noted that:

> Although not every family who gave evidence to us felt the same way, the majority undoubtedly believed that reform of past practices was necessary. As we noted in our preliminary report, those families who have been through the trauma of discovering that organs or tissue have been taken from their relatives without their knowledge or agreement did not dispute the value of medical education and research. Rather they objected strongly to the fact that this had been done without their knowledge and agreement.[6]

In the view of the relatives, beneficence clearly did not justify removing tissue and body parts without their knowledge, even less deliberate deceit. These concerns can be analysed more systematically against wider moral frameworks.

5.2.1 Welfare

Utilitarian and welfarist principles of beneficence could no doubt be invoked to provide a justification for the harvest of human body parts or tissue without consent for the purpose of advancing medical research for the collective benefit of society. However, the limitations of the utilitarian moral framework are startlingly highlighted by the Bristol and Alder Hey scandals. From a utilitarian perspective, the grief of relatives and shock from the rest of society are but one factor to be entered into the calculations or scales against the benefits to be enjoyed by future generations. Since the deceased is no longer able to experience suffering (or happiness), his or her feelings cannot be entered into the welfare calculations.[7] On some versions of utilitarianism – such as preference utilitarianism – it might be possible to justify entering the deceased's past wishes into the aggregate calculus if the deceased had expressed a prior wish in respect of the disposal of his or her dead body.[8] But why the deceased's prior views about disposal of his or her own body should carry any special weight as against the views of potential beneficiaries is not something that preference utilitarianism can easily explain.[9] At best, the deceased individual's past preferences are but one set of preferences to be weighed against the totality of society's preferences. At worst, some versions of utilitarianism would require that the individual's past preferences be disregarded altogether (for example, if the preferences were to be gauged as irrational against an 'ideal' or 'rational' standard). In all the versions of utilitarianism, the feelings and experiences of the surviving relatives and friends and the rest of society could certainly be included in the total aggregate. However, the difficulty with reliance on the latter is that it provides only an indirect reason to justify respect for the

---

6   Scottish Executive, 2001.
7   See Smart, 1973; Glover, 1990; Sen and Williams, 1982.
8   See Sen and Williams, 1982; Griffin, 1986.
9   For a compelling discussion of this point see Hursthouse, 1987.

deceased's body. In all the versions of utilitarianism, deceit could be justified if it could be concealed and the overall effect was to promote future aggregate welfare.[10] Finally, both the 'preference' and the 'mental state' versions of utilitarianism raise considerable difficulties about the associated political framework which they presuppose. Neither version is necessarily consistent with liberal democracies which are founded on the primacy of individual rights.[11] Utilitarian theory gives lexical priority to collective welfare. It logically presupposes the primacy of collective welfare over individual rights. In practice, then, utilitarianism could justify the instrumental use of human bodies for the collective benefit of society uncovered by the Bristol and Alder Hey inquiries. As a theory, utilitarianism cannot provide direct reasons to respect the prior wishes or dignity of the deceased.

5.2.2 Autonomy

The weaknesses of utilitarian theory are avoided by deontological, autonomy-centred Kantian or neo-Kantian theories which confer primacy on individual rights as against collective welfare. In Kant's view, each individual person's ability to 'legislate for himself' and make autonomous choices confers a unique value and dignity on that individual. Failure to respect the individual's autonomous choices is morally wrong because it involves treating the individual as something which has value only for others instead of something which has value in itself and is worthy of respect and dignity. In Kant's famous words, 'only that which has value in itself has dignity and is worthy of respect'.[12]

One major difficulty with 'autonomy' centred models is that the individual's ability to make choices for himself or herself *prima facie* ends with death. However, respect for an individual's expressed prior choices could arguably be justified on the grounds that these choices were made by the once autonomous individual and are as much part of the individual's personal history and identity as choices pertaining to the time when the individual was alive. An illustration of this kind of approach may be found in Dworkin's *Life's Dominion*.[13] According to Dworkin, respect for individual autonomy requires respect for the individual's choice as to the timing and manner of his or her death. There is such a thing as a 'fitting' end to a life, namely an end with reflects the individual's own distinctive values and lends integrity to his or her life. Ends will vary depending on the beliefs and values of each individual. What a Catholic will regard as a proper and dignified death will be dramatically different from what a committed atheist would value. On this view, the autonomy principle thus requires respect not only for the wishes of individuals who are alive, but also respect for the autonomous individual's

---

10 Smart, 1973; Glover, 1990; Sen and Williams, 1982.
11 JS Mill sought to espouse both liberalism and utilitarianism in Mill, 1998. But see critiques in Dworkin, 1979 and Rawls, 1973.
12 Kant, 1969.
13 Dworkin, 1993.

prior expressed wishes regarding the manner of his or her death. Dworkin's argument could be extended to disposal and use of body parts after death. Individuals from different religious persuasions will have different beliefs as to what constitutes a fitting disposal and use of their bodies. An expanded view of autonomy requires that the individual's autonomous prior choices should be respected posthumously.

The main problem with autonomy-centred theories is that they have difficulties explaining why any special value or dignity should be conferred on those who never had (and/or will never have) the capacity to formulate rational choices, for example, infants and the mentally handicapped. In the Kantian model, such individuals are not strictly entitled to the dignity and respect which is due to autonomous beings since they lack the capacity to make (rational/autonomous) choices. In Dworkin's alternative theory of autonomy as integrity, reason too has primacy. Individuals who suffer from Alzheimer's or dementia are described as human 'vegetables'. In the event of an inconsistency between the kind of life they now desire (to sit in the sun eating peanut butter and jelly sandwiches) and their past wishes (to be actively involved in the creation of a great book or work of art), the individual's present wishes must be disregarded. In Dworkin's view, the life of an individual who lacks autonomy is not worthy of respect and presumably lacks human dignity. However, civilised societies recognise that small infants, the mentally handicapped, the demented and arguably the dead too retain human dignity. One of the enduring legacies of the Holocaust is to have exploded the myth that human dignity and respect are owed only to those individuals who have the capacity to make choices for themselves. Autonomy-centred theories are unable to explain why a human being who lacks autonomy may nevertheless have dignity and be worthy of respect.

5.2.3 Dignity

The emphasis on autonomy as a basis for respect and dignity may be understandable in the political context in which 17th and 18th century western liberal theories of rights developed to vindicate and secure the liberty of individuals against oppressive monarchies, but an expanded version of human dignity is required to adequately reflect the beliefs and practices of civilised societies towards all human beings, irrespective of their intellectual abilities. As Feldman elegantly argues: 'We must not assume that the idea of dignity is inextricably linked to a liberal-individualist view of human beings as people whose life-choices deserve respect.'[14] At the same time, the concept of human dignity, as was seen in the previous chapter, is essentially underdetermined and open ended in its application. In the case of disposal of human corpses, the concept of human dignity entails that there is a distinctive manner of treating human beings which is appropriate and fitting to them (in a way, for instance, which would be different from the appropriate handling of a material object, a

---

14 Feldman, 1999a, p 685.

mineral, an animal or a plant).[15] However, what is considered fitting or appropriate will depend both on individual and societal values. It cannot be a set of determinate qualities such as the ability to reason or think or feel or have this or that emotion, since an individual human being may at any one time may lack any or all of these qualities during his or her lifetime and yet continue to retain his or her dignity. When Anthony Bland[16] was lying in a persistent vegetative state (PVS) in bed, unable to see, hear or feel anything, his brain reduced to a watery mess, many thought that the constant invasion of his body by the medical team to keep him alive was an affront to his dignity. Others disagreed. To those who believe that autonomy is central to human dignity, the continuing invasion of Anthony Bland's body was seen as a degrading affront to Bland's dignity because it reduced his existence to that of a well-tended vegetable. To those who believe that the only prerequisite for human dignity is human life, procedures used to maintain a body alive cannot *per se* constitute an affront to his or her dignity, although they may become so if conducted in a certain inappropriate manner (in the same way as the feeding of a demented and incapacitated old person need not, in itself, divest the individual of dignity but could do so if conducted in a certain uncaring, unkind or disrespectful manner). Thus it has been said that dignity 'is rather an expression of an attitude to life which we as humans should value when we see it in others as an expression of something which gives particular point and poignancy to the human condition'.[17]

'Human dignity' in relation to human corpses is thus essentially an underdetermined concept whose specification reflects the diversity of anthropological, cultural and ethical practices of a given society (atheists, Muslims and Hindus will have different concepts of what respect for the dignity of the dead specifically requires). At the same time, implied in all the different specifications and concrete determinations of the concept of human dignity is the idea that when we ascribe human dignity to an individual, we do not take a slice of the individual's life at a given point in time and ask whether it instantiates a determinate set of mental attributes, but we think about what the life meant to the individual himself or herself (overarching goals, projects, achievements, etc) and to others (family, friends, colleagues) over time. All these aspects of a human life confer a meaning and value on an individual human life, which in turn relates to the meaning of a human being's death and the appropriate burial and disposal of the individual's body after his or her death.[18] What dignity and respect require in the disposal of a human corpse is thus deeply related to social beliefs about the meaning and value of human life. No such beliefs attach to the handling of physical objects from a scientific perspective.

---

15   Aristotle, 1954.
16   *Airedale v Bland* [1992] 1 All ER 821.
17   Feldman, 1999a, p 687.
18   Similar point made by Feldman, 1999a, p 688.

5.3   ENGLISH COMMON LAW

5.3.1 No property in a corpse

Given the fundamental difference between human corpses and other physical objects, one would expect the ordering of legal duties and rights vis à vis human corpses to be based on rules other than those ordinarily governing legal rights and duties over (mere) physical objects and things. The principle of English law that 'there is no property in a corpse' (*Williams v Williams*) arguably reflects this fundamental distinction.[19] Horses, carriages and land may be owned and therefore be bought and sold, retained or destroyed at the will of the owner. Human bodies can't. The relatives and executors of the estate have no right to retain the body and use or dispose of it as they wish. The common law imposes a duty on the person who is in possession of the body or the executor or administrator (*Rees v Hughes* (1946)) to dispose of the body by lawful means.[20] Failure to discharge the duty is a criminal offence (*Halsbury's Laws of England*, Disposal of dead bodies, Failure to discharge duty (p 904)). It is stated in *Russell on Crime* that to prevent the burial of a dead body is an indictable misdemeanour and the authority cited is the unreported case of *R v Young* referred to in *R v Lynn* (1788). In *R v Hunter* (1973) the accused were charged with conspiracy to prevent burial of a corpse.

5.3.2 Justification of the rule

The justification for the principle that there can be no property in the human body is not explored in the cases, and the historical foundation of the principle itself has been claimed to be shaky, the suggestion being that the principle originated in a misunderstanding of the old cases.[21] Be that as it may, the above analysis suggests that the 'no property' legal principle can legitimately be grounded in the deep conceptual differences between the human body and other physical objects/things, and in the related distinct normative values expressing society's perception and expression of the special status and dignity of the dead (through the diverse practices relating to burial and disposal of a dead body). If so, then the purpose of the legal principle that there can be no property in the human body would be to provide a legal basis on which to secure protection for the dignity of the dead.

---

19   (1882) 20 Ch D 659. See also Clerk and Lindsell, 1995, p 653, para 13–50.

20   Right/duty of disposal of body lies with executor or administrator. In *Holtham v Arnold* [1986] 2 BMLR 123, Ch D, claimant had lived with deceased for past two years – estranged wife wanted different burial – deceased had not left a will – wife as legal administrator had right to dispose of body.

21   See Skegg, 1975; Matthews, 1983.

Such a justification would in turn explain the exception to the principle created by English courts in *R v Kelly* (1999) that there can be no property in the human body. In *Kelly*, the Court of Appeal held that 'parts of a corpse are capable of being property within s 4 of the Theft Act 1968 if they have acquired different attributes by virtue of the application of skill, such as dissection or preservation techniques, for exhibition or teaching purposes'. The defendants had removed without permission and kept body parts which were retained for teaching purposes by the College of Surgeons under s 1(2) of the Anatomy Act 1984. The defendants, who had been charged with stealing the body parts under the Theft Act 1968, contended that the College did not have lawful possession of the parts at the time, as the body parts had been retained by the College beyond the period of time authorised by the Anatomy Act 1984. Notwithstanding this, the Court of Appeal concurred with the Crown Court that the college could be held to have possession of the collection of human body parts for the purposes of the Theft Act 1968. The Court of Appeal in *Kelly* also said *obiter* that:

> It may be that, if on some future occasion, the question arises, the courts will hold that human body parts are capable of being property for the purposes of s 4, even without the acquisition of different attributes, if they have a use or significance beyond their mere existence. This may be so if, for example, they are intended for use in an organ transplant operation, for the extraction of DNA or, for that matter, as an exhibit in a trial.

5.3.3 Inconsistencies and loopholes

The court's finding that body parts could, on the facts of the case, constitute property for the purposes of the Theft Act 1968 could be explained on the basis that strict adherence to the principle that there can be no property in the human body would in the circumstances have produced a perverse result by allowing the defendants to go unpunished after having appropriated body parts without authorisation and consent and disposed of them at their own will. However, understandable as the ruling in *Kelly* may be, it does nevertheless create further loopholes and uncertainties in the existing law:

- First, it presupposes that the College originally came into possession of the body parts by lawful means, in this instance by collecting the parts in accordance with the provisions of the Anatomy Act 1984. However, as the Bristol inquiry highlighted, the Anatomy Act 1984 itself is unclear as to what constitutes lawful possession.[22]

- Secondly, *Kelly* does not address the question of who would have had rights over the body parts in the event of the removal procedures having been found to have been evaded or avoided by the college (for example, evasion of the consent requirements in the Human Tissue Act 1961).

- Thirdly, the decision leaves the law in an unsatisfactory state because in order to find the defendants guilty of theft, the court had to construe as lawful the

---

22 The Bristol Royal Infirmary Inquiry, *Interim Report: Removal and Retention of Human Material*, Annex B, July 2001.

retention of body parts by the College which was in clear contravention of the procedures contained in the Theft Act 1968. In the light of the recent abuses from the medical profession exposed by the Bristol inquiry, such a benevolent judicial attitude to the medical profession is unlikely to be acceptable in the future.

- Finally, the decision has enormous implications for the conduct of biomedical research as it opens the way for the commercial exploitation of body parts, a distinct issue which raises complex and related but nonetheless quite different questions.

By contrast, the same court in the earlier case of *Dobson and Another v North Tyneside HA and Another* (1996) rejected the claimant's contention that body parts or tissue could be an object of ownership if they had been altered by the application of special skill. Gibson LJ, delivering the main judgment (Thorpe and Butler-Sloss LLJ agreeing), held that brain tissue fixed in paraffin after a *post mortem* is not rendered an item of possession, the right to which was vested in the claimants. The claimant was a relative of the deceased. The claimant wanted to recover samples of brain tissue which had been taken to establish the cause of death. The claimant's motive was to have further tests conducted on the tissue sample to provide evidence for a possible action in negligence against the hospital. The tests ordered by the coroner had been duly performed and the samples disposed of in accordance with the Coroners Rules 1984.[23] The crucial issue was whether the brain samples could be an object of property or an object to which the claimant had a right of possession. The claimant relied on a *dictum* of the High Court of Australia in *Doodeward v Spence* (1908), where Griffiths J had said that when someone had so 'dealt with a human body or part of a human body in his lawful possession that it has acquired some attributes differentiating it from a mere corpse awaiting burial, he acquires a right to retain possession of it, at least as against any person not entitled to have it delivered to him for the purpose of burial'. Clerk and Lindsell had, in their authoritative modern textbook on torts, relied on the *dictum* to suggest that it might be authority for the proposition that an unburied corpse can be subject of property if it has acquired attributes through the lawful exercise of work or skill. Gibson LJ disagreed. In Gibson's LJ's view, Griffiths's *dictum* in *Doodeward v Spence* was confined to a stillborn, two-headed child who had been preserved for 40 years by the defendant. In no way did the *dictum* cast doubt on the authority of the principle that there can be no property in the human body. *Doodeward v Spence* was a majority decision. Higgins J had dissented on the grounds that no one could have property in another human being. Barton J had agreed only that a stillborn foetus could be the subject of property, but did not want to cast doubt on the general rule that an unburied corpse cannot be the subject of property.

---

23 *Per* Gibson LJ: 'Dr Perry was under an obligation imposed by r 9 of the Coroners Rules 1984, SI 1984/552, to make provision for the preservation of material which in his opinion bore upon the cause of death, but only for such period as the coroner thought fit. It is not alleged that Dr Perry was in breach of that obligation ... once the cause of death had been determined by the coroner ... there could be no continuing obligation under the rule to preserve the material.'

Prima facie, Kelly and *Dobson* are inconsistent with each other since, according to *Dobson*, the exception to the general principle that there is no property in the human body is confined to exceptional cases such as *Doodeward* where the human body in question is almost categorised as a member of a different genus altogether (in the court's view, a 'freak'). By contrast, *Kelly* admits of an exception to the principle when the body or body parts have been *lawfully* transformed by the application of special skill. *Kelly* opens the way for lawful trade and commerce in human tissue and body parts which had been resisted only two years earlier by the same court in *Dobson*.

The ruling in *Dobson* could superficially be read to imply greater respect for the dignity of the human body. However, the strict adherence to the principle that there can be no property in the human body in *Dobson*, coupled with the loopholes in the Anatomy Act 1984 regarding the legal status of the parts once the cause of the death has been determined, has the effect of divesting relatives of the deceased of any rights over the body whilst at the same time impliedly conferring on hospitals and scientists a relatively unchecked right of use and disposal of human tissue and body parts, albeit a right stopping short of the right to derive a financial benefit from the commercial exploitation of the parts (*contra Kelly*).

When the uncertainties in the common law are set against the lacunae in the Human Tissue Act 1961 and Anatomy Act 1984 uncovered by the Bristol inquiry, it is clear that there is a pressing need to revise the law regulating the use of human tissue and body parts.

5.4   MODELS FOR REFORM

5.4.1 The property model

One suggestion for legal reform canvassed in various forms by several commentators is to drop the legal principle that there can be no property in the human body and replace it with the principle that the human body or its parts may be owned, the *prima facie* owner being the person whose body it is. The reasons cited range from the shaky historical basis of the rule to it having produced perverse legal results and allowed parties other than the individual whose body (parts) have been used to derive a commercial benefit at the exclusion of the individual himself or herself. Thus, whilst Mason and Laurie concede that the aim of the no property in the body principle or rule may well have been:

> to emphasise an intuitive belief that some sort – and, perhaps a considerable sort – of human dignity remained in the body after death and that to allow trading in a body was the ultimate indignity,[24]

nevertheless, the rule has backfired, since there cannot be theft of the human body[25] or body parts nor paradoxically can a person dispose of their own body by will.[26]

---

24 Mason and Laurie, 2001.
25 See cases discussed above and Mason and Laurie's own analysis, at p 714.
26 *Williams v Williams* (1882) 15 Cox CC 39.

The 'property' model, it is suggested, would fill the deficiencies of the consent model, as it would allow the person whose body it is (or the relatives or executors) to have proprietary or possessory rights over the body and dispose of it at will; it would protect the financial interests of the body 'owner' by allowing him or her a claim for a fair share in the commercial benefits accrued by those who have and exploited his or her body parts/tissue; and it would rationalise current law which in any event, it is argued, presupposes a proprietary model of the body whilst depriving the individual whose body parts/tissue are presumed to have been 'abandoned' or given as gifts to receive any financial benefits for the use or commercial exploitation of those parts/tissue.[27]

However, the body as property model is philosophically problematic. Whilst the supposed 'owner' and his or her body (parts) may be conceptually distinct, there is a limit to how far owner and body can be separated in reality.[28] We can make sense of the claim that the 'owner' of the body or 'I' continues to exist without a finger or a leg, but what happens to an 'owner' who has fallen into a PVS state or indeed someone who has temporarily lost consciousness? The alleged 'owner' in those cases is in no position in reality to make any decisions about 'his' or 'her' body (parts). Presumably, the 'owner' also ceases to exist after death (at least for the purposes of making decisions about 'his' or 'her' body, irrespective of religious views one may have about life after death). In practice then, the extension of the property model to the human body would involve the creation of legal fictional 'owners' of bodies in the case of the mentally incompetent or dead. The model would also not circumvent the need to specify decision-making procedures and possibly even substantive limits relating to removal, use and disposal of the body parts/tissue of 'owners' of bodies who have expressed no prior wishes and who are no longer mentally competent or alive. Finally, even in respect of individuals who are mentally competent, a legal model of the body as property would have to contain substantive limits on use and disposal of bodies (or parts/tissue) by their 'owners' to reflect society's concerns about risks of economic exploitation and abuse.

5.4.2 The consent model

The Scottish and English official inquiries into the removal and retention of human tissue and body parts have both attributed the source of the medical profession's widespread evasion of the law to lacunae and deficiencies in the relevant legislation, particularly the Human Tissue Act 1961. The Act confers on relatives a mere right to object (but not consent) to interference with the body of a deceased.[29] The pathologist is under a statutory duty to make 'reasonable' inquiries, but the standard of 'reasonableness' is not specified. Neither does the Act carry any deterrent value, as there are no penalties attached to failure on the

---

27 For instance, Mason and Laurie cite the Nuffield Foundation recommendation that bits of body parts which are left after an operation should be treated as 'abandoned' or as 'gifts'.

28 The 'property' model is likely to be based on dualist conceptions of the person. For a critique of dualism see Wittgenstein, 1984 and Rorty, 1981.

29 Human Tissue Act 1961, s 1(2)(b).

part of the pathologist to comply with the statutory requirements. Unsurprisingly then, much of the focus of the English official inquiry has been to explore the drafting of alternative informed 'consent' requirements by relatives together with the imposition of civil or criminal penalties as a means of controlling abuse.[30]

The 'consent' approach, however, is not itself without difficulties. The Scottish inquiry rejected it partly on the basis that the term 'consent' is most appropriately used in relation to individuals who have the capacity to make informed decisions, or alternatively their proxies whose decisions are then limited by the 'best interest' requirement, a notion whose application seems uneasy in the case of the dead.[31] Further, the ethical underpinning of the consent requirement in law (most commonly in the context of medical treatment) is thought to lie in the autonomy principle.[32] However, a relative's 'consent' to the use of human tissue and body parts from the deceased need not necessarily support the deceased's (prior) autonomy, as relatives may well have different views from the deceased as to what should happen to his or her body. Hence, to confer on relatives legal authority to consent to removal and use of the deceased's body may no doubt empower relatives of the deceased vis à vis pathologists, but nevertheless still fail to ensure respect for the (prior) autonomy of the deceased. In the view of the Scottish review: 'Where a competent adult has left written instructions on this matter, these wishes should be respected, irrespective of the views of surviving relatives ... It must be clear that the relatives have no legal role in circumstances where the deceased has made known, and not retracted his or her wishes.'[33]

In this light, the suggestion advanced by the Scottish review that changes to the legislation should be framed in terms of 'authorisation' rather than 'consent' carries some force. The use of the word 'authorisation' rather than 'consent', it is claimed:

> ... strengthens the role of parents in decision-making about the way in which their children should be dealt with and clarifies the scope of the (legally valid) decision-making powers which they have in respect of such children in these circumstances. Equally, the use of the term 'authorisation' rather than consent meets the concerns of those parents who do not wish to receive information about post-mortem examination and/or the subsequent removal and retention of organs or tissue, but who do not object to this.[34]

---

30   See the Bristol Royal Infirmary Inquiry, *op cit*, fn 1.

31   *Independent Review Group on Retention of Organs at Post-Mortem: Final Report*, 2001, Scottish Executive. Summary of recommendations: 'We are aware that the use of the word "consent" as currently legally understood is inappropriate and misleading, in the context of post-mortem examination and the removal, retention and use of organs/tissue. Accordingly we recommend that this should be replaced by the word "authorisation". The limitations of the terminology of consent are particularly acute in the case of the death of a child, in that parents are given lawful authority to consent only where the decision is "in the best interests" of the child. It is difficult to apply the best interests concept in the circumstances of this report' (para 3).

32   Mason and Laurie, 2001.

33   Paragraph 27.

34   Paragraph 17, s 1, *Independent Review Group of Organs at Post-mortem: Final Report*, 2001, Scottish Executive.

Nevertheless, the advantages of using the term 'authorisation' are arguably outweighed by the lowering of protection which could result from the implied relaxation of rules or standards on disclosure of information. Such a relaxation would in turn sit ill at ease with the official inquiries' finding that the nature and quality of information disclosed to the surviving relatives of the dead had been overwhelmingly inadequate and the main cause of the relatives' huge distress. To frame new legislation in terms which would make adequate disclosure of information an option rather than a legal imperative would risk perpetuating the paternalistic culture of the profession which was expressly called into question in the public enquiries. In addition, neither would use of the term 'authorisation' without further qualification ensure that the legal representative gives effect to the prior expressed wishes of the deceased. In short, use of the term 'authorisation' would not, by itself, remedy the shortcomings of existing legislation and would, in any event, need to be accompanied by a specification of the duties of legal representatives and the medical profession, in order to ensure that changes to the legislation do achieve their intended aim of securing better control and protection of the deceased.

In reality, the legal articulation of both the consent and the property models would require a specification and determination of procedures and limits on removal and use of body parts which would need to strike a balance between the need to ensure respect for the deceased's prior autonomy, the need to respect the dignity of the dead and society's legitimate interest in the advancement of science. It may be that in the specification of procedures and substantive legal limits to achieve these aims there is much more convergence than divergence between the property and consent models. In the remainder of this chapter I suggest that the articulation of the relevant principles may be best secured through a human rights framework.

5.5   A HUMAN RIGHTS PERSPECTIVE

5.5.1 Scope of the European Convention on Human Rights (ECHR)

A possible model of a legal instrument which attempts to foreclose the potential loopholes opened by the term 'authorisation' may be found in the Council of Europe's Convention on Human Rights & Biomedicine (CHRB) in the related context of participation of (live) mentally incapacitated persons in research. The CHRB uses the language of authorisation rather than consent in respect of the powers vested on the legal representative of a mentally incapacitated person (Art 18), but imposes an explicit and separate requirement that 'adequate information' be given to the legal representative prior to authorisation (Art 19). The wider background of rights contained in the Convention and the primacy of the value of human dignity also act as limiting concepts on removal and retention of human tissue and organs from the dead. Before exploring the possible application of a (legal) human rights framework to the removal and retention of human organs and tissue, it is helpful to explore the moral basis of such rights and the related value of human dignity to determine how different moral perspectives could bear on existing and future law.

One possible area of difficulty with the suggestion that rights may be vested on an individual who *ex hypothesis* is no longer alive is that such an individual cannot and will never be able to assert or claim the rights in question. However, the same is true to a lesser extent of individuals who are in a permanent coma, mentally retarded or brain damaged, and there is no question of divesting these individuals of their rights.[35] The accepted way forward in such cases is for the law to confer legal authority and powers on a representative to represent the interests of those who are mentally incapacitated.[36] The Covenant on Civil and Political Rights (1966) recognises that: 'The mentally retarded person has a right to a qualified guardian when this is required to protect his personal well-being and interests' (Art 5). The CHRB also recognises the need for law to make provision for the appointment of a legal representative to make decisions on behalf of the mentally incapacitated in respect of medical interventions (Art 6(3)). The right to a legal representative could by analogy be extended to the deceased.

It may be argued that the analogy does not work, for whilst the mentally incapacitated retain some interests which could or should be protected by law, it is not clear that the dead retain any interests at all. To this it may be answered that the interests of a dead person lie in respect for that person's (prior) autonomy and/or dignity. Further, even those who have suggested that a person in a PVS state may have no interests left at all (*per* Lord Mustill in *Bland*) have stopped short of denying such individuals – whilst still alive – a right to a legal representative. Finally, English law already confers legal authority on executors to act on behalf of a deceased in relation to the disposal of the deceased's estate and, to a limited extent, in respect of decisions concerning the form of burial. Arguably there is no conceptual gulf to be bridged in extending the powers of legal executors to encompass disposal of the deceased's body as well as his or her estate. In either case, the purpose of the power is either to protect the (prior) autonomy and/or dignity of the deceased, and/or to protect the interests of surviving relatives or beneficiaries.

The more serious difficulty lies in specifying how the values of (prior) autonomy and dignity of the dead could find a determinate expression in the specific substantive rights recognised in international instruments such as the ECHR. All the major international instruments on human rights contain declarations recognising the fundamental importance of respect for human dignity. Human dignity is expressly mentioned in the preambles to the Charter of the United Nations (1945),[37] to the Universal Declaration on Human Rights (1948), to the International Covenant on Economic, Social and Cultural Rights (1966) and the International Covenant on Civil and Political Rights (1966)[38] and in the

---

35 For a critique of 'claims' theories of rights see Waldron, 1993 and Simmonds, 2002.

36 The position in English law is anomalous as it currently lacks a procedure to confer legal authority on others to make decisions on behalf of mentally incapacitated adults: *Re F* [1990] 2 AC 1.

37 'We the peoples of the United Nations determined to save succeeding generations from the scourge of war, which twice in our lifetime has brought untold sorrow to mankind, and to reaffirm faith in fundamental human rights, in the dignity and worth of the human person ... have resolved to combine our efforts to accomplish these aims.'

38 '... in accordance with the principles in the Charter of the UN, recognition of the inherent dignity and of the equal and inalienable rights of all members of the human family is the foundation of freedom, justice and peace in the world ... these rights derive from the inherent dignity of the human person.'

reference to the preamble to the UN Declaration in the ECHR. The European Court of Human Rights (ECtHR) has also reiterated on numerous occasions the fundamental importance of human dignity, most recently in *Pretty v UK*: 'The very essence of the Convention is respect for human dignity and human freedom.'[39] The Council of Europe's CHRB, which represents the most recent and comprehensive attempt to state the range of rights in biomedicine, also begins with a declaration of the importance of ensuring the dignity of the human being in the preamble, and then an explicit requirement in Art 1 that the parties to the Convention 'shall protect the dignity and identity of all human beings'. The CHRB does not address the issue of removal and use of human tissue for research purposes from the dead.[40] But the ECHR does contain prohibitions on degrading treatment and privacy which have hitherto been presumed to apply to the living only but could arguably be extended to the dead. If, as suggested by Feldman,[41] human dignity it is not a separate right in itself but rather an overarching value which underpins specific rights such as the right to privacy (Art 8) or the right to freedom from degrading treatment (Art 3), the key question then is whether Convention Articles which articulate how human dignity is to be protected in specific areas (for example, degrading treatment, privacy) could have their presumed field of application to the living extended to the dead. To what extent could substantive rights protected by the ECHR be extended to human beings who are no longer alive? In what follows, I shall suggest that such an extension is possible in respect of several Articles and, furthermore, is warranted and consistent with the ideal of the Convention as a 'living document'.

5.5.2   Article 2

The first point to note is that the nature of the rights protected by some of the Articles in the Convention precludes their application to human beings who are no longer alive. For instance, the right to life protected by Art 2 can only meaningfully be ascribed to human beings who are (still) alive[42] or, alternatively, to individuals who have lost their lives in circumstances where the State was under an obligation to protect the individual's life. For instance, Art 2 could be engaged when a patient is refused life-saving treatment by a health authority when the treatment is available on the NHS and in that particular instance has a reasonable chance of succeeding. Alternatively, the ECtHR has also determined that the right to life protected by Art 2 imposes on States a positive obligation to take steps to prevent killings (*Osman v UK* (1990)). So Art 2 may be invoked on behalf of an individual who is no longer alive but has lost his or her life as a result

---

39   *Pretty v UK* (2002) 35 EHRR 1 at 65.

40   An Additional Protocol to the Convention on Human Rights & Biomedicine, on Transplantation of Organs & Tissues of Human Origin, was adopted by the Council of Europe in 2002, but has not yet entered into force. The Protocol contains a chapter (IV) on organ and tissue removal from deceased persons. Article 17 requires prior consent or authorisation as required by law and Art 18 requires the human body to be treated with respect.

41   Feldman, 1999a.

42   Eg, *R v Cambridge Health Authority ex p B* [1995] 1 WLR 898 and *Pretty v UK* [2002] 2 FLR 45.

of a breach of the State's obligation to protect life (although here too the proportionality test may be invoked to gauge the reasonableness of policy decisions regarding the deployment and use of limited police forces). In short, the main interest protected by Art 2 is the life of the individual. The interests or rights that an individual may have over removal or disposal of his or her body or parts thereof when dead cannot be construed as engaging the right to life anymore than the right to life could be extended to embrace the right to die (*Pretty v UK*).

5.5.3   Article 8

In the case of other Articles in the Convention, it is not always clear whether the application of the Article to individuals who are no longer alive is definitely excluded. For instance, in respect of the right to family life protected by Art 8, it could be argued that the right could only meaningfully be ascribed to individuals who are *de facto* able to found a family, which, *ex hypothesi*, would seem to require the individual in question to be alive. It might be suggested that the idea of an individual having a right to found a family *post mortem* is simply conceptually incongruent. But what if the right in question concretises into the right to have one's sperm used to facilitate conception *post mortem*? Here, the public controversy and academic commentaries which followed the *Blood* case suggest that there is no clear moral consensus on this point.[43] Arguably, this lack of consensus could be invoked to refute the claim that the interests affected have the status of fundamental rights. Alternatively, in the event of a 'rights claim' being recognised as legitimate in this context, curtailment of the right in question by the State in the form of a prohibition of insemination *post mortem* could be seen as a legitimate and proportionate use of State power if the aim of the proposed derogation was, for instance, to protect the psychological well-being of the child to be born. In short, the question of whether Art 8 is engaged or not in this context need not necessarily depend on whether the possible bearer of the rights is (still) alive or dead.

In some respects, the possible application of Convention Articles to the removal and use of organs/parts/tissue *post mortem* is less difficult to conceptualise because of the high level of congruence in the public's outrage about the removal and use of body parts without consent.

A broad interpretation of the (moral) principle of self-determination/ autonomy requires that an individual's prior expressed views about the manner of disposal of his or her body *post mortem* should be respected. Domestic English case law already recognises one form of extension of the principle of self-determination, namely its application to advanced refusals of life-saving treatment. In *Bland*,[44] the House of Lords conceded that the right to self-determination requires an individual's prior express wishes in respect of medical treatment to be respected in the event of the individual subsequently losing his or her mental competence. The same principle has been accepted in other common law jurisdictions.[45] Arguably, the principle could be consistently extended at

---

43   See Lee and Morgan, 2001.
44   *Airedale NHS Trust v Bland* [1993] 1 All ER 821.
45   Eg, in the US, *Nancy Cruzan v Missouri Department of Health* 58 LW 4916 (US 1990).

common law to protect the prior autonomy of an individual who is no longer alive in respect of expressed choices regarding interference with and disposal of his or her body.

Similarly, the fundamental importance of the principle of self-determination has recently been acknowledged by the ECtHR in *Pretty v UK* (2002), where it was said that:

Although no previous case has established as such any right to self-determination as being contained in Art 8 of the Convention, the Court considers that the notion of personal autonomy is an important principle underlying the interpretation of its guarantees.

Diane Pretty had argued that she had a right to determine whether or not to remain alive and to receive assistance in ending her own life. She argued that the criminal prohibitions on assisted suicide constituted a violation of her right which was protected by Arts 2, 3, 8 and 9. The ECtHR rejected her claim that the right to life protected by Art 2 encompassed the right to die, on the grounds that such an interpretation involves a contradiction in terms. The Court also rejected her claim that the prohibition on assisted suicide forced her into an undignified and cruel death (Art 3).

On the other hand, the Court determined that she could found a valid claim under Art 8. She had a right to self-determination, which extended to choosing the manner and time of her death. The Court stressed that the concept of 'private life' protected by Art 8 is very broad: it covers the physical and psychological integrity of a person (at para 61).

Since Art 8 was engaged, the question was whether the UK's criminalisation of assisted suicide constituted a necessary and proportionate limitation on Ms Pretty's right. The Court determined that the limitation was necessary and proportionate, the aim being to protect vulnerable groups who could be put at risk of having their life ended. The reasoning in *Pretty* gives a fairly clear indication of how a claim regarding the removal of body parts without consent could proceed on the basis of Art 8.

When the person is no longer alive but had expressed prior wishes regarding the manner of disposal of his or her body *post mortem*, those wishes are arguably analogous to advance directives relating to medical treatment whose legal binding force the ECtHR has recognised as lying in the principle of self-determination protected by Art 8 of the Convention.[46] On this interpretation, Art 8 imposes on the State an obligation to ensure that the prior known wishes of a deceased human being as to the manner of disposal of their body are respected. Removal of body parts and tissue for research purposes against the express wishes of the deceased or his or her representatives could thus constitute a violation of the individual's right to self-determination protected by Art 8.

---

46 'In the sphere of medical treatment, the refusal to accept a particular treatment might, inevitably, lead to a fatal outcome, yet the imposition of medical treatment, without the consent of a mentally competent adult patient, would interfere with a person's physical integrity in a manner capable of engaging the rights protected under Art 8(1) of the Convention. As recognised in domestic case law, a person may claim to exercise a choice to die by declining to consent to treatment which might have the effect of prolonging his life' (at para 63).

Nevertheless, as was made clear in *Pretty*, the right protected by Art 8 is not absolute. A State may lawfully limit from this obligation if it is necessary in order to fulfil aims which comply with the legitimacy and proportionality requirements in a democratic society. Hence, it might be justifiable in exceptional circumstances to override the express wishes of an individual for purposes such as the protection of public health or morals. Similarly, the deceased's desired form of burial might for instance be legitimately prohibited if the condition of the body would pose a serious risk to public health. Exceptionally, it might even be legitimate to remove some body tissue when, for instance, the individual died of a condition which is particularly virulent and whose study might benefit others.

If prior express wishes cannot be ascertained, either because the individual never expressed a choice in this matter or because he or she lacked the capacity to make choices when alive, then respect for human dignity still requires that the body of the deceased should nevertheless be handled in an appropriate manner in recognition of the special meaning and status of that body as distinct from other purely physical objects. The operative concept of human dignity here cannot be the same as autonomy-centred Kantian or neo-Kantian concepts of dignity since, *ex hypothesi*, there is no agent to express a choice and when the agent was alive no choice was expressed and/or the agent lacked the capacity to make a choice. Human dignity in this context cannot be synonymous with autonomy, but as indicated earlier operates to limit and constrain the range of morally acceptable conduct vis à vis a human corpse on the basis of its distinctive humanity. The principle of respect for human dignity arguably puts the State under an obligation to ensure that the individual's body and its parts are not handled as commodities, but are disposed of with the respect and dignity owed to the dead. In what follows, I shall suggest how the rights in question could come within the sphere of protection of Art 3.

5.5.4 Article 3

Article 3 has been described by the ECtHR as 'one of the most fundamental provisions of the Convention and as enshrining core values of the democratic societies making up the Council of Europe's values of democratic societies' (*Soering v UK* (1989)). Article 3 proscribes any treatment of individuals which is 'inhuman or degrading'. The prohibition is absolute and, unlike Art 8, admits of no limitation. At its minimum, the prohibition on inhuman or degrading treatment imposes on Member States a negative obligation to refrain from inflicting serious harm on persons within their jurisdiction (for example, *Ireland v UK* (1978)). A positive obligation on State authorities to protect the health of persons deprived of liberty or to take steps to protect individuals from being subjected to inhuman or degrading treatment has also been said to arise in *S v UK* (2001) and *Keenan v UK* (2001).

The main difficulty in bringing unauthorised interference with a deceased body under the sphere of protection of Art 3 lies in ascertaining the precise scope of the concept of 'inhuman or degrading treatment'. If the concept is to be construed narrowly as confined solely to instances of conduct which – whether by omission or commission – cause physical or psychological harm to an individual, then Art 3 would have no application as a corpse cannot, *ex hypothesi*, suffer harm. A corpse cannot feel anything at all and therefore cannot literally suffer harm, whether serious or not. On the other hand, if the concept of inhuman or degrading treatment is given a wider meaning to include conduct which constitutes an attaint on the individual's right to physical integrity and human dignity,[47] then unauthorised interference with a corpse could arguably come within the scope of Art 3. The fact that the individual who is the subject of the degrading and inhuman treatment is not mentally competent or indeed even conscious should not necessarily preclude application of Art 3, otherwise small infants and in general vulnerable populations could not benefit from protection under the Article (*contra, S and Others v UK*). Such an exception would also be inconsistent with Art 6 of the International Covenant on Civil and Political Rights (1966), which prescribes that 'The mentally retarded person has a right to protection from exploitation, abuse and degrading treatment'.

Assuming Art 3 is applicable, then the more difficult issue would be that of circumscribing the range of conduct and nature of interference with a corpse in a manner which is sufficiently broad to allow legitimate biomedical research to take place, whilst nevertheless protecting the dignity of the dead. Arguably, and in the light of the above discussion, the limiting concept in this case would have to be articulated through the concepts of authorisation or approval by lawful authority/executor/representative.

5.6   BALANCING INDIVIDUAL v SOCIETAL INTERESTS

The adoption of a human rights perspective on removal and use of human tissue and body parts from the diseased allows legislators and policy makers to conduct a balancing exercise between the rights of the individual and the interests of society. As discussed previously, Art 8, in particular, allows for departures and exceptions to the principle of respect for autonomy and physical integrity when interference with the right is necessary in a democratic society, in the interests of national security, public safety or the economic well-being of the country, for the prevention of disorder or crime, for the protection of health or morals, or for the protection of the rights and freedoms of others.

On this basis, there is no doubt that the rights of the deceased could legitimately be balanced against the interests of society in the conduct of scientific research on human tissue or organs. It is precisely such societal interest that critics of the original Human Tissue Bill thought were being compromised.[48] By the time the Bill had reached its third reading in the Commons on 28 June 2004, there had been 99 amendments to the original Bill and the Government had listened to

---

47   *X v Germany* (1983) 7 EHRR 152. The applicant had been force fed by prison authorities whilst being on hunger strike. The ECtHR held force feeding did constitute an attaint to the individual's dignity, but no violation because the aim was to preserve life which the State had an obligation do under Art 2.

48   See McKie, 2004.

representations from members of the scientific and medical research communities and tabled amendments with a view to securing their support. A discussion of the Bill before its final adoption is beyond the scope of this chapter. However, an examination of the overarching principles and rights involved in the removal and use of tissue and body parts from the dead may assist in the final evaluation of the legislation. When defending the tabled amendments, the Health Minister Rosie Winterton had said that: 'The purpose of the Human Tissue Bill continues to be to protect the rights and expectations of patients and families, whilst ensuring a framework in which research can flourish.'[49] After all, the Human Tissue Bill expressly purports to be compliant with the ECHR.

---

49 'Concerns spark tissue bill change', BBC News, 24 June 2004.

CHAPTER 6

RESEARCH IN DEVELOPING COUNTRIES: NEW ETHICS AND NEW THREATS TO HUMAN RIGHTS

6.1 INTRODUCTION

The global AIDS epidemic has prompted some critical rethinking of the ethical obligations of the research community and sponsoring industry to human participants in medical research. Developing countries are facing a humanitarian crisis of catastrophic proportions caused by the AIDS epidemic. Over 40 million people throughout the world are currently infected with HIV/AIDS.[1] The overwhelming majority (95%) live in developing countries. The World Health Organisation (WHO) and the Joint United Nations Programme on HIV/AIDS (UNAIDS) estimate that at least 6 million of these have advanced stage HIV and are in urgent need of antiretroviral (ARV) treatment now. Four million live in sub-Saharan Africa but in 2002 fewer than 50,000 (under 2%) of HIV positive people in Africa received antiretroviral therapy, whilst 95% had no access to testing and remained unaware of their HIV status.[2] And yet, where available, highly active antiretroviral therapy (HAART) has reduced mortality by 90% and dramatically improved quality of life.[3] In November 2003, the WHO and UNAIDS declared the AIDS epidemic a public health emergency and launched the 3 x 5 Initiative to treat 3 million sufferers by 2005.[4] The unprecedented scale of the international effort required from 'resource-rich' countries to meet these targets may be gleaned from the lack of progress on the targets set in the 2001 Declaration of Commitment by UNAIDS.[5] At the launch of the 3 x 5 Initiative, Peter Biot, Executive Director of UNAIDS, talked about the need to overcome the 'formidable barrier of creating sufficient operational capacity to expand access to HIV treatment'.[6] Lee Jong Wook, Director-General of the WHO, said that this massive challenge could only be met if 'we change the way we think and change the way we act'.[7] The 3 x 5 Initiative aims to 'advance the UN goals of promoting human rights as codified in the UN Declaration of Human Rights, as expressed in the WHO Constitution in

---

1   *Epidemic Update*, December 2003, UNAIDS, www.unaids.org.
2   Mukherjee, Farmer, Niyizonkiza, McCorkle, Vanderwarker, Teixeira and Kim, 2003.
3   *Ibid*, at p 1105.
4   WHO and UNAIDS, 2003.
5   Two years later, Kofi Annan, Secretary General of the UN, warned that: 'we have the commitment. Our resources are increasing. But the action is still far short of what is needed ... By 2005, we should have cut by a quarter the number of young people infected with HIV in the worst affected countries; we should have halved the rate at which infants become infected; and we should have comprehensive care programmes in place everywhere. At the current rate, we will not achieve any of those targets by 2005.' Press Release SG/SM/9014 AIDS/65 OBV/393.
6   WHO and UNAIDS, 2003, p 1.
7   *Ibid*.

seeking the attainment of the highest possible standards of health, and clarified in the Declaration of Commitment of the UN General Assembly Special Session on HIV/AIDS in 2001'.[8] This chapter reviews and compares the 2000 revision of Helsinki with new ethical guidelines on research in developing countries, including the Council for International Organisations of Medical Science (CIOMS) and European Group on Ethics (EGE) guidelines. The options canvassed by the World Medical Association (WMA) in response to the continuing controversy over the text of the 2000 revision are analysed, and the legal implications of the rift from Helsinki evaluated. The last section analyses the compatibility of the new guidelines with human rights law as codified in the Council of Europe's Convention on Human Rights & Biomedicine (CHRB) (1997) and the European Convention on Human Rights (ECHR) (1950) and considers the extent to which the new guidelines are consistent with the fundamental principle of international human rights law of respect for the equal dignity of all human beings and the prohibition on discrimination. The chapter concludes with some reflections on the issues which need to be addressed in the future to achieve transnational justice.

6.2 THE ETHICS OF AZT TRIALS: ETHICAL IMPERIALISM AND ETHICAL CONFLICT

In 1997, distinguished academics, scientists and members of the US human rights watchdog Public Citizen Health Research Group sent a letter to the US Department of Health & Human Services (HHS) concerning public funding by the National Institutes of Health (NIH) of trials in Asian, African and Caribbean countries which, they argued, were unethical because they involved testing new or shorter regimens of antiviral HIV drugs against placebos.[9] Altogether 17,000 women were involved in the trials. The authors argued that the deaths of several thousand children could have been prevented if, instead of the placebos, the control arm of the groups had been given the antiviral drug AZT (076) which in NIH sponsored trials three years earlier had been shown to reduce HIV transmission from mother to child by approximately two-thirds. The results had been so dramatic that the study was stopped before completion.

The use of a placebo in the new studies would have been prohibited in the US. The writers of the letter accused US researchers and the NIH of double standards in funding studies that routinely provide life-saving drugs to Americans whilst denying these drugs to thousands of citizens of developing countries, thus conveying to the international community the impression that the US government places less value on the life of non-Americans.[10] The experiments were said to be in 'clear violation of all of the major international, ethical guidelines'[11] including at least four principles of the Nuremberg Code and most particularly the WMA's

---

8   *Ibid*, p 10.
9   Lurie, Wolfe, Jordan, Annas, Grodin and Silver, 1997.
10 *Ibid*, p 2.
11 *Ibid*, p 2.

Declaration of Helsinki which, at the time, stated unequivocally that in each medical study 'every patient – including those of a control group, if any ... should be given the best proven diagnostic and therapeutic method'.[12] If anything, the authors of the letter argued, ethical safeguards in developing countries should be greater than those in the industrialised world, as people in developing countries are likely to be more vulnerable.[13]

The authors recognised that, as industrialised countries celebrated the successes of AZT, it had become quickly apparent that the exorbitant and prohibitive cost of the drugs, together with logistical difficulties, meant that the vast majority of women in developing countries would never have access to the treatment. Thus, the authors stressed that '... we are, therefore, not opposed to research that modifies the regimen provided in Protocol 076 in order to identify a simpler, less expensive, similarly effective or more cost-effective intervention'.[14] However, whilst it was true that many of the strategies being tested in the studies were less expensive than in Protocol 076, they could still be unaffordable in developing countries and there was no guarantee that the women and infants in those countries would benefit from the knowledge gained from the research. In these circumstances, the AZT trials amounted to exploitation: 'If the underdeveloped country could not afford to spend $50 any more than it could spend $800, then it could not possibly derive information that would be of any benefit to its population. This is the definition of exploitation.'[15]

There followed a fierce exchange over the interpretation and application of ethical international guidelines on research in developing countries between supporters of the trials and their critics, conducted mainly through the pages of the *New England Journal of Medicine (NEJM)*.[16]

Supporters of the trials, which included researchers in both developing countries and resource-rich countries, argued that affordable treatment was urgently needed in the face of the appalling number of deaths and placebo controlled trials could deliver a faster, scientifically more reliable answer than the use of active controls which would result in a substantial increase in expense as well as a loss of efficiency.[17] Furthermore, the cost of the AZT 076 regimen at the time was $800 per patient or 10 times the cost of the short-duration regimen under test. In the sub-Saharan countries where the trials were carried out, the typical annual per capita allocation for health was less than $10. The 076 regimen could not therefore represent a sustainable standard in these countries. Placebo controlled trials thus addressed best and were most responsive to the health needs of resource-poor host countries. Whilst it was regrettable that developing

---

12   *Ibid*, p 2.
13   *Ibid*, p 2.
14   *Ibid*, p 3.
15   Glantz, Annas, Grodin and Mariner, 1998, p 40.
16   The exchange led to the resignation of one of the editors of the *New England Journal of Medicine*.
17   Levine, 1999.

countries could not afford the best available treatment available in industrialised countries, they should be allowed to develop treatments and preventive interventions that they could afford: 'research sponsors, both industrial and governmental, in industrialised countries should not be prevented from assisting developing countries in their efforts in this regard'[18] through misconceived appeals to international ethical guidelines such as the Declaration of Helsinki which are routinely violated with impunity. To do so was no less than 'ethical imperialism'.[19]

Accusations of 'ethical imperialism' had paradoxically originally been raised by critics of the placebo controlled studies.[20] In a controversial editorial in the NEJM,[21] Angell had expressed concern at the spectre of 'a general retreat' from the clear principles enunciated in the Nuremberg Code and the Declaration of Helsinki as applied to research in developing countries, where the ethical imperative to give priority to the welfare of the individual is being displaced by the utilitarian research goal to benefit large numbers of individuals in the future. The danger was that, with the most altruistic of motives, researchers may find themselves slipping across the line which prohibits treating human subjects as a means to an end.[22] The risk was particularly serious in the light of the growing competitive global environment:

> The fact remains that many studies are done in the Third World that simply could not be done in the countries sponsoring the work. Clinical trials have become a big business, with many of the same imperatives. To survive, it is necessary to get the work done as quickly as possible, with a minimum of obstacles. When these considerations prevail, it seems as if we have not come very far from Tuskegee after all.[23]

However, critics thought that advocates of the 'local' standard of care were confused over the status of ethical guidelines. 'Local standard', they argued, is a descriptive concept which denotes existing standards of care in a given place at a given time. By contrast, the standard set by ethical guidelines is normative and intended to prescribe universal ideals of conduct.[24] The setting of ethical guidelines requires the adoption of a normative, not a descriptive standard. The (ideal) standard should be universal and not relative to existing, regrettably low, standards in developing countries, and should put the interests of the individual participant in the research over those of the wider community.[25] Trials conducted

---

18 Levine, 1999, p 533.
19 Letter by K Mbidde, Chairman of the AIDS Research Committee of the Uganda Cancer Institute, to the Director of the NIH, 8 May 1997, stating that it is 'ethical imperialism' for outsiders to dictate to Ugandan researchers and IRBs what sort of research is ethical or unethical for Ugandans to carry out on their own people.
20 Angell, 1988.
21 Ibid.
22 Angell, 1997. Figures cited in the Nuffield Council Report and the NBAC report show a tenfold increase in research in developing countries.
23 Ibid.
24 Annas and Grodin, 1997.
25 Schuklenk and Ashcroft, 2000, p 158.

for 'economic' reasons only, in order to find cheaper forms of treatment, were unethical and should not be conducted on individuals in developing countries unless the researchers/sponsors can conclusively establish before the trial that the cheaper treatments, if shown to be successful, would be made available to populations in the developing host countries.

Macklin convincingly suggests that the differences between supporters and critics of the AZT trials point to deeper differences in underlying key values, including conceptions of exploitation and the requirements of distributive justice.[26] None of the players want exploitation and yet critics of the AZT trials think that the adoption of a local standard involves exploitation, whilst supporters think not. In addition, critics think that justice requires the application of a universal standard, whereas supporters say that justice requires adjustment or responsiveness to local conditions.

The 2000 revision to the Declaration of Helsinki, far from settling the matter, has given rise to further controversy. According to Macklin, this is because the 2000 revision 'simply does not address other aspects of international research about which people disagree'[27] including what is owed to the community or country where the research is conducted after the trial is over. Is this right?

6.3 CONTROVERSY OVER HELSINKI STANDARDS

6.3.1 Placebo controls: best 'current' v best 'proven'

The latest (2000) revision of the Declaration of Helsinki replaces the previous requirement that the control group be provided with the best 'proven' diagnostic and therapeutic method with the best 'current' method instead. Paragraph 29 provides that:

> The benefits, risks, burdens and effectiveness of a new method should be tested against those of the best *current* prophylactic, diagnostic, and therapeutic methods. This does not exclude the use of placebo, or no treatment, in studies where no proven prophylactic, diagnostic or therapeutic method exists.

Does best 'current' denote a universal standard, determined purely by clinical factors, or does the standard denote whatever treatment is currently available locally, in which case the standard may be relative to the local, social and economic conditions which may vary from one locality to another? If the former, the best 'current' standard would prohibit the use of placebo controls in resource poor countries. If the latter, placebo controls could legitimately be used under Helsinki rules in developing countries when participants in the same trial in developed countries would be given whatever state of the art treatment is available locally instead of a placebo.

---

26 Macklin, 2001.
27 *Ibid*, fn 27.

In the immediate aftermath of the 2000 revision, there was concern amongst some critics that the new formulation replacing best 'proven' by best 'current' methods was ambiguous. Public comments made by Dr Delon Human, Secretary General of the WMA, about the intention of the drafting committee did not satisfy those who found the formulation ambiguous. Dr Human had acknowledged that 'it is extremely difficult' to define the term, but he claimed the drafting committee had intended 'to give the patient access to the ... potential or possible or current treatment of the day'.[28] The phrasing of the provision, however, was said by critics to 'obfuscate' the committee's intent.[29]

On the other hand, Levine, a leading supporter of placebo control trials and their use in under-resourced countries, was left in no doubt about the meaning of the revised formulation which, in his view, continued to perpetrate the flaw of the earlier formulation, namely the 'excessively rigid proscription of placebo controls'.[30] In his view it was regrettable that 'The Declaration's absolute proscription remains intact for placebo controls in clinical trials designed to evaluate therapies for diseases or conditions for which there already exists a therapy known to be at least partially effective'.[31] Levine is thus continuing to campaign for a fundamental revision of Helsinki standards to allow placebo controls to be used in countries where the alternative best current clinical treatment is neither available nor sustainable.[32]

The reading of the best 'current' standard as denoting a universal, purely clinical standard is probably correct, particularly in the light of the footnote to para 29, added by the WMA in an unprecedented move to settle the controversy barely two years after the new formulation had been adopted. The footnote states that: 'The WMA hereby reaffirms its position that extreme care must be taken in making use of a placebo controlled trial and that in general this methodology should only be used in the absence of existing *proven* therapy ...'

6.3.2   Post-trial benefits to participants

Another source of controversy with the 2000 revision of Helsinki is the addition of a provision in para 30 requiring that: 'At the conclusion of the study, every patient entered into the study should be assured of access to the best proven prophylactic, diagnostic and therapeutic methods identified by the study.'

The provision was added to avoid exploitation of vulnerable populations in under-resourced countries and to ensure that the poor and sick would not become cheap guinea pigs for those who could afford to pay for the drugs or treatment which had been tested successfully.

But it is now clear that para 30 will not be adhered to by major US and international pharmaceutical corporations, as the US Food & Drug Administration

---

28   Vastag, 2000.
29   Forster, Emmanuel and Grady, 2001.
30   Levine, 2002.
31   *Ibid.*
32   *Ibid.*

(FDA) has refused to recognise the 2000 revision of Helsinki. The FDA carries considerable international muscle because it has the power to withhold licences for drugs which do not comply with its rules. The FDA, which unsuccessfully sought a revision of Helsinki in 2000 to allow for use of placebos in control groups, is now seeking a change to para 30 which, it claims, is unrealistic, could not be implemented and would deter sponsors from badly needed research.

The WMA has spent the past two years considering whether para 30 of the Declaration should be revised again since, the WMA conceded, the wording 'was not perfect'.[33] The WMA finally decided in January 2004 that it would be inappropriate to revise the Declaration so soon after the 2000 revision, partly because it was thought that there was general agreement with the spirit of para 30, and partly because it would be difficult to achieve 75% approval for any change. It was also thought that the need for stability dictated that the Declaration should only be revised when absolutely necessary.

6.3.3 WMA proposed new revisions

In this light, it is therefore surprising to find that, far from the matter having now been closed and settled, the WMA has also decided to seek consultation[34] on whether other alternative approaches should be followed, including the possibility of:

(1) adding a preamble explaining that the Declaration of Helsinki is a set of ethical guidelines, not laws or regulations;

(2) adding a note of clarification that reaffirms the intention of para 30 but avoids the possibility of misinterpretation;

(3) making no changes or additions to the Declaration.

A serious difficulty with option 2 is that the proposed 'clarification', whilst formally or technically falling short of the proposed new 'revision' rejected by the WMA, would in practice nonetheless involve some alteration to the Declaration, thus raising the very difficulties about the stability and, ultimately, authority of the Declaration, which the WMA was quite reasonably seeking to avoid. In addition, there is a real danger that any 'additional' clarification may raise different or new doubts as to the interpretation and scope of application of para 30 and/or questions regarding the consistency of para 30 with any additional clarification, as illustrated by Dr Human's comments on para 30 after its adoption. Dr Human said that the aim of para 30 is 'to guarantee that research participants are not worse off after a study than they are during the study'. However, this appears to restrict the application of para 30 in the case of experiments where some of the participants are part of a control group receiving a placebo. The natural reading of para 30 is that at the end of the experiment all the participants in the trial should

---

33 WMA, news release, 30 January 2004.
34 *Ibid*.

receive the successfully tested treatment. By contrast, under Dr Human's expanded version, there would be no obligation on the research sponsors/scientists to offer the tested treatment to the participants in the control group receiving the placebo, since these participants will not be worse off after the study than they were during the study (they were only getting a placebo).

Option 1 reads as an attempt to limit the effect of the Declaration in countries which have adopted laws or regulations which are inconsistent with the Declaration, by impliedly relegating the Declaration to the (lesser) status of ethical guidelines. At one level, the proposed insertion seems totally innocuous as it appears to do nothing more than state the obvious, namely that the Declaration is not a legally enforceable instrument but a statement of ethical ideals. On the other hand, if the implied suggestion is that the Declaration carries only moral or ethical force but no legal force whatsoever, then the suggestion is misleading and mistaken. The Declaration of Helsinki, along with the Nuremberg Code, is an internationally recognised guideline on human experimentation.[35] Although the Declaration and the Code have no direct legal force, they nevertheless constitute a form of 'soft law' in that they may be relied upon by courts as sources of what international lawyers call 'the accepted custom or practice of nations'.[36] This is reflected in the fact that Helsinki has been regularly invoked and carried influential weight with Canadian and US courts in litigation involving claims from participants in research programmes against research sponsors and co-ordinators.[37]

The persuasive weight of the Declaration in legal proceedings lies in the fact that it purports to, and has hitherto been seen as, setting an internationally agreed standard of conduct which is universal and not relative to local, economic or social conditions. From a legal perspective, there is a real danger that the persuasive weight of the Declaration will be seriously diminished if it impliedly sets itself as having less authority than local laws which exact less demanding standards. Hence there is much to be said for the WMA resisting pressure to dilute standards or allowing the application of differential, less exacting standards to vulnerable populations in resource poor countries.

On the other hand, the legal weight carried by the Declaration depends on its being recognised as a rule of customary international law. This in turn requires that the rules or principles contained in the Declaration should be supported by (i) general and consistent State practice and (ii) evidence that the general and

---

35 Some have even argued that the Nuremberg Code is an international legal document: see Annas, 1992.

36 Campbell and Cranley Glass, 2001. See also Fidler, 2001; Arnold and Sprumont, 1998.

37 *Abdullahi v Pfizer Inc* 2002 WL 31082956 (SDNY, 17 September 2002) (NO 01 CIV 8118), *Robertson ex rel Robertson v McGee* 2002 WL 535045 (ND Okla, 28 January 2002) (NO 01CV60), *Grimes v Kennedy Krieger Institute Inc* 366 Md 29, 782 A 2d 807 (Md, 16 August 2001) (NO 128 SEPT TERM 2000, 129 SEPT TERM 2000), *Johnson v Arthur*, 65 Ark App 220, 986 SW 2d 874 (Ark App, 3 March 1999) (NO CA98-660, CA98-661), *Whitlock v Duke University* 637 F Supp 1463, 33 Ed Law Rep 1082 (MDNC, 16 June 1986) (NO C-84-149-D), *Pierce v Ortho Pharmaceutical Corp* 84 NJ 58, 417 A 2d 505, 115 LRRM (BNA) 3044, 12 ALR 4th 520, 101 Lab Cas P 55,477, 1 IER Cases 109 (NJ, 28 July 1980).

consistent State practice is followed out of a sense of legal obligation.[38] From a legal perspective, the US FDA withdrawal of support for the 2000 revision of the Helsinki Declaration constitutes the most serious threat to date to the authority of the Declaration because it introduces dissent where previously there was international consensus, and in this way carries the potential to emasculate the Declaration of any, albeit indirect, legal force.

In this light, option 3 does nothing to address the considerable pressure on the WMA to achieve a consensus on the 2000 revision, particularly in the light of the emergence of new international ethical codes on research in developing countries, all of which are pointing away from Helsinki.

6.4   THE INTERNATIONAL DRIFT AWAY FROM HELSINKI

An additional threat to the authority of the Declaration of Helsinki is the growing drift in new national, regional and international guidelines on research in developing countries. On the question of the use of placebos in the control arm of an experiment in resource-poor countries when effective treatment is available in developed countries, the US National Bioethics Advisory Commission (NBAC),[39] the Nuffield Council on Bioethics, the European Group on Ethics, CIOMS and UNAIDS have not only adopted ambiguous positions, but recommendations which are *prima facie* inconsistent with the Helsinki requirement that the best *current* treatment be provided instead of a placebo.

6.5   'EFFECTIVE' v 'BEST "CURRENT"' TREATMENT

6.5.1   UNAIDS and NBAC

The UNAIDS (2000) guidelines state that the use of a placebo is ethically acceptable as long as there is no known *effective* HIV preventive vaccine,[40] echoing the NBAC guidelines which also recommended that researchers and sponsors should design clinical trials that provide members of any control group with an 'established *effective* treatment, whether or not such treatment is available in the host country'.[41]

However, as the NBAC itself noted, the criterion of 'effectiveness' here falls short of the Helsinki requirement of best '*current*' treatment. The NBAC took the latter to denote purely clinical considerations, whilst the former may also involve socio-economic factors. The NBAC justified this departure on the grounds that the concept of what constitutes 'the best current treatment' is ambiguous and admits of different possible answers. Whilst this is no doubt true, however, the NBAC's

---

38   Brownlie, 1998, pp 5–8.
39   Now defunct and replaced by President Bush with a President's Council.
40   Guidance point 11.
41   US National Bioethics Advisory Commission, 2001, Recommendation 2.2.

alternative formulation is equally open to different interpretations, not least the view that where the host country does not have an 'established' effective treatment, it is permissible for a research sponsor to deny participants in a research trial the benefit of effective treatments established in other countries. Such an interpretation at first glance seemed to have been ruled out by the NBAC's explanation that established effective treatments are not limited to what is routinely available in the country in which research is being conducted, as:

> the phrase an *established effective treatment* (is used) to refer to a treatment that is *established* (it has achieved universal acceptance by the global medical profession) and *effective* (it is as successful as any in treating the disease or condition).[42]

However, the NBAC report also adds that the 'effectiveness' of a treatment may depend on the 'locally available medical or social resources needed for a successful intervention'.[43]

6.5.2 CIOMS

The new guidelines of the WHO sponsored Council for International Organizations of Medical Sciences (CIOMS) similarly obfuscate the meaning of their alternative formulation that placebos may be used when there is no 'established effective intervention'. The latest revision of the guidelines provides that placebos may be used 'when there is no established effective intervention'.[44]

CIOMS itself acknowledges in the Introduction to the Guidelines that the formula departs from the terminology of Helsinki which refers to the best 'current' rather than the 'most effective' intervention. But it is then implied that the meaning of the two formulations may in fact coincide, as clinicians may disagree on what is the best 'current' intervention is and:

> In other circumstances in which there are several established 'current' interventions some clinicians recognise one as superior to the rest. Some commonly prescribe another because the superior intervention may be locally unavailable, for example, or prohibitively expensive ...

The explanatory comments in the Introduction to the Guidelines state that the expression 'established effective intervention' is intended to refer to all such interventions. At the same time, the explanatory comments also envisage, *contra* Helsinki, that it may be ethically acceptable to use an established effective intervention as a comparator even when such an intervention is not considered the best 'current' intervention. The comments on Guideline 11 depart even further from Helsinki in contemplating circumstances in which it may be ethically acceptable to use a placebo 'in a country in which an established effective intervention is not available and is unlikely in the foreseeable future to become available, usually for economic or logistic reasons'. The control mechanisms in such circumstances would include the requirement that the proposed

---

42   National Bioethics Advisory Commission, 2001, Executive Summary.
43   *Ibid.*
44   Council for International Organizations of Medical Sciences, 2002, Guideline 11.

investigational intervention should be responsive to the health needs of the population from which the research subjects are drawn *and* that 'there must be an assurance that, if it proves to be safe and effective, it will be made reasonably available to that population'.

6.5.3 EGE

Whether the stipulated constraints can achieve the stated aim of protecting vulnerable populations in poor countries from exploitation is undoubtedly the crucial question. Before returning to this question, it is worth noting that the recommendations of the EGE in the report *Ethical Aspects of Clinical Research in Developing Countries*[45] are equally ambivalent and equivocal. The EGE expressly acknowledges that the use of a placebo for the purpose of developing cheaper treatments could mean accepting a double standard for poor and rich countries, whereby research in developing countries leads to new treatments which are patented in rich countries and cannot be afforded by poor countries. However, the EGE recommendations state on the one hand that the same rules as those applying to the use of placebos in European countries should apply to developing countries (presumably Helsinki). But, on the other hand, exceptions to depart from the best current standard may be justified, 'an obvious one being where the standard treatment is not available for logistic reasons or cost'.[46] In order to avoid exploitation, the report stresses the need for trials to address specific health conditions of the host countries, for instance, tropical diseases or developing a new treatment cheaper than those already existing,[47] and states that there should be an obligation that the clinical trial benefits the community that contributed to the development of the drug. This can be, for example, to guarantee a supply of the drug at an affordable price for the community or under the form of capacity building.[48]

6.5.4 Nuffield Council on Bioethics

The recommendations of the Nuffield Council on Bioethics are arguably the least congruent with Helsinki. Whilst claiming agreement with UNAIDS on the desirability of aiming for a universal standard of care, this standard is qualified as being applicable only where 'appropriate',[49] a worryingly elusive concept,

---

45 EGE, 2003. The ethical basis is wider: The fundamental ethical principles applicable are those already recognised in former opinions of the EGE, and more specifically: the principle of respect for human dignity and the principles of non-exploitation, non-discrimination and non-instrumentalisation, the principle of individual autonomy (entailing the giving of free and informed consent and respect for privacy and confidentiality of personal data), the principle of justice and the principle of beneficence and non-maleficence, namely with regard to the improvement and protection of health, the principle of proportionality (including that research methods are necessary to the aims pursued and that no alternative more acceptable methods are available).

46 *Ibid*, para 2.10.

47 *Ibid*, para 2.5.

48 *Ibid*, Recommendation 2.13.

49 Nuffield Council on Bioethics, 2001, para 10.33.

particularly in the light of the further statement that 'Where it is not appropriate to offer a universal standard of care, the minimum standard of care that should be offered to the control group is the best intervention available for that disease as part of the national public health system'.[50] In practice, as the evidence canvassed by the Nuffield Council itself on the economics of health inequalities shows, in sub-Saharan African countries that means no treatment.

In short, as noted by other commentators, despite agreement on general principles on the ethics of research in developing countries and in particular on the justice requirement to avoid exploitation of the poor by the wealthy, there is deep disagreement over the understanding and application of what justice requires.[51] Most disturbingly, there is an increasing rift between Helsinki standards, as defined in the 2000 revision, and the new emerging guidelines from other international or regional organisations on research in developing countries.

6.6   WHO BENEFITS? INDIVIDUAL v SOCIETY

Whether the departure from Helsinki can ultimately be justified arguably depends on whether the introduction of double standards will not have the effect of leaving research subjects in developing countries exposed to burdens and risks for the benefit of others in more affluent countries. The control mechanisms to avoid exploitation in all the guidelines are therefore absolutely crucial. These usually require that (i) the research should be responsive to the health needs of the local population and (ii) that participants in the research and/or the community should be offered the treatment if successful.

There are several difficulties about the reach of these requirements.

6.6.1   Responsiveness to local health needs

The first control mechanism undoubtedly precludes research sponsors from using participants from developing countries as guinea pigs for treatments which are only relevant to the health needs of developed countries. However, the formulation of the principle does not guarantee protection of the *individual* research participant in a developing country in accordance with the hitherto internationally accepted principle that the interests of the individual should prevail over those of science/society.

The UNAIDS guidelines require that:

The outcome of research should potentially benefit the *population* from which research participants are drawn.[52]

---

50   *Ibid.*
51   Macklin, 2001.
52   *Ibid*, guidance point 4.

Similarly, the NBAC had in the previous year recommended that clinical trials in developing countries should be limited to studies that are responsive to the health needs of the host country.[53]

The EGE guidelines, whilst stopping short of directing that the research should address the health needs of the local population/community, require that attention should be paid to the relevance of the research to the health priorities of the host country (2.9). But there is no express requirement that the interests of the individual should prevail over those of science/society.

The CIOMS guidelines require that the research is responsive to the health needs and priorities of the *population or community* in which it is carried out (Guideline 10). But here too there is no express adherence in the rest of the text to the principle that the interests of the individual should prevail over those of society.

In short, the requirement that the research should address the health needs of the local population is a double-edged sword which could potentially undercut the protection afforded to participants in medical research. In the absence of any express indication to the contrary, it is potentially inconsistent with the hitherto accepted principle that 'considerations related to the well-being of the human subject should take precedence over the interests of science and society'.

6.6.2 Availability of treatment

The 2000 revision of Helsinki seeks to avoid this utilitarian outcome with the addition in para 30 of the requirement that every patient entered in a study should be assured of access to the best proven intervention identified in the study. The UNAIDS guidelines too require that:

> A successful vaccine should be made available as soon as possible to all participants in the trials in which it was tested, as well as in the populations at high risk of HIV infection.[54]

NBAC adopts a less directive approach and requires instead that researchers and sponsors should make reasonable, good faith efforts before the initiation of a trial to secure at its conclusion, continued access for all participants to needed experimental interventions that have been proven effective for the participants.[55]

The EGE recommendations adopt the stronger language of 'obligation' to supply the successfully tested drug to *all participants* in the trial. Guideline 2.13 states that:

> In industrialised countries, free supply of a proven beneficial new drug to all the participants of a trial after the trial is ended is the rule as long as it is not yet available through the normal health care system. In developing countries, the same rule must be

---

53 National Bioethics Advisory Commission, 2001.
54 *Ibid*, guidance point 2.
55 National Bioethics Advisory Commission, 2001, Recommendation 4.1.

applicable even if this implies supplying the drug for a lifetime if necessary. Moreover, there should be an obligation that the clinical trial benefits the community that contributed to the development of the drug.

However, the EGE suggests that the requirement can be discharged 'under the form of capacity building' which arguably may or may not confer any benefit at all to individual participants in the trial.

Guideline 10 of CIOMS simply requires that 'the successful treatment be made reasonably available "for the benefit of that *population or community*"'[56] (emphasis added). There is no express requirement that the treatment should be made available to the individual *participants*.

One source of concern with the more expansive formulation adopted by the CIOMS guidelines to make treatment available to whole populations, rather than the more limited Helsinki requirement to make the treatment available to participants in the research, is that under the more expansive principle it is theoretically possible for a research subject to be entered into an experiment in which he or she may be exposed to risks and from which he or she does not stand to derive any personal potential benefit, even though the local community might. This theoretical scenario is not only incompatible with Helsinki but represents an inversion of the fundamental ethical principle that the interests of the individual should take precedence over those of society. At the very least, the CIOMS guidelines create a theoretical tension and conflict between the fundamental ethical principle which requires that in medical experiments, the interests and rights of the individual should take precedence over those of society and the utilitarian principle to maximise social welfare.

6.7   CONTROLLING ABUSE

In addition, there are compelling reasons to doubt that the framework of guidance offered by the guidelines may be sufficient to prevent abuses in practice. One major source of concern is the absence of overarching regulatory mechanisms to monitor and control adherence to the guidelines, even less to exact compliance and impose penalties for breach. The guidelines assume that Research Ethics Committees (RECs) may be entrusted with the task of scrutinising research protocols to weed out those which do not comply with the new requirements. But whether RECs can adequately discharge this responsibility is doubtful. In the first instance, the creation of RECs is still relatively recent even in industrialised countries where they now standardly operate within defined administrative or regulatory frameworks.[57] In developing countries, where research infrastructures are practically non-existent, there are no RECs to review research protocols.[58]

---

56 Guideline 10.

57 See Brazier, 2003; Mason, McCall Smith and Laurie, 2001; Montgomery, 2001.

58 In reality, the research will be authorised by a government department, which may or may not have the requisite expertise to prevent abuses. See DHSS Office of Inspector General, 2001.

6.7.1   The role of RECs

Even where RECs are in place, in view of the open and divergent wording of the various guidelines, difficulties of interpretation over the scope and precise meaning of the guidelines are inevitable. Consider, for instance, the requirement that sponsors should undertake in advance of the trial to make the proven intervention reasonably available post-trial. One possible interpretation is that the sponsors should undertake in advance of the trial to supply the proven effective intervention at a price which can be afforded by the host country. The EGE guidelines seem to go further in contemplating a 'guarantee' that the drug will be supplied at an affordable price. However, as mentioned above, the EGE guidelines also consider that this obligation may be discharged 'under the form of capacity building', an option favoured by some academic commentators who consider that other alternatives could include some other form of benefit to the community, such as assistance in building research capacity or constructing a water sanitation plant in a community that lacks clean water.[59] In short, as supporters of prior agreements themselves are prepared to acknowledge, the question of what counts as making an effective intervention reasonably available, and more generally whether 'derivative' benefits which may accrue to research participants from benefits conferred on host populations do qualify under the requirement, poses real difficulties of interpretation.

Setting aside difficulties over construction and interpretation of the various guidelines, there are also serious question marks about the level of oversight which can realistically be expected of these committees. Research protocols do not currently require sponsors and researchers to state in advance of a trial pricing policies for distribution of any successful drug post-trial, even less to have negotiated and agreed the final price with relevant national agencies. Assuming research protocols were to be modified to allow for the inclusion of statements from sponsors and researchers on pricing and availability of drugs post-trial, it is unclear what level of scrutiny and oversight over this matter could realistically be expected of RECs. Are they to take statements made by sponsors and researchers about prior agreements at face value, without further inquiry? Or are RECs expected to show a higher level of scrutiny and inquire into evidence of any arrangements or discussions on pricing? If the latter, what criteria are they to use to determine whether a prior agreement is adequate for the purposes of allowing the trial to proceed, and how can an REC ensure that the agreement is enforceable (or that it does not legally amount to an empty promise)? As the ongoing controversy over Trade Related Aspects of Intellectual Property Rights (TRIPS) and intellectual property rights on pharmaceuticals marketed in developing countries makes abundantly clear, policy development in this area requires a grasp of complex and highly technical legal questions. Arguably, RECs have neither the competence nor the authority to oversee the legitimacy and/or legality of any hypothetical bargaining arrangements between a sponsor and a national agency in a developing country.

---

59   Page, 2002.

In light of the above, it seems inevitable that the practical implementation of the guidelines will of necessity fall far short of the stated aim to avoid exploitation of the poor by the rich. The absence of a clear and determinate framework of rules to guide RECs in the application of the guidelines militates against any certain, uniform and therefore fair application of the guidelines. Neither will RECs be able adequately to scrutinise the existence and adequacy of any bargaining arrangements on pricing and availability of drugs post-trials. As a result, the practical effect of the guidelines could be exactly the opposite of that intended, namely to lower the standards of research owed to individual research subjects in developing countries without any guarantee of direct benefits accruing to them or the local community. Unscrupulous corporations could be licensed to lower research standards and conduct cheaper trials in developing countries on the basis of empty promises regarding availability and pricing of drugs post-trial.

Finally, it is unclear why it is thought that even the more scrupulously inclined corporations should decide to invest in research in developing countries to develop products which could turn out to be considerably less profitable than other products tested in developed countries without the same pricing and marketing constraints. The NBAC report noted that some observers believe that market forces have already pressured private organisations to become more efficient in the conduct of research with the potential compromise this implies for the protection of research participants.[60] The NBAC report concluded that although the extent, relevance and force of these pressures are widely debated, it is clear that such pressures can exist regardless of the funding source. From an economic perspective there must be a real danger that the new guidelines will be considered too onerous by research sponsors and will have the effect of driving away investment from resource poor countries.[61] In addition, there is certainly no indication that the FDA, which is opposed to the considerably more limited Helsinki principle that proven interventions should be made available to the pool of participants in a trial, will be any more inclined to agree to the provision of the treatment to a whole community at a 'reasonable' price.

Because of the potentially detrimental effect of the new guidelines on vulnerable research subjects in developing countries, it is imperative that the guidelines themselves be kept under review in the light of information regarding their actual operation and implementation. In particular, the CIOMS and the WHO should ensure that implementation of the guidelines by local RECs is monitored, and information about their actual working analysed and fed into future reviews.

6.8 THE CONVENTION ON HUMAN RIGHTS & BIOMEDICINE (CHRB)

Unlike international and regional ethical guidelines such as Helsinki, CIOMS and UNAIDS, the CHRB is a legal instrument which defines the scope of protection of

---

60 Chang, 2002.
61 Similar concerns have been expressed by Diamant, 2002.

the rights protected by the European Convention on Human Rights (ECHR) in the field of biomedicine. Applicants who believe their rights have been violated may appeal to the European Court of Human Rights (ECtHR) which has jurisdiction to determine whether Member States have breached their obligations under the Convention. In an action alleging breach of human rights in the field of biomedicine, the ECtHR would look to the CHRB to guide its interpretation of the Articles in the main Treaty.[62] The CHRB thus carries considerable legal weight.

Significantly, there are no specific provisions in the CHRB on research in developing countries. *Prima facie*, such research would thus have to be conducted on the same terms and principles which are applicable to all research, whatever their geographical location. The level of protection owed to participants would thus remain the same whether they belonged to resource rich or resource poor countries. In particular, in addition to the specific requirements on consent, risks/benefit ratios and REC approval contained in Arts 15–17 on scientific research, the research would have to comply with the fundamental principle stated in Art 2 of the CHRB that: 'The interests and welfare of the human being shall prevail over the sole interest of society or science.'

Article 2 thus clearly rules out research which puts the interests of a community over and above those of individual research participants. However, since some of the speculative scenarios canvassed above indicate that an inversion of Art 2 may be possible under the CIOMS, UNAIDS and EGE guidelines, it would seem at first hand that the new guidelines may not be compliant with human rights law as defined by the CHRB.

However, a broader reading of the CHRB suggests another, less conclusive interpretation. First of all, the chapter on 'General Provisions' in the CHRB also contains an article on professional standards which requires that 'Any intervention in the health field, including research, must be carried out in accordance with relevant professional obligations and standards' (Art 4). Included amongst the relevant professional obligations would be adherence to recognised international and regional guidelines such as the CIOMS and the EGE, which do allow research participants to be denied a proven treatment when no 'effective' treatment is available locally and the research has the capacity to confer a benefit on the community as a whole (or if the successful treatment is made reasonably available to the community). There is therefore an underlying potential tension in the application of Arts 2 and 4 of the CHRB which surfaces in the controversy over standards of research in developing countries. Since both Articles have the same weight, the resolution of any putative conflict between the two Articles would have to appeal to the aims and overarching and fundamental principles of the CHRB. I shall return to this point later.

---

62 See Plomer, 2001a. The CHRB has for the first time been invoked in the case of *Glass v UK* [2004] 1 FLR 1019.

6.8.1 Council of Europe Protocol on medical biomedical research

Before doing so, it is worth noting that the Council of Europe has recently adopted an Additional Protocol on Biomedical Research (June 2004) which is not yet in force but which, unlike the main text of the CHRB, does contain some provisions on research in developing countries.[63] The provisions contained in the Protocol are indicative of a shift in the direction of thinking of the framers of the Convention.

The relevant provisions are contained in Art 23 whose heading, deceptively, does not specifically refer to research in developing countries but adopts instead the general formulation: 'Non-interference with necessary clinical interventions.' Article 23 states that:

1   Research shall not delay nor deprive participants of medically necessary preventive, diagnostic or therapeutic procedures.

2   In research associated with prevention, diagnosis or treatment, participants assigned to control groups shall be assured of proven methods of prevention, diagnosis or treatment.

3   The use of placebo is permissible where there are no methods of proven effectiveness, or where withdrawal or withholding of such methods does not present an unacceptable risk or burden.

Paragraph 2 is almost a verbatim rendering of the pre-2000 version of Helsinki, which has traditionally been interpreted as pointing to a strictly clinical, universal standard, unaffected by local socio-economic considerations. Under the Additional Protocol, the control group is to receive, if not the *best*, at least a *proven* treatment and not a placebo. When read with para 1 which prohibits delay of medically necessary interventions, the natural interpretation is that Art 23 prohibits the use of placebos when there is a proven treatment, irrespective of the participants' locality. However, it seems that this natural reading of the text is at odds with that envisaged by the Explanatory Report, which explains that as regards 'proven' methods of intervention: 'It is expected that a proven method of treatment *that is available in the country or region* concerned be utilised'[64] (emphasis added).

Even when 'region' is given a wide meaning to include neighbouring countries (as suggested by the Explanatory Report), the construction suggested by the report points to a local rather than a universal standard.

On the other hand, para 3 clearly authorises the use of placebos where there are no methods of proven 'effectiveness', a term which, as already seen, has been consciously adopted by the new guidelines in contradistinction to the expression 'proven treatment' in the pre-2000 version of Helsinki, to allow for adjustments of clinical standards by social and economic factors which may vary from one locality to another. In effect then, Art 23 appears to seek an amalgamation of the pre-2000 and 2000 version of Helsinki together with some of the post-Helsinki criteria in the new guidelines. Superficially, such an amalgamation may be

---

63   At least four Member States must express their consent to be bound by the Protocol before it can enter into force (Art 37).

64   At para 120.

semantically possible but, in view of the real conceptual tension between the adequacy of universal versus relative standards underlying the use of terms such as 'proven' and 'effective', the text fails to resolve the ongoing controversy.

Furthermore, the last part of para 3 introduces a separate exception to the provision of proven treatment(s) for control group(s), aside from considerations relating to local availability, by also authorising the use of placebos in the alternative 'when this would not present an unacceptable burden or risk'.

The wording of this section implies that it might conceivably be permissible to withhold from a patient a proven treatment *even if* it is available in the region, providing this does not present an unacceptable burden or risk. The restriction on unacceptable burdens or risks would definitely rule out the Tuskegee refugees type of experiment, but it doesn't rule out other less burdensome experiments. The Explanatory Report indicates that it is expected that the level of risk or burden which is acceptable would have to be judged by RECs. However, the range of considerations which may be relevant to this balancing exercise is not spelt out and examples are not given (by contrast, for instance, to the lengthy Explanatory Report section of the meaning of 'minimal risk' in Art 17 of the CHRB). It does not help either that neither para 3 nor the Explanatory Report makes clear whether a volunteer who is suffering from a condition for which there is no treatment available locally is to be deemed not to have been exposed to unacceptable burdens or risks by being placed in a placebo control group. Overall then, the wording of Art 23 is ambiguous and creates considerable uncertainty as to the precise scope of exceptions to the rule that control groups should be provided with proven treatments rather than placebos.

In practice, and until the Additional Protocol on Biomedical Research enters into force, the ambiguity and uncertainty surrounding the meaning and scope of Art 23 is largely a matter of academic interest. For the time being, therefore, the legally binding provisions on research are those contained in the CHRB. As mentioned earlier, the CHRB does not authorise different and lower levels of protection for participants in developing countries, although there could be a potential tension between the requirement in Art 2 that the interests of the individual prevail over those of science or society and the growth of new professional guidelines prescribing differential standards which may conflict with Art 2. How would the ECtHR resolve the potential conflict?

I suggested earlier that in order to assist its construction, the court would look to the purpose and overarching principles of the CHRB. These are stated in the text itself and in the preamble, and include the fundamental principles and values adopted in other international legal instruments which are expressly endorsed in the CHRB.

6.8.2 The primacy of equal dignity

As far the purpose of the CHRB is concerned, Art 1 defines the object of the CHRB as follows:

> Parties to this Convention shall protect the dignity and identity of all human beings and guarantee everyone, without discrimination, respect for their integrity and other rights and fundamental freedoms with regard to the application of biology and medicine. Each Party shall take in its internal law the necessary measures to give effect to the provisions of this Convention.

The fundamental value asserted here is that all human beings are equal in dignity and therefore deserving of equal protection and respect for their dignity and integrity.

In acknowledging the equality of all human beings, the CHRB is echoing the endorsement of these values, most notably in the Universal Declaration of Human Rights proclaimed by the General Assembly of the United Nations (1948) and in the ECHR, which are expressly endorsed in the preamble to the CHRB.

The principle that all human beings are equal in dignity and entitled to equal rights is a fundamental overarching value underlying all international human rights instruments. It is expressly stated in the preamble of the Universal Declaration of Human Rights, which begins with a recognition of 'the inherent dignity and ... equal and inalienable rights of the members of the human family'. Article 1 of the Universal Declaration of Human Rights further states that 'All human beings are born free and equal in dignity and rights', whilst Art 2 states that:

> Everyone is entitled to all the rights and freedoms set forth in this Declaration, without distinction of any kind, such as race colour, sex, language, religion, political or other opinion, national or social origins, property, birth or other status.

6.8.3 Prohibition on discrimination

Article 2 is reproduced almost *verbatim* in the ECHR in Art 14, entitled 'Prohibition of Discrimination':

> The enjoyment of the rights and freedoms set forth in this Convention shall be secured without discrimination on any ground such as sex, race, colour, language, religion, political or other opinion, *national or social origin*, association with a national minority, property, birth or *other status*. [emphasis added]

Since the CHRB could only be invoked in the context of an application for breach of an Article in the ECHR, the prohibition on discrimination would have a fundamental role to play in the determination of the legality of differential placebo control trials involving participants from developing countries.[65] From this perspective, the crucial question then is whether differential treatment of research participants in developing countries could represent a violation of the fundamental right of all human beings to equal treatment and non-discrimination.

The first thing to note is that not all differential treatment need necessarily amount to unequal treatment and discrimination. Differential treatment may be permissible, but differences must be relevant and justified. In some cases, failure to

---

65 Note that Art 14 is only actionable in conjunction with breach of another Article in the Convention.

differentiate and take into account the relevant individual circumstances may even constitute discriminatory treatment. In *Thlimmenos v Greece*,[66] the Grand Chamber of the ECtHR held unanimously that the applicant had suffered discrimination under Art 14 in respect of his right to freedom of religion (protected by Art 9). The Grand Chamber considered that:

> The Court has so far considered that the right under Art 14 not to be discriminated against in the enjoyment of the rights guaranteed under the Convention is violated when States treat differently persons in analogous situations without providing an objective and reasonable justification [see *Inse v Austria* A 126 (1987)].

However, the Court also considered that:

> ... this is not the only facet of the prohibition of discrimination in Art 14. The right not to be discriminated against in the enjoyment of the rights guaranteed under the Convention is also violated when States without an objective and reasonable justification fail to treat differently persons whose situations are significantly different.

On this basis, whether or not the use of a placebo and the withholding of a proven treatment from a control group constitutes a violation of the individual's right to non-discrimination would depend on whether there are objective, reasonable justifications for the differential treatment.

As regards the use of placebos, it could conceivably be acceptable to test a new treatment against a placebo in a developing country, when the proven treatment is not available locally either because the requisite health infrastructure is missing or because it cannot be afforded by the country *and* the aim is to develop a new treatment which addresses the health needs of the community and seeks to overcome the local obstacles to the provision of treatment (for example, by circumventing the demands on health infrastructures and/or the development of cheaper alternatives which could be afforded locally). However, there would be a clear violation of the non-discrimination principle if, in a multicentre international trial, participants in a control group in developed countries received a proven treatment, whilst their counterparts in developing countries received a placebo instead and the reason for the withholding the treatment was for the sponsor to save costs. The differential treatment here would be discriminatory because it would be based on the socio-economic and national status of the participants, which cannot be relevant considerations for denying individual research participants the fundamental rights enjoyed by other participants.

Arguably, it may also be equally discriminatory for a research sponsor to single out a group of participants in developing countries to test a new treatment against a placebo when the tested treatment, if proved successful, could not be made available locally, either because the health infrastructure is inadequate or because the cost would be prohibitive. Further, it would also be equally discriminatory in such circumstances to withhold free supply of a successfully tested treatment post-trial to the participants in developing countries. Again this would have the hallmarks of discrimination, as the use of placebos and withholding of proven treatments in such circumstances would appear to be

---

66 Judgment of 6 April 2000.

based on the socio-economic status of the participants contrary to the non-discrimination prohibition in Art 14.

Finally, to the extent that the CIOMS guidelines allow sponsors to deny a benefit which is usually conferred on individual participants in industrialised countries to individual participants in developing countries and shift the benefit instead to the local community, the guidelines could be seen as discriminatory. There is therefore a real question mark as to whether the CIOMS guidelines and other similar ones are compliant with the fundamental principle of equal respect in human rights law.

6.9   THE FUTURE OF HUMAN RIGHTS IN BIOMEDICAL RESEARCH

Whilst it is possible to identify fundamental values in regional and international human rights instruments which raise doubts as to compliance of the new ethical guidelines on research in developing countries with the right of each and everyone to equal treatment and non-discrimination, it is nevertheless clear that claimants would have to overcome significant and in some cases fatal hurdles before they could obtain a remedy in a court of law.

6.10   DEFICIENCIES IN EUROPEAN HUMAN RIGHTS LAW

6.10.1 Uncertainty on the scope of Arts 2, 3 and 8

In the case of a legal suit relying on the CHRB, as noted previously, the action would have to be based on a breach of one or more of the rights protected by the ECHR. However, Art 14 of the ECHR on non-discrimination is not actionable *per se* but requires the applicant to establish that discrimination has occurred in respect of one of the other substantive rights protected by the Convention. For instance, the applicant would have to establish that participation in the experiments engaged his or her right to life (Art 2) or right to freedom from cruel treatment (Art 3) or the right to self-determination (Art 8), and that he or she has suffered discrimination in the protection of that right.[67]

As seen in the discussion of the possible reach of these Articles in other contexts in previous chapters, there is considerable uncertainty regarding the legal reach of Arts 2, 3 and 8. As regards the possible application of these Articles in the context of research in developing countries, whilst there are no judgments of the ECtHR directly on the point, academic analyses of the possible reach of the right to life and other relevant rights in biomedical research in international human rights instruments shows that potential applicants would face considerable difficulties.[68] For instance, as regards the right to life, the applicant would have to

---

67   *Belgian Linguistic* Case No 2 A 6 (1968).
68   See the excellent discussion of Fidler, 2001. Also Orlowski, 2003, p 381.

convince the ECtHR that Art 2 should be construed as imposing a positive obligation on States to ensure that participants in a research trial are given access to a successfully tested life-saving treatment post-trial. Fidler's discussion of the right to life in other international human rights instruments shows the difficulties involved in the exercise.[69]

Similar difficulties arise in respect of the extension of other human rights to biomedical research.[70] Hence, in order to help applicants secure a remedy, substantive, normative links have to be developed and specified between the general rights protected by the ECHR and the rights contained in the CHRB. The discussion in previous chapters has explored some possible avenues. This line of work has now to be pursued more systematically across all areas of biomedical research in the future.

6.11   PROCEDURAL LIMITS

The bridging of normative and substantive gaps between the ECHR and the CHRB will not, however, be sufficient to secure remedies for participants in research trials. Applicants also face considerable procedural hurdles which in the case of research involving participants in developing countries are most likely to be fatal and preclude a case reaching trial.

The jurisdiction of the ECtHR is limited to claims based on the ECHR which are brought by applicants who are residents of Member States. This *de facto* excludes claims from research participants in developing countries. Furthermore, even in cases where the jurisdiction of the court is not in question, where the violation of a right has been committed by a private corporation, the applicant would also have to establish that the Convention has horizontal and not only vertical effect.[71] In short, there are enormous substantive and procedural difficulties in the way of securing justice.[72]

6.12   TOWARDS TRANSNATIONAL JUSTICE

The move from ethics driven regulation of biomedical research towards human rights driven regulation through the CHRB is a landmark achievement which has the potential to bring greater justice to participants in research trials. However, for the potential to be realised, further advances are needed. On the one hand the normative gap between the CHRB and the ECHR has to be filled. On the other hand fundamental, procedural limitations on enforcement have to be lifted. Only then will transnational justice be truly achieved.

---

69   Fidler, 2001.
70   See Scott, 2001.
71   See Chinkin, 1999; Sornaraja, 2001.
72   For an excellent discussion of the limitations of international human rights instruments see Ford and Tomossy, 2004.

BIBLIOGRAPHY

Advisory Committee on Human Radiation Experiments (ACHRE), *Final Report of the Advisory Committee on Human Radiation Experiments*, 1996, New York: OUP

The American Heritage Stedman's Medical Dictionary, 1995, Boston, MA: Houghton Mifflin

Andorno, R, 'La dignidad humana como nocion clave en la Declaracion de la UNESCO sobre el genoma humano' (2001) 14 *Rev Der Gen H* 41–53

Angell, M, 'Ethical Imperialism? Ethics in international collaborative clinical research' (1988) 16 *New England Journal of Medicine* 1081–83

Angell, M, 'The ethics of clinical research in the third world' (1997) 337(12) *New England Journal of Medicine* 847–49

Annas, G, 'The changing landscape of human experimentation: Nuremberg, Helsinki, and beyond' (1992) 2 *Health Matrix* 119

Annas, G and Grodin, M (eds), *The Nazi Doctors and the Nuremberg Code, Human Rights in Human Experimentation*, 1992, New York: OUP

Annas, G and Grodin, M, 'An apology is not enough' *Boston Globe*, 18 May 1997, C1–C2

Annas, GJ, Caplan, A and Elias, S, 'Stem cell politics, ethics and medical progress' (1999) 5(12) *Nat Med* 1339–41

Aristotle, *Nicomachean Ethics*, 1954, trans Ross, Sir David, London: OUP

Arnold, P and Sprumont, D, 'The "Nuremberg Code": rules of public international law', in Trohler, U and Reiter-Theil, S (eds), *Ethics Codes in Medicine: Foundations and Achievements of Codification Since 1947*, 1998, Brookfield, VT: Ashgate

Baker, R, 'A theory of international bioethics: multiculturalism, postmodernism, and the bankruptcy of fundamentalism' (1998a) 8(2) *Kennedy Institute of Ethics Journal* 201–31

Baker, R, 'A theory of international bioethics: the negotiable and the non-negotiable' (1998b) 8(3) *Kennedy Institute of Ethics Journal* 233–74

Beauchamp, T and Childress, J, *Principles of Biomedical Ethics*, 1979, NY: OUP

Beauchamp, TL, 'The mettle of moral fundamentalism: a reply to Baker' (1998) 8 *Kennedy Institute of Ethics Journal* 4

Berlin, I, *Four Essays on Liberty*, 1969, London: OUP

Bernard, C, *An Introduction to the Study of Experimental Medicine*, 1865, trans Greene, H and reprinted in Reiser, SJ, Dyck, AJ and Curran, WJ (eds), *Ethics in Medicine*, 1977, Cambridge, MA: MIT Press, pp 137–39

Beyleveld, D and Brownsword, R, *Human Dignity in Bioethics and Biolaw*, 2001, Oxford: OUP

Bland, JM, 'Fifth revision of Declaration of Helsinki. Ethics and money are not good bedfellows' (2002) 324(7343) *BMJ* 975–76

Brazier, B and Miola, J (2000) 'Bye-bye *Bolam*: a medical litigation revolution? 8(1) *Med L Rev* 85–114

Brazier, M, *Doctors, Patients and the Law*, 3rd edn, 2003, London: Penguin

Brazier, M, Campbell, A and Golombok, S, *Surrogacy: Report of the Review Team*, Cm 4068, 1998, London: HMSO

Brennan, T, 'Proposed revisions to the Declaration of Helsinki – will they weaken the ethical principles underlying human research?' (1999) 341 *New England Journal of Medicine* 527–31

Brownlie, I, *Principles of Public International Law*, 5th edn, 1998, New York: Clarendon, pp 5–8

Brownsword, R, 'Bioethics today, bioethics tomorrow: stem cell research and the "Dignitarian Alliance"' (2003) 17 *Notre Dame Journal of Law, Ethics and Public Policy* 15

Brownsword, R, 'Regulating human genetics: new dilemmas for a new millennium' (2004) 12 *Med L Rev* 14–39

Byk, C, 'A map to a new Treasure Island: the human genome and the concept of common heritage' (1998) 3 *Journal of Medicine and Philosophy* 235

Byk, C and Memeteau, G, *Le Droit des Comités d'Ethique*, 1996, Paris: Eska

Campbell, A and Cranley Glass, K, 'The legal status of clinical ethics policies, codes, and guidelines in medical practice and research' (2001) 46 *McGill LJ* 473

Cane, P, 'A warning about causation' (1999) 115 *LQR* 21

Chang, E, 'Fitting a square peg into a round hole? Imposing informed consent and post-trial obligations on US sponsored clinical trials in developing countries' (2002) 11 *S Cal Interdisc LJ* 339

Chinkin, C, 'A critique of the public/private dimension' (1999) 10 *European Journal of International Law* 387

Clerk and Lindsell on Torts, 17th edn, 1995, London: Sweet & Maxwell

Coleman, C, 'Procreative liberty and contemporaneous choice: an inalienable rights approach to frozen embryo disputes' (1999) 84(1) *Minn L Rev* 55–128

CORDIS NEWS, *Beyond 2002, Inter-institutional Debate on Stem Cell Research Reveals Extent of Ethical Split Within Europe* 2003-04-25

Council for International Organizations of Medical Sciences, *International Ethical Guidelines for Biomedical Research Involving Human Research*, 2002, Geneva

Council of Europe Steering Committee on Bioethics (CDBI), *Preparatory Work on the Convention*, Strasbourg, 28 June 2000 CDBI/INF (2000) 1 [cdbi/plénier/docs publics/inf/travaux préparatoires Conv (2000.1)a] Provisional (CAHBI 24-27/03/92)

Council of Europe, *Convention on Human Rights & Biomedicine: Chart of Signatures & Ratifications*, status on 2 July 2004

Crisp, R and Slote, M, *Virtue Ethics*, 1997, Oxford: OUP

Crouch, R and Arras, J, 'AZT trials and tribulations' (1998) 28(6) *Hastings Center Report* 26–34

Dalla-Vorgia, WA, Plomer, A *et al*, 'Overview of European legislation on informed consent for neonatal research' (2001) 84 *Arch Dis Child Fetal Neonatal Ed* 70–73

De Zulueta, P, 'Randomised placebo-controlled trials and HIV-infected pregnant women in developing countries: ethical imperialism or unethical exploitation?' (2001) 15(4) *Bioethics* 289

Dehmel, JM, 'To have or not to have: whose procreative rights prevail in disputes over dispositions of frozen embryos?' (1995) 27 *Conn L Rev* 1377

Delkeskamp-Hayes, C, 'Respecting, protecting persons, humans and conceptual muddles in the Bioethics Convention' (2000) 25(2) *Journal of Medicine and Philosophy* 147–80

DHHS Office of Inspector General, *The Globalization of Clinical Trials. A Growing Challenge in Protecting Human Subjects*, Rep No OEI-01-00-00190, 2001, Boston: Office of Evaluation and Inspections

Diamant, J, 'The revised Declaration of Helsinki – is justice served?' (2002) 40 *Int J Clin Pharmacol Ther* 76–83

Duffy, PJ, 'Article 3 of the European Convention on Human Rights' (1983) 32 *ICLQ* 316–46

Dworkin, R, *Law's Empire*, 1986, Cambridge: Harvard University Press

Dworkin, R, *Life's Dominion: An Argument about Abortion, Euthanasia and Individual Freedom*, 1993, New York: Knopf

Dworkin, R, *Taking Rights Seriously*, 1977, London: Duckworth

Ethics Committee of the American Fertility Society *Ethical Considerations of Assisted Reproductive Technologies, Fertility and Sterility*, Supp 1 November 1994, 29S–30S

'Europe dithers over regulations for stem-cell research' (2003) *Nature*, 11 December

European Commission, *Commission Staff Working Paper Report on Human Embryonic Stem Cell Research*, SEC 441, 2003

European Group on Ethics & New Technologies (EGE) Opinion No 15, *Ethical Aspects of Human Stem Cell Research and Use*, 14 November 2000

European Group on Ethics in Science & New Technologies (EGE) Opinion No 16, *Ethical Aspects of Patenting Inventions Involving Human Stem Cells*, 7 May 2002

European Group on Ethics in Science & New Technologies (EGE) Opinion No 17, *Ethical Aspects of Clinical Research in Developing Countries*, 4 February 2003

Evans, R, *Gassed: British Chemical Warfare Experiments on Humans at Porton Down*, 2000, London: House of Stratus

Feinberg, J, *Harmless Wrongdoing: The Moral Limits of the Criminal Law*, Vol iv, 1988, Oxford: OUP

Feldman, D, 'Human dignity as a legal value' (Part 1) [1999a] 2 *PL* 682–702

Feldman, D, 'Human dignity as a legal value' (Part 2) [1999b] 3 *PL* 61–76

Feldman, D, *Civil Liberties and Human Rights in England and Wales*, 2nd edn, 2002, Oxford: OUP

Fidler, D, 'Geographic morality revisited: international relations, international law, and the controversy over placebo-controlled HIV clinical trials in developing countries' (2001) 42 *Harvard International Law Journal* 2–29

Ford, J and Tomossy, G, 'Clinical trials in developing countries: the claimant's challenge' (2004) 1 *Law, Social Justice & Global Development* 1–14

Forster, H, 'The legal and ethical debate surrounding the storage and destruction of frozen human embryos: a reaction to the mass disposal in Britain and the lack of law in the United States' (1998) 76 *Wash ULQ* 759

Forster, H, Emmanuel, E and Grady, C, 'The 2000 revision of the Declaration of Helsinki: a step forward or more confusion?' (2001) *The Lancet*, 27 October, 1449–53

Friele, M, 'Do committees rule in the bio-political culture? On the democratic legitimacy of bioethics committees' (2003) 17(4) *Bioethics* 301–18

Giesen, D, 'Civil liability of physicians for new methods of treatment and experimentation: a comparative examination' (1995) 3 *Med L Rev* 22

Glantz, L, Annas, G, Grodin, M and Mariner, W, 'Research in developing countries: taking "benefit seriously"' (1998) 28(6) *Hastings Center Report* 38–42

Glasa, J, *Ethics Committees in Central & Eastern Europe*, 2000, Strasbourg: Council of Europe

Glover, J, *Causing Deaths and Saving Lives*, 1977, Harmondsworth: Penguin

Glover, J, *Utilitarianism and its Critics*, 1990, New York: Macmillan

Gostin, LO and Lazzarini, Z, *Human Rights and Public Health in the AIDS Pandemic*, 1998, New York: OUP

Griffin, J, *Well-being, Its Meaning, Measurement and Moral Importance*, 1986, Oxford: Clarendon

Grobstein, C, 'Human development from fertilisation to birth', in Reich, WT (ed), *Encyclopedia of Bioethics*, 1995, New York: Macmillan, p 847

Halsbury's Laws of England, Lord Hailsham (ed), 4th edn, 1973, London: Butterworths

Hare, R, *Moral Thinking*, 1981, Oxford: Clarendon

Harris, D and Mowbray, A, *Cases and Materials on the European Convention on Human Rights*, 2001, London: Butterworths

Harris, J, 'Clones, genes and human rights', in Burley, J (ed), *The Genetic Revolution and Human Rights* 1999, Oxford: OUP

Harris, J, *The Value of Life*, 1985, London: Routledge & Kegan Paul

Hart, HLA, *The Concept of Law*, 2nd edn, 2004, Bulloch, P and Raz, J (eds), Oxford: Clarendon

Hegel, GWF, *Philosophy of Right*, 1949, trans Knox, TM, London: OUP

Held, D, *Models of Democracy*, 2nd edn, 1996, Stanford: Stanford UP

Henkin, L, *The Age of Rights*, 1990, New York: Columbia University Press

Hinsliff, G and McKie, R, 'Doctors beat curbs on tissue research' (2004) *The Observer*, 6 June

Hobbes, T, *Leviathan*, 1997, Oakeshott, M (ed), New York: Simon & Schuster

Holden, C, 'Stem cell lines: NIH's list of 64 leaves questions' (2001) 293(535) *Science* 1567

Honderich, T, *Violence for Equality: Inquiries in Political Philosophy*, 1980, Harmondsworth: Penguin

Hume, D, 'Of suicide', in Miller, E (ed), *Essays Moral, Political and Literary*, 1985, Indianapolis, IN: Liberty Classics

Hume, D, *A Treatise Concerning Human Nature*, Norton, D and Norton, J (eds), 2000, New York: OUP

Hursthouse, R, *Beginning Lives*, 1987, Oxford: Basil Blackwell in association with Open University

Husserl, E, *The Crisis of European Sciences and Transcendental Phenomenology: An Introduction to Phenomenological Philosophy*, 1970a, trans Carr, Evanston: North Western UP

Husserl, E, *Logical Investigations*, 1970b, trans Findlay, London: Routledge & Kegan Paul

Independent Review Group on Retention of Organs at Post-Mortem: Final Report, November 2001, Scottish Executive

Interim Report: Removal and Retention of Human Material, Bristol Royal Infirmary Inquiry, May 2000

Jonas, H, *The Future of Human Nature*, 2003, London: Polity

Jonas, H, *The Imperative of Responsibility*, 1984, Chicago: Chicago UP

Jonsen, AR, *The Birth of Bioethics*, 1998, NY: OUP

Kahn, JP, Mastroianni, AC and Sugarman, J, *Beyond Consent – Seeking Justice in Research*, 1998, New York: OUP

Kant, I, *Foundations of the Metaphysics of Morals*, 1969, trans White Beck, L, with critical essays edited by Wolf, RP, Indianapolis: Bobbs-Merrill

Kant, I, *Kant's Political Writings*, 1970, Reiss, H (ed), trans Nisbet, HH, Cambridge: CUP

Kass, L, 'Preventing a brave new world or why we should ban human cloning now' (2001) *The New Republic*, 21 May

Kass, L, 'The wisdom of repugnance: why we should ban the cloning of humans', in McGee, G (ed), *The Human Cloning Debate*, 2000, Berkeley, California: Berkeley Hills Books

Katz, DA, 'My egg, your sperm, whose pre-embryo? A proposal for deciding which party receives custody of frozen pre-embryos' (1998) 5(42) *Va J Soc Pol'y & L* 623

Kennedy, I and Grubb, A, *Medical Law*, 2000, London: Butterworths

Kuhn, T, *The Structure of Scientific Revolutions*, 1996, Chicago: Chicago UP

Kutukdjian, G, 'Remember your humanity', Proceedings of the 47th Pugwash Conference on Science and World Affairs, 1999

Lee, R and Morgan, D, *Human Fertilisation and Embryology*, 2001, London: Blackstone

Lenoir, N and Mathieu, B, *Les Normes Internationals de la Bioethique*, 1998, Paris: PUF

Levine, R, 'The "best proven therapeutic method" standard in clinical trials in technologically developing countries' (1998) 20(1) *IRB* 5–9

Levine, R, 'The need to revise the Declaration of Helsinki' (1999) 341(7) *New England Journal of Medicine* 531–34

Levine, R, 'International codes of research ethics: current controversies and the future' (2002) 35 *Ind L Rev* 557

Locke, J, *An Essay Concerning Human Understanding*, 1975, Nidditch, P (ed), Oxford: Clarendon

Locke, J, *Two Treatises of Government*, 1988, Laslett, P (ed), Cambridge: CUP

Lovejoy, AO, *The Great Chain of Being*, 1970, Cambridge, MA: Harvard UP

Lurie, P and Wolfe, SM, 'Unethical trials of interventions to reduce perinatal transmission of the human immunodeficiency virus in developing countries' (1997) 337(12) *New England Journal of Medicine* 853–56

Lurie, P, Wolfe, S, Jordan, W, Annas, GJ, Grodin, M and Silver, G, 'Letter to the Department of HHS concerning funding of unethical trials which administer placebos to HIV infected pregnant women through NIH and the Centre for Disease Control' (1997) Health Research Group Publication, 22 April, available at www.citizen.org/publications

MacIntyre, A, *After Virtue and Justice*, 1981, London: Duckworth

Macklin, R, 'A defense of fundamental principles and human rights: a reply to Baker' (1998) 8(4) *Kennedy Institute of Ethics Journal* 403–22

Macklin, R, 'After Helsinki: unresolved issues in international research' (2001) 11(1) *Kennedy Inst Ethics J* 17–36

Marx, K, *Economic and Philosophic Manuscripts*, 1977a, London: Lawrence and Wishart

Marx, K, *Capital: A Critique of Political Economy*, 1977b, Harmondsworth: Penguin

Mason, JK and Laurie, G, 'Consent or property – dealing with the body and its parts in the shadow of Bristol and Alder Hey' (2001) 64(5) *Modern Law Review* 710–29

Mason, K, McCall Smith, RA and Laurie, G, *Law and Medical Ethics*, 2001, London: Butterworths

Mason, S and Megone, C (eds), *European Neonatal Research: Consent, Ethics Committees and Law*, 2001, Aldershot: Ashgate

Matthews, P, 'Whose body? People as property' (1983) 36 *CLP* 193

McGinn, PR, 'World Medical Association adopts new research standards that puts patients at risk' (2000) *AM News*, 18 December

McGinn, PR, 'Painstaking process of revising WMA's Declaration of Helsinki' (2001) *AM News*, 8 January

McKie, R, 'Bill on removal of organs will "paralyse" life-saving research' (2004) *The Observer*, 8 February

McIntyre, A, *After Virtue*, 1981, London: Duckworth

Merleau-Ponty, M, *The Phenomenology of Perception*, 2002, trans Smith, C, London: Routledge

Mill, JS, *Collected Works*, 1984, Robson, J (ed), Toronto: Toronto UP

Mill, JS, *Utilitarianism*, 1998, Crisp, R (ed), Oxford: OUP

Montgomery, J, *Health Care Law*, 2nd edn, 2001, Oxford: OUP

Mowbray, A, *The Development of Positive Obligations under the European Convention on Human Rights by the European Court of Human Rights*, 2004, Oxford: Hart

Morin, K, 'The standard of disclosure in human subject experimentation' (1998) 19 *J Leg Med* 157

Mukherjee, JS, Farmer, PE, Niyizonkiza, D, McCorkle, L, Vanderwarker, C, Teixeira, P and Kim, JY, 'Tackling HIV in resource poor countries' (2003) 327 *BMJ* 1104–06

National Bioethics Advisory Commission (NBAC) *Ethical Issues in Human Stem Cell Research: Executive Summary*, 1999, Rockville, MD: NBAC

National Bioethics Advisory Commission (NBAC), *Ethical and Policy Issues in International Research: Clinical Trials in Developing Countries Report and Recommendations*, April 2001, Bethesda, MD: NBAC, available at www.georgetown.edu/research/nrcbl/nbac/execsumm.pdf

Nicholson, RH and Crawley, FP, 'Revising the Declaration of Helsinki: a fresh start' (1999) 151 *Bull Med Ethics* 13–17

Nuffield Council on Bioethics, *The Ethics of Research Related to Healthcare in Developing Countries*, 2001, London: Nuffield Council on Bioethics

Orlowski, V, 'Promising protection through internationally derived duties' (2003) 36 *Cornell International Law Journal* 381–414

Page, AK, 'Prior agreements in international clinical trials: ensuring the benefits of research to developing countries' (2002) 3 *Yale J Health Pol'y L & Ethics* 35

Parry, B, Zimmern, R, Hall, A and Liddell, K, 'A critique of the human tissue bill' Discussion paper, 2004, Cambridge Genetics Knowledge Park

Pellegrino, E, 'The origins and evolution of bioethics: some personal reflections' (1999) 9(1) *Kennedy Institute of Ethics Journal* 73–88

Plomer, A, 'Participation of children in clinical trials: UK, European and international legal perspectives on consent' (2000) 5 *Medical Law International* 1–24

Plomer, A, 'Medical research, consent and the ECHRB', in Garwood-Gowers, A *et al*, *Healthcare Law: The Impact of the Human Rights Act 1998*, 2001a, London: Cavendish Publishing, pp 313–30

Plomer, A, 'Protecting the rights of human subjects in emergency research' (2001b) 8 *European Journal of Health Law* 333–52

Plomer, A, 'Principles underlying the regulation of clinical trials with children: international bioethics or moral bankruptcy', in Mason, S and Megone, C (eds), *European Neonatal Research: Consent, Ethics Committees and Law*, 2001c, Aldershot: Ashgate

Plomer, A, 'Beyond the HFE Act 1990: the regulation of stem cell research in the UK', (2002) 10(2) *Medical Law Review* 132–64

President's Council on Bioethics, *Human Cloning and Human Dignity: An Ethical Inquiry*, July 2002, Washington, DC

Rawls, J, *A Theory of Justice*, 1972, Oxford: Clarendon

Report of a Census of Organs and Tissue Retained by Pathology Services in England, 2001, Advice from the Chief Medical Officer, London: Department of Health

Report of Content Analysis of NHS Trust Policies and Protocols on Consent to Organ and Tissue Retention at Post-mortem Examination and Disposal of Human Materials in the Chief Medical Officer's Census of NHS Pathology Services, Health Services Directorate, 2000, London: Department of Health

Report of the IBC on the Possibility of Elaborating a Universal Instrument on Bioethics, 2003, 13 June, Paris: IBC

Report of the Independent Review Group on the Retention of Organs at Post-mortem, McLean Report, January 2001

Report of the Royal Liverpool Children's (Alder Hey) Inquiry, Redfern Report, HC, January 2001

Riedel, E, 'Global responsibilities and bioethics: reflections on the Council of Europe Bioethics Convention' (1997) 5(1) *Indiana Journal of Global Legal Studies* 179–90

Robertson, JA, 'In the beginning: the legal status of early embryos' (1990a) 76 *Va L Rev* 437

Robertson, JA, 'Prior agreements for disposition of frozen embryos' (1990b) 51 *Ohio St LJ* 407

Roman, J, 'US medical research in the developing world: ignoring Nuremberg' (2002) 11(2) *Cornell J Law Public Policy* 441–60

Rorty, R, *Philosophy and the Mirror of Nature*, 1981, Oxford: Blackwell

Rosenau, H, 'Legal prerequisites for clinical trials under the revised Declaration of Helsinki and the European Convention on Human Rights and Biomedicine' (2000) 7(2) *Eur J Health Law* 105–21

Rothman, DJ, *Strangers at the Bedside: A History of How Law and Bioethics Transformed Medical Decision Making*, 1991, NY: Basic Books

Russell, Sir WO, *Russell on Crime*, Cecil Turner, JW (ed), 12th edn, 1964, London: Stevens, Vol 2

Sandel, M, *Liberalism and the Limits of Justice*, 1982, Cambridge: CUP

Schiermeier, Q, 'German bioethics inquiry could hold up essential changes' (1999) 402 *Nature* 331–32

Schmidt, K, 'The concealed and the revealed: bioethical issues in Europe at the end of the millennium' (2000) 25(2) *Journal of Medicine and Philosophy* 123–32

Schuklenk, U, 'Unethical perinatal HIV transmission trials establish bad precedent' (1998) 12 *Bioethics* 312–19

Schuklenk, U and Ashcroft, R, 'International research ethics' (2000) 14(2) *Bioethics* 158–72

Scott, C (ed), *Torture as Tort: Comparative Perspectives on the Development of Transnational Human Rights Litigation*, 2001, Oxford: Hart

Sen, A and Williams, B, *Utilitarianism and Beyond*, 1982, Cambridge: CUP

Sheinbach, D, 'Examining disputes over ownership rights to frozen embryos: will prior consent documents survive if challenged by State law and/or constitutional principles?' (1999) 48 *Cath U L Rev* 989

Simmonds, NE, *Central Issues in Jurisprudence: Justice, Law and Rights*, 2002, London: Sweet & Maxwell

Singer, P, *Practical Ethics*, 1993, Cambridge: CUP

Singer, P and Kuhse, H (eds), *Unsanctifying Human Life*, 2002, Oxford: Blackwell

Singer, PA and Benatar, SR, 'Beyond Helsinki: a vision for global health ethics' (2001) 322(7289) *BMJ* 747–48

Skegg, PDG, 'Human corpses, medical specimens and the law of property' (1975) *Anglo-Amer L Rev* 412

Smart, JJC, *Utilitarianism, For and Against*, 1973, Cambridge: CUP

Sornaraja, M, 'State responsibility for harms by corporate nationals abroad', in Scott, C (ed), *Torture as Tort: Comparative Perspectives on the Development of Transnational Human Rights Litigation*, 2001, Oxford: Hart

Sprumont, D, 'Legal protection of human research in Europe' (1999) 6 *European Journal of Health Law* 25–43

Stauch, M, 'Taking the consequences for failure to warn of medical risks' (2000) 63 *MLR* 261

Steinberg, D, 'Divergent conceptions: procreational rights and disputes over the fate of frozen embryos' (1998) 7 *BU Pub Int LJ* 315

Sunstein, C, *Legal Reasoning and Political Conflict*, 1966, New York: OUP

Syal, R, 'Porton Down used soldiers for Sarin gas tests in 1983' (2002) *Sunday Telegraph*, 13 October

Taylor, AL, 'Globalisation and biotechnology: Unesco and an international strategy to advance human rights and public health' (1999) 25 *American Journal of Law & Medicine* 451–79

Ter Meulen, R, Arts, W and Muffels, R (eds), *Solidarity in Health and Social Care in Europe*, 2001, Dordrecht and Boston: Kluwer

The Removal, Retention and Use of Human Organs and Tissue from Post-mortem Examination, Advice from the Chief Medical Officer, 2001, London: Department of Health

Todres, J, 'Can research subjects of clinical trials in developing countries sue physician-investigators for human rights violations?' (2000) 16(3) *NY Law Sch J Hum Rights* 737–68

UNAIDS, *Ethical Considerations in HIV Preventive Vaccine Research*, 2000, Geneva: Joint United Nations Programme on HIV/AIDS

UNAIDS, *Epidemic Update*, December 2003

UNESCO, Statutes of International Bioethics Committee, 1998, Unesco Press

UNESCO, *The Use of Embryonic Stem Cells in Therapeutic Research: Report of the IRC on Ethical Aspects of Human Embryonic Stem Cell Research*, rapporteurs: McCall Smith, A and Revel, M, 2001, Paris: Unesco Press

UNESCO, *The IBC: Ten Years of Activity*, 2003, UnescoPress

Van Dijk, P and Van Hoof, GJH, *Theory and Practice of the European Convention on Human Rights*, 1998, The Hague: Kluwer Law International

Vasak, K 'Les differentes categories des droits de l'homme', in *Les Dimensions Universelles des Droits de l'Homme*, 1990, Brussels: Bruylant, p 302

Vastag, B, 'Helsinki discord? A controversial declaration' (2000) 284(23) *JAMA* 2983–85

Waldron, J, *Law and Disagreement*, 1999, Oxford: Clarendon

Waldron, J, *Liberal Rights: Collected Papers 1981–1991*, 1993, Cambridge: CUP

Walter, P, 'His, hers, or theirs – custody, control and contracts: allocating decisional authority over frozen embryos' (1999) 29 *Seton Hall L Rev* 937

Wellcome Trust, 'Medical research under threat from new bill', press release, 14 January 2004

Wendler, D, 'Informed consent, exploitation and whether it is possible to conduct human subjects research without either one' (2001) 15(4) *Bioethics* 289–311

WHO, *Surveying and Evaluating Ethical Review Practices*, 2000, Geneva: WHO

WHO & UNAIDS, *Making it Happen: The WHO and UNAIDS Global Initiative to Provide Antiretroviral Therapy to 3 Million People with HIV/AIDS in Developing Countries by the End of 2005*, 2003

Wittgenstein, L, *Philosophical Investigations*, 1984, trans Anscombe, GEM, Oxford: Basil Blackwell

WMA, *Declaration of Helsinki: Ethical Principles for Medical Research Involving Human Subjects*, 1964 (revised 1975, 1983, 1989, 1996 and 2000)

WMA, 'International code of medical ethics' (1949) 1(3) *World Medical Association Bulletin* 109

WMA, *Public Consultation Begins on the Declaration of Helsinki*, press release, 16 February 2000

Woolf (Lord) 'Are the courts excessively deferential to the medical profession?' (2001) 9(1) *Med L Rev* 1–16

Zilgalvis, P, 'The European Convention on Human Rights and Biomedicine: its past, present and future', in Garwood-Gowers, A *et al, Healthcare Law: The Impact of the Human Rights Act 1998*, 2001, London: Cavendish Publishing

INDEX